WORKHOUSE

The People • The Places • The Life Behind Doors

WORKHOUSE

The People • The Places • The Life Behind Doors

SIMON FOWLER

the national archives

First published in 2007 by

The National Archives
Kew, Richmond, Surrey, TW9 4DU, UK

www.nationalarchives.gov.uk

The National Archives brings together the Public Record Office,
Historical Manuscripts Commission, Office of Public Sector
Information and Her Majesty's Stationery Office.

A catalogue card for this book is available from the British Library.

ISBN 978 1 905615 03 2

Jacket front: Halifax workhouse, Yorkshire, 1901
(Mary Evans Picture Library); poor boy, 1875 (TNA: PRO COPY 1/29)
Jacket back: contemporary photograph of Southwell workhouse,
Nottinghamshire (NTPL/Andrew Butler)

Jacket design by Briony Chappell
Picture research by Gwen Campbell
Printed in Great Britain by Biddles Ltd, King's Lynn

Contents

Metric and decimal equivalents

Victorian England remained relentlessly imperial, even though (or perhaps because) the metric system was being adopted across Europe. Here are some common imperial measurements, referred to in the text, with their metric equivalents:

Weight	1lb (pound) = 454g
	1oz (ounce) = 28g
Liquid	1 pint (20 fluid ounces) = 568ml
Length	One foot = 305mm
Land	1 acre = 4,046 square metres

Monetary values

Before 1971 the pound was divided into twenty shillings (abbreviated as s) and subdivided again into twelve pennies (d). There were thus 240 pennies to the pound. Occasionally you might come across a reference to a guinea, which was worth 21s, although few paupers would ever have seen one.

It is almost impossible to give any idea of what this was worth in modern terms. A mid-Victorian labourer might hope to earn between 20s and 30s per week, but of course many had to support their families on much less, particularly in times of economic distress. By contrast the minimum wage rate for workers over 22 today is just over £5 an hour. When Mary Higgs and her friend spent a week visiting lodging houses and casual wards in the north of England in the early 1900s, they each took just 2s 6d to last a whole week. It was claimed that a beggar or loafer in London and other big cities might make up to five shillings a day through a combination of begging and doing odd jobs such as holding horses or taking messages.

The National Archives' website has a currency calculator at www.nationalarchives.gov.uk/currency.

The Problem of the Poor

I have seen the men gnaw the bones, they broke the pig chap bones to
pick the fat and gristle out… The men were very glad to get hold
of them, they were so hungry.

John Wells, Andover workhouse, 1845

WHEN people of my parents' generation were growing up, they were
often threatened with the workhouse for being wasteful or profligate with precious resources. It was largely a reflex action, but for my
grandparents, and particularly for my great grandparents, the workhouse
and the world of the Poor Law was one which they strenuously, and as far as
I know successfully, avoided. This book is an attempt to find out why they
reacted that way, and to answer two other questions.

Most people learn about the workhouse at school or by visiting museums
and living history sites such as the Norfolk Rural Life Museum at Gressenhall
or the National Trust's restored workhouse at Southwell near Newark in
Nottinghamshire. It can be a harrowing process. The horrors at Andover
workhouse in Hampshire, where in 1845 starving paupers were discovered
eating rotting marrow from the bones they were meant to be crushing, shocks
modern students just as it did the readers of the newspapers at the time. But
was every workhouse as bad? And were the paupers who dwelt there the
innocent victims of a cruel and misguided policy, forced into dreadful workhouses where the children were beaten and their parents neglected?

The Andover scandal is worth mentioning here as it starkly illustrates
the problems of the workhouse system. And the starving inmates who fought

over bones had a far-reaching impact. Two very public inquiries, together with detailed and stomach-turning revelations in *The Times*, revealed a sorry story of complacency, neglect, brutality and maladministration – both locally and nationally – that horrified the nation.

At the centre of the scandal was the workhouse master, Colin McDougal – a career soldier, drunkard and a bully. The Parliamentary inquiry concluded that his behaviour was 'utterly deficient in many of the qualities which are of essential importance in the difficult position which he filled viz fairness and impartiality, a due sense of truth, a well regulated temper, and proper habits of self-control'. Yet his behaviour was condoned by the complacency of the local board of guardians and its chairman, the Rev. Christopher Dodson, another bully with little regard for his poorer parishioners. Dodson and his colleagues were solely concerned in keeping the poor rate as low as possible, for which they won numerous plaudits from the local ratepayers.

The worst problem was that the food provided was clearly not sufficient, but this did not worry the workhouse guardians. One of the MPs asked Leonard Lyewood, who had then become chairman of the guardians, 'Were you aware that the dietary was insufficient?' to which he replied, 'No. I considered it sufficient, for this very reason, whenever any pauper applied to the board and said that he had not a sufficiency of food, the question was always put to Mr Westlake [the Medical Officer] "Mr Westlake what is your opinion?" He invariably answered, "I do not doubt they could eat more, but it is amply sufficient to keep them in health." That was his answer.'

Inmate after inmate was interviewed by the commissions of inquiry, and their statements bear testament to their dignity and to their mistreatment. One of them, John Wells, told MPs: 'I have seen the men gnaw the bones, they broke the pig chap bones to pick the fat and gristle out. I have seen them eat the marrow out of the bones. Some of the bones were stinking bones. They were got very high sometimes. The men were very glad to get hold of them, they were so hungry.'

The scandal was only exposed after rumours about conditions came to the notice of the local MP, Thomas Wakeley. He persuaded the government to set up an inquiry, which largely found in favour of the guardians. A further investigation by a select committee of MPs was rather more rigorous. In 25,619 questions and over 2,000 pages, they systematically dissected the Poor Law system and its operation both in Whitehall, and at Andover.

In the aftermath of the report, the Poor Law Commission was abolished and replaced by the Poor Law Board with a minister in Parliament directly responsible for its activities. Conditions in workhouses began to improve, if for no other reason that few guardians wanted their unions exposed in the same way. Over the protests of many guardians, bone-crushing as a task offered to pauper inmates was banned by Whitehall. And Colin McDougal was sacked.

Yet the system endured. Workhouses existed, in some shape and form, for over two and a half centuries, and they did develop and evolve over that time. This book largely covers the period between 1834, which saw the introduction of the New Poor Law, and the First World War, by which time the workhouse in traditional form was becoming a historical curiosity. There is the occasional reference to the world of the Old Poor Law, which was largely discredited by the 1830s. Although it was abandoned in 1834, however, some of the old ways still lingered on – not least because the workhouse and many of the ideas that lay behind it were developed by the men who administered the Old Poor Law.

Workhouse also explores how the institution appeared to contemporaries, from writers such as Charles Dickens, Thomas Hardy and George Orwell to those who ran, inhabited or strove to avoid them. Florence Nightingale and other celebrities condemned them, and many fine words of outrage were expended on behalf of those who had nowhere else to turn. The views of most late Victorians are summarized in the poem 'In the Workhouse, Christmas Day' – which first appeared in *The Dagonet Ballads* by the dramatist and journalist George R. Sims (1847–1922). Now mocked for its cloying sentimentality, it was originally a powerful attack on the workhouse system and the people incarcerated within it. Coincidentally, the year of the poem's publication, 1877, saw the first signs of reforms to improve the operation of the Poor Law, and by 1900 the workhouse of which Sims wrote had largely been transformed. However, people still liked the monologue, recited for generations in public bars and living rooms across the country, and it remained popular at least until the Second World War. The poem tells the story of a pauper who rejects his Christmas meal – a rare moment of indulgence in the spartan daily regime – as he recalls with horror the disastrous events of a year ago that have brought him to such a place. Poignant and full of drama, it is worth quoting at length.

It is Christmas Day in the Workhouse,
And the cold bare walls are bright
With garlands of green and holly,
And the place is a pleasant sight:
For with clear-washed hands and faces
In a long and hungry line
The paupers sit at the tables,
For this is the hour they dine.

And the guardians and their ladies,
Although the wind is east,
Have come in their furs and wrappers,
To watch their charges feast:
To smile and be condescending,
Put puddings on pauper plates,
To be hosts at the workhouse banquet
They've paid for – with the rates.

Oh, the paupers are meek and lowly
With their 'Thank'ee kindly, mum's';
So long as they fill their stomachs
What matters it whence it comes?
But one of the old men mutters,
And pushes his plate aside:
'Great God!' he cries; 'but it chokes me!
For this is the day she died.'

The guardians gazed in horror
The master's face went white;
'Did a pauper refuse his pudding?'
'Could their ears believe aright?'
Then the ladies clutched their husbands,
Thinking the man might die
Struck by a bolt, or something,
By the outraged One on high.

10

Even after 130 years the poem still affects how we perceive the workhouse – and as we shall see, it contains more than a glimmer of truth which speaks across the centuries.

Sims' poem became famous, but if this book had a dedication it would be to an anonymous pauper author, discovered completely by chance. I was browsing the shelves of the London Library, beginning the research for this book, when I came across a slim volume hidden behind a much larger book. It was in poor condition and it was clear that since its publication, 120 years ago, the book had never been borrowed. *Indoor Paupers by One of Them* was published in 1885, and it offers a remarkable insight into life in the workhouse of the 1880s.

Researchers into the history of the Poor Law and destitution quickly learn that firsthand accounts are written with an audience in mind. Even the greatest of the explorers into Victorian poverty, Henry Mayhew, was not beyond fictionalizing the experiences of the men and women he talked to in order to 'sex up' their stories. Yet much of *Indoor Paupers* has a ring of truth to it. The author is not above sentimentalizing situations in the workhouse and some of the characters he met to meet the expectations of his middle-class readership. It is clear that he comes from the middle class himself; which is in itself unusual, although by no means unique. Even so, his is a powerful voice from a near-forgotten time, with enough bitter experience and common sense to give the reader an idea of what it was like: the camaraderie, as well as the horrors and the tedium. 'The Indoor Pauper' recurs throughout the book; I thought you should know why.

CHAPTER ONE

The World of the Workhouse

The real object of [the New Poor Law] ... is to lower wages
and punish poverty as a crime.
Richard Oastler, *The Northern Star*, 1838

THE word 'workhouse' has resonance: unfeeling, mean and bleak, casting a terrifying shadow over ordinary lives. It appears a deeply inhuman institution, and today we shudder at photographs of rooms full of identically dressed elderly men and women with no spark of life in their eyes. The scandal at Andover workhouse in Hampshire was not unique, but rather the most shocking of several that erupted in the 1840s. Newspaper exposés later in the century and the writings of Jack London, Beatrice Webb and others have given a pretty bleak picture and shaped the workhouse's legacy.

For much of the 19th century, however, it did not seem like this to practitioners. Foreign social workers were impressed with the provision that the State made for the poor, compared with what was available on the Continent or in the United States, where care was largely left in the hands of charities or the Church. It is also clear that the Poor Law guardians – the men (and from the 1880s women) who were responsible for administering and supervising the workhouse and their staff – were not always as unimaginative and penny-pinching as they have often been made out to be. Great efforts were made to care for children in the workhouse to ensure that they did not repeat the mistakes made by their parents. Passages were paid for paupers, both adults and children, to give them new opportunities in Australia and Canada, and from the 1880s unemployment schemes were created to help the jobless.

And yet, for every enlightened union with imaginative guardians and dedicated staff, there were perhaps half-a-dozen places where the guardians were more concerned with keeping the rates low and the staff unresponsive to the conditions of those in their charge. Most workhouses, of course, fell somewhere between the two. Just one imaginative and determined guardian, together with a dedicated master and matron, could make a big difference to the care offered. A significant problem facing the central authorities was that standards of food and accommodation, let alone the medical care or schooling offered to the children, varied tremendously, even between neighbouring workhouses. The British government had few real powers; officials in Whitehall might argue, persuade and on occasion embarrass, but, particularly before the 1870s, they could be – and often were – ignored.

Poor laws and paupers

The greatest of all the paradoxes associated with the New Poor Law and the workhouse is that the institutions were largely designed for a pool of able-bodied idlers and shirkers. However, this group hardly existed outside the imagination of a generation of political economists. Their theories were based on an increasing number of unemployed and semi-employed men, women and children who had always existed on the margins of society, but whose numbers soared during the economic downturn after the end of the Napoleonic Wars in the mid-1810s. Changing agricultural practices in southern England, which required fewer workers on the land, exacerbated the problems they faced. To understand why the economists' view gained such a hold, we need to look at the origins of the New Poor Law.

The Poor Law originated in the dying days of Elizabeth I's reign, and it remained much the same until the early 1830s. Each parish became responsible for looking after those who were too ill, young or old to work, and the costs of so doing had to be paid for by a tax or rate on the property of the wealthier in the parish. Overseers of the poor were elected by the ratepayers each year to administer the system and maintain the accounts. The first 'workhouse' premises were built in the late 16th century, although parishes were not obliged to provide them. An early workhouse opened in Exeter in the 1670s; it was a bequest of Canon John Bury, who in 1667 left the sum of £40 per annum to the parish of St Sidwell in the city so that 'All ye poore people of that Parish that should be able to work should be maintained therein and kept to work.' In 1697 Exeter became one of the first places in England to be incorporated under a special Act of Parliament to administer its own poor relief:

> Whereas it is found by experience, that the Poor in the City of Exon do daily multiply, and Idleness and Debauchery amongst the meaner sort doth greatly increase for the want of Workhouses to set them to work, and a sufficient Authority to compel them thereto, as well to the charge of the Inhabitants, and grief of the charitable and honest citizens of the said City, as the great distress of the poor themselves; for which sufficient redress hath not yet been provided.

The workhouse was administered by a corporation comprised of 'the Mayor and Alderman and of forty other persons' elected by payers of the poor rate.

This Poor Law and its processes worked well enough in the stable conditions of the 17th and 18th centuries, but as the population increased it came under enormous strain. Under what was known as the Speenhamland system (after the Berkshire village where it was first introduced), local magistrates or overseers of the poor often made up the wages of agricultural labourers from the poor rate or insisted that local farmers take on the unemployed. What initially seemed like an act of social solidarity soon became a nightmare for farmers and local payers of the poor rates, as more and more men and their families sought relief. Urban areas were also affected. The poor law authorities in towns came increasingly under pressure as people poured in from agricultural areas seeking employment in the new factories and mills. When they were unable to find work, they naturally approached the parish for help.

By the 1830s widespread abuse of the system was suspected. Partly as a consequence of this, the government established a Royal Commission on the Poor Law in 1832, to investigate the situation and make recommendations for change. Witness after witness gave evidence of apparent abuse, which seemed to be occurring across the country. From the Essex village of Great Henny, for example, William Newport, a churchwarden, and Edward Cook, the overseer, reported that:

> A man of bad character, on account of which he is not employed, having two children or more, applies to the parish at the end of the week for relief, through loss of time, and has the same money given him as the honest labourer receives of his master for his labour for the same week.

In London the authorities were also overwhelmed by the numbers seeking relief, and again there was a feeling that the system was being abused. Samuel Miller, assistant overseer of the parish of St Sepulchre in the City, declared that:

> With respect to the out-door relief, there must, from the very nature of it, be an immense deal of fraud. There is no industry, no inspection, no human skill, which will prevent gross impositions belonging to this mode of relief. By far the greater proportion of our new paupers are persons brought upon the parish by habits in intemperance... After relief has been received at our board, a great proportion of them proceed with the money to the palaces or gin-shops, which abound in the neighbourhood.

The solution appeared to lie in reducing the number of people seeking support from the parish. Financial concerns were complemented by a favourite moral argument of the time – that the receipt of relief was corrupting the independent nature of the poor. To illustrate this, the Commission found a number of parishes where the outdoor relief had either been cut substantially or abolished altogether – and instead there was a proud and independent workforce. One such village was Thurgarton near Southwell in Nottinghamshire, where Assistant Commissioner Cowell noted that:

> The non-intervention of the poor laws constrained them [the labourers] to be habitually provident, thrifty and industrious... I cannot help thinking that had the whole body of labourers throughout England been left alone during the last 40 years – had there been no laws of relief whatever ... no scale nor other similar interventions regulating wages – their general condition would be highly flourishing.

The reason why the parish authorities were able to abolish out-relief was because Thurgarton was both fairly prosperous (it had a long-established savings bank and every family had a garden in which to grow food) and located close to the rapidly growing markets of Nottingham. This was in stark contrast to many overpopulated villages in the south and southwest of Britain.

The other way to reduce the poor rate was to establish workhouses – places to which the poor would be forced to move or face having their relief cut off. The first ones, often called poorhouses or houses of industry, had been established in the late 16th century and they had a significant impact. In Beverley in east Yorkshire, for example, a new workhouse opened in 1727 capable of housing 100 people. A year later the overseers reported that they had given:

> notice to all the Poor that the Weekly Allowances were to cease at Midsummer: that such as were not able to maintain themselves and their families must apply to the governors of the workhouse to be by them provided for. And though before the opening of the house 116 received the parish allowance, not above 8 came in at first and we have never exceeded 26 in the house all this winter.

Particularly during the 18th century many parishes established workhouses of varying degrees of salubriousness. At Gressenhall, in Norfolk, the unemployed from 60 local parishes were placed in a 'house of industry' where they could live and be employed in fruitful labour. Sir Frederick Eden, who visited in 1795, found that the men were either farming the adjoining land or combing wool, dressing flax and hemp and weaving them for use in the house. The women and children (more than half of the 530 inmates were under 14) spun worsted for manufacturers in Norwich. Such a hive of industry sounds encouraging, but the parson and diarist James Woodforde, who visited in 1781, was not impressed: 'a very large building at present tho' there wants another wing. About 380 Poor in it now, but they don't look either happy or cheerful, a greater Number die there, 27 have died since Christmas last.'

By the 1830s most parishes had at least one such building, and the overseers of the poor managed it in their own way. Some were harshly run, but most were organized humanely, at least by later standards. The commissioners appointed in 1832 to investigate the Old Poor Law, for example, were very impressed with the standard of the beer brewed at the workhouse at St Martin's, Reading, Berkshire. However, most were too small to cope with the demands. Most overseers of the poor, however, preferred to support the unemployed outside the workhouse because they cost less to the ratepayers and it was better for them that they continued to live in their cottages.

Theorists such as the Rev. J.T. Becher, who was behind the establishment of what became the Southwell workhouse in Nottinghamshire, argued that workhouses should act as a deterrent to the poor, rather than as a long-term solution. In his pamphlet *The Anti-pauper System* (1828) Becher wrote: 'Let it be remembered that the advantages resulting from a workhouse must arise not from keeping the poor in the house, but from keeping them out of it.'

Influenced by Becher and others, the Commission members had largely made up their minds about what had to be done, even before they met. Critically, they had persuaded themselves that, in the main, those who sought work could find it. This view came not from studying Britain's economy as a whole, but from selected parishes where rigour in the administration of the Poor Law was being practised. They thus concluded that it was relatively easy for men and women whose relief was withdrawn to find other work, noting that: 'One of the most encouraging of the results of our inquiry is the degree to which the existing pauperism arises from fraud, indolence or improvidence.' In 1834 the Commission recommended that outrelief be abolished and all paupers should live in workhouses where conditions were to be worse and more humiliating than to be found outside. This was to become known as 'the workhouse test'. The idea was that the poor would not wish to endure such conditions and would either find gainful employment or turn to charities and each other for support.

The new rules were introduced on 1 June 1835, and their impact was swift. Eight days later the New Poor Law Commission, the department which administered the system, received this petition from nearly a hundred bewildered agricultural labourers from Haverhill:

We the undersignants the poor inhabitants of the parish of Haverhill in the County of Suffolk are in a very low condition through the reduction of wages and for the want of employment which when having employment

17

our wages are from 7 to 8 shillings per week which us with large families are made up to 1s 3d per head per week to support ourselves and family, which out of this small sum we have to find cloths and working tools and to pay from 3 to 4 [£] per year rent for our cottage.

Which it may be considered by you Gentlemen to be a starving condition, therefore we should be very thankful if you could grant us any further assistance, which we have made application to the Gentlemen the Guardians and [visitor of] the parish for more assistance or an order for the workhouse and they refuse us, therefore we apply to your worship to do something for us.

Their petition was ignored. It is not known what happened to most of the petitioners, but it is probable that most of them were soon forced to leave the land in search of work elsewhere.

Mr J. Boreham, vice-chairman of Risbridge Union (which included Haverhill), told a Select Committee of the Poor Law in 1838:

Where the great number of unemployed labourers have gone, or how employed, I cannot imagine… At this time (December [1837]) there is not an able-bodied labourer out of employ nor has there been more than one or two for several months. The parish of Steeple Bumstead had nearly 50 men and boys unemployed. Now, with what have migrated without the interference of the guardians there are not men enough to cultivate the land in that parish.

Those that remained were in a pitiable state. *The Times*, in December 1838, reported that a petition from the Rev. R. Roberts of Haverhill 'and the whole of the gentry and ratepayers of the Union' had been presented to the guardians urging an increase in the out-relief offered to the poor. But the guardians refused, citing orders from the Commissioners in London that forbade 'all out-door relief to the able-bodied labourer, no matter however poignant his and his family's suffering might be'.

The Times also cited the case of Edmund Basham (one of the signatories of the petition of 1835) who was forced through illness to enter with his wife into Haverhill workhouse. His cottage was taken and given to a pauper family with seven children, under decidedly questionable motives. 'A happy thought seemed to strike [the guardians]: "we will put them into

Basham's cottage and force Basham in here and this man and his family will be off our hands".' The correspondent noted that Basham had worked hard for 30 years and had never received any parish assistance.

Charles Dickens wrote that the alternatives were 'of being starved by a gradual process in the house or by a quick one out of it'. Many preferred to beg, borrow or steal, or simply to expire in some wretched room in the East End, as did 69-year-old William May, a former sailor. May was found dead and very emaciated in December 1842. He had recently fled a workhouse, shouting: 'They want to kill me.' Asked to return, he had replied, 'No, it is of no use, as I should have nothing but porridge, porridge for breakfast, porridge for drink.'

Respectable artisans such as Joseph Gutteridge, a silk weaver and free-thinker from Coventry, refused to have anything to do with the Poor Law and the shame it brought. Thrown out of work, he and his young family were close to starvation: 'I was severely blamed that I did not apply to the parish for relief, but I would rather have died from sheer starvation than, being so young, have degraded myself by making such an application.'

A decade after the introduction of the New Poor Law, *The Times* continued to report outbreaks of the burning of ricks and other property belonging to farmers in Norfolk and Suffolk, which its correspondent attributed to the workhouse. He asked a labourer what was the cause of the fires, and he replied: 'If there had been no Union, in my opinion there would have been no fires, and everybody says the same that I hear. The Union distresses people and drives them mad.' Many out-of-work labourers refused to enter the workhouse, and those who tried were defeated by the need to get a ticket signed by local farmers indicating that they could not employ the individual.

Friedrich Engels was undoubtedly right when, in 1844, he described the authors of the 1834 Poor Law report as wishing 'to force the poor into the Procrustean bed of their preconceived doctrines. To do this they treated the poor with incredible savagery.'

Historians have pointed out that the New Poor Law was largely designed to solve the problems of over-population in rural parishes south of the Wash. It had less relevance in the industrial north. This lay behind the considerable opposition to the establishment of Poor Law Unions in the north, where they were seen as an attack on the poor and their rights. Many parishes here had already adopted the workhouse as a deterrent to the idle and dissolute. Others made relief to the able-bodied dependent on the performance of tasks. In Huddersfield, for example, paupers in the workhouse were employed in street cleaning. One of the leaders of the protests, Richard Oastler, wrote in the *Northern Star* in 1838 that 'the real object of [the New Poor Law] ... is to lower wages and punish poverty as a crime. Remember also that children and parents are lying frequently in the same Bastille without seeing one another or knowing the other's fate.'

There were also regional differences in social conditions: the poor in the north were more independent and relatively wealthy compared with their cousins in the south and the midlands. The poor rate was also lower in the north. The Huddersfield historian Hilary Marland suggests that this was due in part to the large number of voluntary organizations and friendly societies (which supported men out of employment), and a greater tendency for the poor to rely on druggists and quacks for medical treatment.

Rich man, poor man, beggar man, thief

The Victorian middle and upper classes were fond of quoting the biblical phrase that the 'poor are always with us'. And indeed they were. Novelists such as Charles Dickens and Thomas Hardy described their lives for middle-class readers. Although Benjamin Disraeli in *Sybil* (1845) wrote of the polarization of rich and poor: 'Two nations between whom there is no intercourse and no sympathy; who are ignorant of each other's habits, thoughts and feelings, as if they were dwellers in different zones or inhabitants of different planets', actually the poor were a highly-visible problem that the middle classes could not ignore. Labourers toiled in every field and every factory, almost every household had its share of half-starved servant girls, and the streets teemed with men and women with no means of support. It was obvious who they were by the clothes they wore. Before exploring the slums of the East End for a book, the American writer and radical Jack London had to change into tattered clothing: 'No sooner was I out on the streets than I was impressed by the difference in status effected by my clothes. All servility vanished from the demeanour of the common people with whom I came in contact... My frayed and out-at-elbows jacket was the badge and advertisement of my class, which was their class.'

And there were so many of them. The Victorian social investigator Seebohm Rowntree found that 30 per cent of the population of York at the end of the 19th century lived below what he called the 'poverty line'. He divided them into rather judgemental categories of 'primary poverty', (that is, 'families whose total earnings are insufficient to obtain the minimum necessaries for the maintenance of merely physical efficiency'), and 'secondary poverty', (that is 'families whose total earnings would be sufficient for the maintenance of merely physical efficiency were it not that some expenditure of it is absorbed by other expenditure either useful or wasteful'). A decade earlier Charles Booth had found much the same proportion under the 'poverty line' in the East End of London.

In explaining why a country as rich as England should have so much poverty, the Victorians tended to ignore economic reasons in favour of psychological ones. The historian G.D.H. Cole argued that the Victorian philanthropist's weakness (and it applied just as much to Poor Law theorists) lay in a tendency to look 'much less at the causes than the effects'. The poor were poor, it was argued, because of character defects. Those who wanted to improve could do so by following the examples of the men in Samuel Smiles' *Self-Help*, whose chief object was 'to stimulate youths to apply themselves diligently to the right pursuits ... and to rely upon their own efforts in life, rather than depend upon the help or patronage of others'.

Such a view permeates the whole debate about the poor, who they were and what could – or should – be done with them. As early as 1788 one of the local guardians, Edward Parry, wrote a report on Gressenhall workhouse in Norfolk for the Society for Bettering the Conditions of the Poor, in which he considered the adult inmates to be 'profligate men who through idleness and debauchery ... [had] reduced their families to depend on the establishment for their support'. Little had changed a hundred years later, when Charles Booth, in his 1889 survey of admissions to the Stepney workhouse, blamed drink (an eighth of admissions), immorality and laziness, as well as old age and sickness, as causes. He added: 'Unwillingness to work is closely connected with self-indulgence in other ways and there is no known cure except the pressure of "neither shall he eat".'

The problem was not the indolent and feckless nature of the working classes, but an economic system which produced both huge unemployment and underemployment. Not until the First World War was there full employment – for the first time. As a result, it was difficult, even for the hard-working and the motivated, to earn enough to keep body and soul together. It was not uncommon to be thrown out of work or suffer some other calamity, such as illness in the family, which started the downward spiral to the workhouse. And once there, it became increasingly difficult to return to normal life.

An endemic problem was underemployment. Labouring work, whether on the land or in towns, was irregular and depended on the seasons and the fickleness of the British weather. A bad winter would throw thousands onto the street, as women could no longer pick vegetables in the fields and men were unable to find temporary labouring jobs. As Mayhew realized: 'In almost all occupations there is … a superfluity of labourers and this alone would tend to render the employment of a vast number of the hands of a casual rather than a regular character.'

Most poor people undertook a variety of different jobs in order to make ends meet. In his study of 18th-century beggars, Tim Hitchcock argues that men, women and children, as well as begging on the streets, sought to keep heads above water by 'selling ballads or their bodies, by working as shoe blacks and chimney sweeps, cinder sifters and errand boys, as criers and hawkers, sellers of mackerel and cabbage nets'. Inevitably, they also sought support from charities and the Poor Law, although this was met with fury when they were caught.

In his report to the Poor Law Commission for 1838, Mr Tufnell, the Assistant Commissioner for Kent and Sussex, noted:

> I am disposed to think that the poorer classes are more frequently above the charity of the rich than the latter imagine, and that this arises from the impossibility of detecting the numerous sources of income that are enjoyed by the labourer, besides the simple receipt of the money wages of the head of the family which are usually all that are taken into account and what is not seen is supposed not to exist. While the Uckfield labourers were supposed to be starving, they were dancing at 2s 6d per head.

Not all workhouse inmates were innocent victims, of course. The institution could provide protection for petty criminals on the run. 'The Indoor Pauper' said that in his workhouse there were a number of professional thieves, 'at the bottom of their profession as a rule', who sought 'the house' to avoid the police, or when their victims became aware that they were being preyed upon.

Employment was often a seasonal phenomenon, in town as well as in the country. Even in a normal year there was a huge pool of men who could be employed on a casual basis, day by day, in the ports of Liverpool and London or in factories elsewhere. On good days good money might be earned, but for most families bad weeks were the norm. As a result, city streets were full of shabby men looking for work, referred to as 'loafers' or 'shirkers' by the gainfully employed middle classes. Many were too weak – through near starvation or the ill-effects of drink – to earn much, except the odd tip for carrying a bag or hailing a taxi. From such people inevitably came the truly destitute men and women who ended up in the workhouse.

Guarding the guardians

The workhouse was the most public face of the Poor Law, where both central government and 680 or so local Poor Law Unions had separate responsibilities. The 1834 Royal Commission on the Poor Law recommended:

> The appointment of a central board to control the administration of the poor laws ... empowered and directed to frame and enforce regulations for the government of workhouses, and as to the nature and amount of relief to be given and the labour to be enacted in them, and that such regulations shall, as far as may be practicable, be uniform throughout the country.

The result was the creation of the Poor Law Commission, which was replaced in due course by the Poor Law Board (1847–71), the Local Government Board (1871–1919) and the Ministry of Health (1919 until the Poor Law was abolished). Their duties were to administer the legislation, particularly the Poor Law Amendment Act of 1834, and to ensure paupers across England and Wales were treated in as equal way as possible. (Scotland and Ireland had separate Poor Law systems.)

The Commissioners (and their successors) did not have a good reputation at the time, and it has not improved in hindsight. The social reformers Sidney and Beatrice Webb saw the Local Government Board as being a reactionary body concerned only to preserve the anachronistic principles of the New Poor Law, and more recent writers, such as the academic Christine Bellamy, have viewed it in a similar light. Its predecessors were not much better, particularly after Edwin Chadwick, the dynamic force behind the introduction of the New Poor Law, was forced to resign in the wake of the Andover scandal.

The prevailing complacent attitude is perhaps best summed up by the evidence given by William Lumley, legal secretary to the Poor Law Board, to the Carnarvon Committee on Conditions in Prisons in 1870. In a statement which bore little resemblance to the reality experienced by most paupers, he said the workhouse inmate was 'generally far too comfortable to prefer going to gaol, where he would be kept to hard labour for a certain time. There is good clothing, there is a warm building and there is attendance in case of any illness; and there is generally speaking some consort and companionship with acquaintances and neighbours.'

Particularly in the days of the Commission and the Poor Law Board, the number of staff was small and their workload prodigious. In 1844 the Poor Law Commission had an establishment of three secretaries, nine assistant commissioners (inspectors) and 31 clerks. By 1864 this had risen to 43 clerks, 12 inspectors and four secretaries. Judging by the surviving correspondence at the National Archives, most letters, often raising complicated points of Poor Law administration, seemed to have been answered almost by return of post. Huge volumes of reports were prepared annually for Parliament, general orders were issued to local Poor Law Unions and inspectors dispatched to investigate potential scandals.

The primary task of the Commission and its successors was the direction of local Poor Law Unions through the issue of orders, through correspondence and by inspection. At its core were the reams of orders and instructions for the Poor Law Unions to follow, ranging from the food to be served at breakfast and the size of cells for vagrants to the treatment to be provided in unusual cases which might present themselves to the guardians. These orders were supposed to be read out at board meetings of the guardians and then implemented. Often, however, they were ignored unless they were considered too important to disregard, or unless a particularly conscientious clerk to the guardians saw to their implementation.

In theory at least, every eventuality was covered. Guides for guardians and Poor Law officials were published which summarized the legislation and the orders that accompanied it. However, in practice the number of letters seeking guidance on particular cases received by the Commissioners and their successors shows that the books can have been little consulted.

In turn, Whitehall at times attempted to 'micro-manage' the affairs of individual boards of guardians. In 1861 and 1879, for example, objections were raised to the request of the guardians of Ludlow in Shropshire to change the day on which they met in order to suit the guardians from outlying villages. And in the late 1850s the Poor Law Board expended considerable effort in order to recover 2s 4d misspent by an officer of the Manchester Union.

Much of our knowledge of the operation of the New Poor Law comes from the tightly bound volumes of correspondence found in series MH 12 at the National Archives. Only letters from individual unions survive; unfortunately, the replies and correspondence after 1900 were lost during the Blitz. Individual boards of guardians, or their clerks, sought advice on difficult cases, returned surveys and requested the approval to recruit (or dismiss) staff. Scribbled draft replies can often be found on the letters: proposals to deviate from the principles of 'less eligibility' were normally quashed, as were ideas about spending ratepayers' money on fripperies; attempts to involve Whitehall in local disputes were brushed aside, and occasionally sound advice was offered on best practice at other unions. In 1871, for example, the Southwell Union wanted to send a pauper family to Canada, but did not know how. The Board in London suggested the clerk approach his colleagues in Sunderland.

The most public form of control came through the Assistant Poor Law Commissioners (later Poor Law Inspectors and Local Government Inspectors), who were the link between Whitehall and individual Poor Law Unions. They were very much the eyes and ears of central government, as well as being the public representatives of it to a much greater extent than such inspectors are expected to be today. Considerable interest was taken in their background and circumstances. The Treasury recommended, in the

1850s, that the inspectors should be worldly-wise and experienced in life; a career was to be discouraged, and appointments were to be made at a salary level which attracted gentlemen. In 1872 James Stansfield, the first President of the Local Government Board, said that he wanted inspectors to be 'men of experience and of tact, accustomed to deal with men, knowing the boards of guardians and having their confidence'. Appointment was generally for life. In 1906 Chief Inspector J.S. Davy was in his thirty-sixth year of service, and in earlier generations both Sir John Walsham and Andrew Doyle spent over thirty years in post. Most had previously been lawyers or came from the landed gentry. However, there were some exceptions: Andrew Doyle (1809–88) had edited *The Times* in the early 1840s and Herbert Preston Thomas (1841–1909) was a pioneering mountaineer and the writer of a popular Edwardian ballad, 'The Cricketer's Carol'.

The work itself could be arduous and individual inspectors were often overworked. Initially there were only nine to cover the whole of England and Wales. One inspector might be responsible for unions in half-a-dozen counties. Generally, they seem to have been a very conscientious body of men (the first women were not appointed until the 1890s, and then only to supervise the schooling of workhouse children). Andrew Doyle, for example, pioneered work on statistics, and his reports were supported by pages of tabulated figures. In a less regulated age, the collection of statistics from farmers was not popular, and when Doyle tried to obtain them from Denbighshire and Shropshire in 1854, many of the forms were burnt. One farmer cut his in pieces and returned it endorsed: 'The idea of such questions. What next!'

The inspectors' main duty was to inspect individual workhouses and report back their findings to the Commissioners in London and the guardians themselves. They were supposed to visit annually, but smaller workhouses were inevitably inspected less frequently.

As their visits were arranged in advance, it was generally possible to present the house in the best possible light. Often the inspector was accompanied by the master and the guardians, which made it difficult for staff, let alone the pauper inmates, to make complaints. In the mid-1860s there were a number of scandals involving the appalling conditions in workhouse sick wards or infirmaries. Poor Law Inspectors were asked to conduct public inquiries. Some of the worst conditions were found at Rotherhithe in south-east London. Matilda Beeton (a nurse at the Rotherhithe Infirmary) was sufficiently appalled to complain to the Poor Law Board. In 1866 she wrote to the Poor Law Inspector Harry Farnall (who conducted the subsequent investigation) that she remembered his visit to the infirmary:

> When there, you asked me about the nursing, the food and other
> things; I think you will recollect I gave you the most favourable answers.
> In this I know I was doing wrong towards you, but I now confess to you
> I was afraid to tell the truth of things to you, through the master being
> with you...
>
> As soon as the Poor Law Inspector passes through the lodge it is
> known all over the house, and one has to run one way and one the other
> to hide such things as perhaps you might want to see; this is done by
> the master's orders and he engages your attention perhaps only for a
> few minutes; this I witnessed on more than one occasion.

The inspectors also advised individual boards of guardians, investigated cases of abuse and prepared reports on a wide range of subjects from vagrancy to the provision of workhouse schools. Perhaps their most difficult task was to persuade local guardians to spend money on improving conditions in the workhouse, particularly when it came to large capital expenditure.

They had few powers of compulsion. Herbert Preston Thomas, who was an inspector in East Anglia and then the southwest in the 1890s, stated bluntly that the only remedy he possessed to deal with inadequate practice was the sledgehammer of sacking the officers.

Where the union chose to ignore the inspector, there was little he could do about it. The master at Rotherhithe grumbled to Matilda Beeton that: 'It's all very well for Mr Farnall to say this is right and the other wrong, but the board do not bind themselves to act up to his suggestions, or they might not have anything else to do.' Indeed, in his report on the scandal at Rotherhithe, Inspector Harry Farnall reproduced the comments he had entered in the visitors' book on 2 January 1865:

> I have this day inspected the workhouse; the house is in precisely the
> same state of cleanliness and order as usual, but I am obliged to add that
> the house is in the same state as regards its defects; these defects I have

frequently pointed out to the guardians, and a reference to the last report written in this book will point out to the guardians what those defects are.

Five years earlier he had written to the Poor Law Board: 'I wish, and very earnestly wish, that I had the power to persuade the guardians to build a new workhouse for this important and rapidly improving parish.'

The people behind the boards

Direct control over the workhouse was exercised by the Poor Law Union. There were 583 individual Poor Law Unions, each made up of a number of parishes which were combined to administer the poor law locally, plus a hundred independent Gilbert Unions (that is, Poor Law authorities that predated the New Poor Law). The unions covered very diverse areas, ranging from rural ones such as Rhayader in mid Wales or Southwell, where a few employees cared for a small number of elderly paupers, to urban Manchester or Poplar in London's East End, which ran an extensive range of institutions including orphanages and infirmaries, looked after thousands of people and employed hundreds of staff, from firemen to matrons.

These Poor Law Unions were a new departure for British administration. The number of parishes within a union varied – in rural areas there could be a dozen or more. Both Mitford and Launditch (Gressenhall) Union in Norfolk and Southwell Union in Nottinghamshire were made up of 60 parishes. In large cities, on the other hand, only two or three parishes might be combined into a union. Poplar was thus made up of Poplar, Blackwall, Bromley and Stratford-by-Bow parishes.

The unions were largely set up between 1834 and 1838 by the Assistant Poor Law Commissioners in association with local landowners and magistrates. The ideal was to have a market town surrounded by smaller rural parishes, which meant it would be easy for paupers and, more importantly, the guardians to get to the workhouse. Bishop's Stortford Union on the borders of Hertfordshire and Essex, for example, consisted of the small town of Bishop's Stortford itself and ten surrounding rural parishes.

In many places local politics intervened to prevent this, particularly the interests of the landed gentry. In Northamptonshire, the Assistant Poor

Law Commissioner Richard Earle drew up the boundaries to suit local magnates. The odd boundaries of the Potterspury Union resulted from lobbying by the Duke of Grafton for all the lands that formed his estate to be the basis of the union.

The unions were managed by boards of guardians, elected by the rate-payers. Each parish sent a number of guardians in proportion to the size of its population, and in many ways they provided a buffer between the central-izing tendencies of Whitehall and the forthright localism that still pervaded local government. Guardians relied on central government for advice about the administration of the Poor Law, but they were not above ignoring, or delaying implementation of, policy laid down by the centre when it suited them. They had much more say over conditions generally and the treat-ment of individual paupers than lay officials have today. The greatest of all workhouse scandals, the one at Andover, was eventually exposed by one of the guardians, Hugh Mundy.

In rural areas the guardians were largely farmers. In Ludlow in 1860, 22 members of the board farmed the land locally, supplemented by six Anglican clergymen, six gentlemen, two lawyers and an auctioneer. In urban areas the guardians were usually tradesmen and small businessmen. George Lansbury, a Socialist politician and one of the first guardians with working-class roots, noted in his autobiography that his fellow Poplar guardians, when he was first elected in 1893, were 'delegates of interests – house agents representing slum landlords or representatives of the dock companies… But most of them were small tradesmen – milkmen, chemists, builders and so on.'

For many ambitious young men and women, serving as a guardian became a convenient way to learn the political ropes before moving onto greater things. The Royal Commission of 1906, which conducted an exten-sive if inconclusive review into the working of the poor laws, was told: 'Many men simply become guardians as a stepping stone to the town council; they wish to gain confidence in speaking and use the boardroom as a prac-tising ground… They are often ignorant and indifferent and stand for other reasons than their knowledge or interest in the poor.'

Until 1894 a property qualification ensured that only reasonably wealthy residents could be elected to the board – the very ones who would benefit most from keeping the poor rate low. After 1894 all adult men and women were eligible for election, provided they paid the poor rate, and this development saw the transformation of many unions, with an increasing number of women and working-class men elected as guardians. The first woman guardian was Martha Merrington in Kensington, London, in 1875, but it was nearly a decade before another woman joined a board of guardians. By 1893 there were 159 women guardians; two years later the number had risen to 875. The arrival of women guardians naturally sparked a mixed reaction among their male colleagues. Some, such as George Bartley, a guardian in Ealing, London, during the 1860s and 1870s, welcomed their arrival in his manual for new guardians, published in 1876: 'It is obvious that a woman even if she has intelligence and education but up to the average standard of a Guardian can inspect many details and quickly see defects which a body of men might overlook for years.' But old attitudes die hard, and as late as 1907 the vice-chairman of Belford Union in Northumberland was complaining to the Local Government Board that women were 'better at home looking after their own work'.

Perhaps of equal importance was the arrival of working-class representatives on boards of guardians. In the 1880s the 'Indoor Pauper' had called for such a development: 'Men who have relatives and former comrades in the house would unquestionably keep a sharp eye on abuses likely to pain their friends and still sharper eye upon them if they felt they themselves were ever likely to "come to the Union".' Two of the earliest were George Lansbury, a veneer-dryer, and Will Crooks, the son of a ship's stoker who had himself spent some time in Poplar workhouse as a child. Both were leading London Socialists and were elected to the Poplar board of guardians in 1893. They stood in order to moderate the effects of the Poor Law on the sick and needy among their neighbours. As Lansbury put it: 'I determined to fight for one policy only, and that was decent treatment for the poor outside the workhouse, and hang the rates.' Another pioneer was Amos Sherriff, who was elected as a guardian in Leicester in 1901. Born in 1856, he had grown up in extreme poverty before becoming a Salvationist, an active member of the Labour Party and a cycle-shop owner.

As guardians, both women and working-class men sought to introduce better conditions in the workhouse. Within six months of her appointment as a Poor Law guardian in Chorlton, Manchester, suffragette Mrs Emmeline Pankhurst had introduced comfortable Windsor chairs with high backs for the elderly to sit on and had made changes to both diet and dress. The bread was cut into slices and buttered with margarine, each person being allowed to eat as much as they desired, the surplus being made into puddings with milk and currants. She chose new material for dresses and bonnets for the girls and women, and she was also successful in persuading the guardians to allow the inmates to go for outings in their own clothes, rather than the degrading workhouse uniforms.

Similar reforms were initiated in Poplar, where pauper clothing was abolished, an improved diet introduced and greater freedoms introduced for inmates. Local officials who mistreated the inmates were either disciplined or pensioned off. In Lansbury's words, 'we revolutionised the place from top to bottom'. Even so, when Jack London spent two nights there in 1902, he found that the workhouse, although better than its neighbours, was still bleak and unwelcoming.

Where there were only one or two women or working-class men on a board, they might have a hard time persuading the other guardians that reforms were necessary. In Leicester, Amos Sherriff led a vocal campaign against the fact that any man in receipt of poor relief was automatically disenfranchised for a year. Instead of accepting bread, he urged the unemployed to demand that the guardians should provide land and workshops where men could earn a living wage. But as Labour was always in a minority on the board, Sheriff was usually frustrated in his ambitions.

In Chorlton, fierce exchanges took place between Mrs Pankhurst and the diehards among the guardians, chief among whom was a boot merchant named Mainwaring. When he realized that his outbursts of rudeness were helping 'the charming Mrs. Pankhurst' to win supporters to her side, he tried to control himself by writing 'Keep your temper!' on the blotting paper in front of him.

However sympathetic they were to the paupers in the workhouse, the new guardians could be as harsh as anyone else on those they deemed to be 'scroungers'. Miss Augusta Brown, a guardian in Camberwell, south London, was asked in 1895 whether women were not too emotional for Poor Law work. She replied that, on the contrary, they were 'not sympathetic enough;

they are too hard and severe, especially to their own sex'. And in his election addresses, George Lansbury regularly called for labour colonies 'for the repression of the habitual casual and repression of the loafer'.

The most important figure in the union was the chairman. Often these men were in post for many years and inevitably gained great influence and expertise. In Congleton in 1857 Randle Wilbraham succeeded his father as chairman, who had been 20 years in the chair. Wilbraham junior in turn served 28 years.

Some were less prepossessing. Joseph Rogers described the chairman of the Strand Union in London in 1854 as being the proprietor of a cookshop, who would 'often come to the house on a Sunday morning dressed in the greasy jacket in which he had been serving *à-la-mode* beef the night before, and unshaven and unshorn he would go into the chapel with the pauper inmates and afterwards go to the Boardroom and had breakfast with the master and matron'.

At the centre of the Andover workhouse scandal of 1847 was the chairman of the guardians, the Rev. Christopher Dodson, rector of Gateley and Penton Mawsey in Hampshire. He dominated meetings of the board with his sarcastic tongue and a bullying manner. Dodson was a popular figure locally because he kept the poor rate low, largely through economies in the workhouse which drove its inmates close to starvation. He also appointed a succession of workhouse masters who proved mostly unsuitable, including Colin McDougal, whose cruelty to the inmates caused a national scandal.

Other chairmen were more sympathetic towards staff and inmates. Joseph Cropper was chairman of Kendal, Cumbria, for nearly 40 years from 1853. Showing decidedly non-Victorian self-doubt, he noted in his diary for April 1873:

> I was in the workhouse again on Friday; just the usual round, and the poor old men and crooning old women and the poor little half-orphaned babies, and bewildered or senseless imbeciles, and the nurse and her cares, and the matron and her contracts for flour and tea, and discussion of servants' behaviour, and the porter's lodge and the vagrant list. I go through it and go through it again, and wonder if I help and if I shall do this and no better work for them or for others, onto the end.

And even after he had left the board, his obituarist noted that on Sundays he would often return to the Poor Law Infirmary 'and anything graphic or stirring was saved to be read aloud on these occasions'.

The guardians met fortnightly, usually in a boardroom at the work-house. A typical workhouse boardroom was described by one observer in the 1860s as being 'a mixture of an Old Bailey court, a small chapel and a third class railway waiting room'. At each meeting the guardians heard reports from the workhouse master, the relieving officer and other officials, and received circulars from Whitehall. They might also interview individ-ual paupers who sought admission or discharge from the workhouse, or discipline those who had caused trouble. Other matters the guardians might want to discuss were the refurbishment of the 'house', setting the poor rate, auditing the union's accounts and non-Poor Law issues, such as the registration of births, marriages and deaths.

There were two matters on which the guardians were notoriously reluc-tant to spend money, despite proddings by Whitehall: buildings and staff. Even minor capital expenditure might be resisted. In the 1920s it took three years for the local Poor Law Inspector to persuade Belford Union to install a telephone, despite its obvious usefulness.

There were often attempts to reduce the pay of the professional officers or to offer new recruits less than the going rate. In 1850, for example, Ludlow guardians tried to cut the wages of the workhouse staff by a fifth in recog-nition of 'the great and general distress under which the agricultural parishes of the Union suffer'. The Poor Law Board disagreed, saying that if wages were cut any lower, they would be unattractive to candidates of the required calibre. The policy of low wages meant that workhouses were often unable to keep good staff and were reduced to employing unsatisfactory men and women.

Another contentious issue was contracting out for the supply of goods to the workhouse, from which a great deal of money could be made by the guardians and their friends. It is clear that this involved much petty corruption, and it was indeed endemic throughout the Poor Law system. George Lansbury noted of the Poplar guardians that 'their ... worst object was merely a trivial corruption over minor contracts. "You scratch my back and I'll scratch yours" was the kind of policy where jobs and contracts were concerned.'

Occasionally guardians might appropriate workhouse property and services for their own good. At Kensington, the guardians in February 1871 were found to have ordered and consumed alcoholic beverages at dinners after board meetings for which they only paid a nominal amount. Across London in Islington, in December 1889, Mr Furlong, the vice-chairman of the Islington guardians, was accused of stealing 'old rags and other refuse' and using workhouse labour to decorate his house, including one pauper Rogers 'who was an artist, painting screens and pictures in the Lavatory'.

The guardians had little training for the responsibilities they held. Few, at least until the 1890s, gave any thought to the underlying causes of poverty. Most shared the view that paupers had largely ended up in the workhouse through their own fault and that there was a rigorous need to discourage pauperism. Nevertheless, this attitude could sometimes be tempered by humanity towards individual paupers.

The guardians' amateurishness was revealed in many ways, not least their dilatory consideration of the cases of paupers brought before them. The 1906 Royal Commission was concerned that 'even when relief is given to the right people, it is too often inadequate in nature and ill adapted to the particular needs of the case'. Ill-informed idiosyncrasies might also result in interference in the work of the professionals they employed. In Norfolk, for example, guardians objected to having maps in the schoolrooms, since geographical knowledge might lead to emigration and a diminution of the reserve of labour that was useful to farmers at harvest time. In the 1840s other guardians elsewhere in the county were concerned about putting the 'torch of knowledge into the hand of the rick-burners' – an ability to read radical publications might provoke further disturbances in an unsettled countryside.

Guardians had a reputation for being unimaginative and mean-spirited that is not entirely deserved. Although many were primarily concerned to keep the poor rate as low as possible, most were also keen to help the men, women and families in their care. Their greatest limitations, perhaps, were an inability to understand the broader causes of pauperism and a lack of power to alleviate poverty in any significant way.

Keeping out of the workhouse

The Poor Law was not the only help available to the destitute; indeed, it was designed to be the last resort. There were alternatives for men and women in temporary difficulties, or for those regarded as respectable (for it was almost as easy for the middle classes to drift into financial difficulties as their poorer cousins).

At a very basic level, friends, neighbours and work colleagues might have a whip-round to help a family in temporary financial trouble. Many observers agreed with Friedrich Engels, who, in the 1840s, said that 'although workers cannot afford to give to charity on the same scale as the middle class, they are nevertheless more charitable in every way'. Sixty years later, the Rev. William Conybeare claimed that it was 'largely the kindness of poor to poor which stands between our current civilisation and revolution'.

Short-term loans could be arranged from pawnbrokers by pawning a handkerchief or an overcoat. It was a staple of many working-class budgets. Alison Backhouse's study of the pledgebook of George Fette, a York pawnbroker in the 1770s, suggests that many of his customers were regulars who pledged small items of bedding or clothing twice a week. And Robert Roberts, the author of *The Classic Slum*, noted that, at a local pawnbroker in Salford in the early years of the 20th century: 'Housewives after washday on Monday pledged what clean clothes could be spared until weekend and returned with cash to buy food.' The items would be redeemed on Saturday nights, so that the family would be dressed in some respectability on the Sabbath.

Shops might be persuaded to offer goods on account for regular customers in temporary difficulties. This was one service which street-corner shops offered that the high-street stores would not, although there was always the risk to the shopkeeper that a customer would default. Robert Robert's mother ran one such shop and sometimes grumbled that she was in effect a banker to the community. But if she had not done this, her customers would have gone elsewhere.

Even the poorest families could share a meagre meal. On a harsh winter's day in Poplar, Will Crooks, the pioneering working-class guardian, came upon the following scene in a slum court:

On the muddy ground in the far corner a woman sat weeping. 'She ain't been living here long, Mr Crooks,' volunteered another woman from her doorstep. 'Her husband's no work, and this morning she were a-sending her four children to school without a bite, so I calls 'em in here and shared out wot we was having for breakfast.' [A loaf was shared between the two families.]

I'm proud of the poor... And I declare it's a dirty insult for outsiders to say that these people are degraded by the feeble efforts I make as a guardian to give bread to the hungry. It's nothing to what they do for each other. That woman sharing her bread is typical of what you'll find in every street and corner of Poplar, where the pinch of hunger is felt.

Most working-class men were members of a friendly society through which, for a few pence a week, you would receive benefits in a period of unemployment or sickness. At the height of the movement, in 1901, just over half the adult male population of England and Wales were members of societies such as the Ancient Order of Foresters, the Oddfellows or the temperance Rechabites. Even a century earlier a third, probably more, were members. Membership was not just the privilege of the more prosperous working class; most societies had unskilled or poorly paid members.

Towards the end of the 19th century, societies typically charged weekly premiums of between fourpence and sixpence for basic sickness and burial benefits. These were amounts that a man in regular employment could afford without great difficulty, but which might well be out of reach for those without jobs or in sporadic employment. Such men found it difficult to maintain regular payments and would thus lose any benefits they might have accrued from membership.

Some succumbed to petty theft to make ends meet, stealing goods from shops and pawning them. The starving Joseph Gutteridge was sorely tempted: 'One morning I stood before a baker's shop where the loaves were temptingly exposed, and never in my life was I so near becoming a thief. The impulse to procure a piece of bread for my starving wife and children was so strong that I could scarcely resist.' Fortunately, the landlord of a neighbouring pub took pity on him and gave him threepence for beer, but Gutteridge again resisted temptation and spent the money on a loaf.

Another alternative was to seek help from a charity. To the Victorians, there were few social ills that could not be cured by a healthy dose of philanthropy. The historian Frank Prochaska has remarked: 'No country on earth can lay claim to a greater philanthropic tradition than Great Britain. Until the twentieth century, philanthropy was widely believed to be the most wholesome and reliable remedy for the nation's ills.' The 1906 Royal Commission on the Poor Law acknowledged:

> No one can have taken part in an enquiry such as ours without being impressed … by the multitude and variety of voluntary organisations established for ameliorating the condition of the poor, the large sums which pass through their hands and the amount of time and effort devoted to them by a veritable army of charitable workers.

The poor had a bewildering choice of charities from which to seek assistance. The social reformer Frederick D'Aeth conducted a survey of Liverpool's charities in 1909 and found 357 bodies, of which just over 300 were engaged in some sort of welfare activity. Although Liverpool was historically particularly well provided for, a glance through any trade or street directory will produce details of dozens of charities in every town, which gave grants and pensions to the poor. Assistance ranged from almshouses to bread and coals for poor widows and small payments to the temporarily destitute and their families.

A generation earlier, in Lambeth, London, there were at least 57 mothers' meetings, 36 temperance societies for children, 25 savings banks or penny banks, 24 Christian endeavour societies, 21 boot, coal, blanket or clothing clubs, and two maternity societies. There were 16 nurses and two part-time doctors, as well as a part-time dentist, who attended the poor, in addition to those sponsored by the provident dispensaries which were closely linked to the churches. Furthermore, there were two 'servants' registries, two lodging registries, two 'industrial societies' which employed women at needlework, one burial guild, one convalescent home, one hostel for the dying, one invalid kitchen, cripples' classes, a children's play school, a day nursery, a 'prostitutes' institute', several libraries and dozens of Sunday schools – in addition to the extensive work of extra-parochial and transdenominational organizations. Almost half the Nonconformist chapels and all the Anglican parishes in the borough also provided relief to the poor in cash or kind.

The geographical distribution of charities, particularly those which attempted to help the very poor, was random. They were concentrated in the older cathedral cities and market towns, with fewer in the newer industrial towns of the midlands and the north. In rural areas, the Anglican parish priest was the first person to whom those in trouble turned.

Charities were also particular about whom they supported. They were there to help the 'deserving poor', that is those who were industrious but had fallen on hard times through no fault of their own, for whom a small grant, loan or donation of bread or coals would, it was felt, help the applicant become self-sufficient again. They were not there to help the indolent 'undeserving', who by definition were fit for nothing but the workhouse. In *Pygmalion* George Bernard Shaw has fun with this concept, when Alfred Doolittle says:

> I am one of the undeserving poor: that's what I am. Think of all that means to a man. It means that he's up agen middle class morality all the time… It's always the same story: 'you are undeserving: so you can't have it.'… I don't need less than a deserving man: I need more. I don't eat less hearty than him; and I drink a lot more… Well they charge me just the same for everything as they charge the deserving.

William Grisewood, secretary of Liverpool's Central Relief Society, spoke for many when he argued that 'the persons aided by the Society belonged to a stratum just above the pauper class, and this is still in measure true, our aim being to prevent, when possible, the indigent from sinking into that class'.

The charities wanted to help people who would benefit quickly (and gratefully) from support, rather than those who might become a drain on resources for many years, or indefinitely. As C.S. Loch, secretary of the Charity Organization Society, said, the question was 'not whether a person was "deserving" or "undeserving", but whether … the distress can be stayed and self-support sustained'.

It is clear that charities helped people who fitted their own perception of the 'deserving poor', such as older Christian men and women or orphaned children of fallen soldiers and sailors. The saying 'cold as charity' reflected the contempt that many people felt for charities and the men and women who ran them. The family of the freethinking Joseph Gutteridge was refused help by a local charity because of his beliefs, or rather lack of them; they were only spared the workhouse – where, ironically, such hypocrisy would have held scant sway, as applicants were judged on their need – by his indignant neighbours.

On the other hand, the system could be abused and not every pauper was a passive recipient of whatever benefits the parish and local charities were prepared to dole out. Those with sharp wits and low cunning could take advantage of the duplication between rival charities and the gullibility of potential donors. For others, this could be the only way to survive. Charles Booth found a widow in the East End who attended every mission hall and every mothers' meeting she could: 'This brings her soup three or four times a week and sometimes a loaf of bread, and so the poor woman keeps her little room and the children with bread.'

It was the regular abuses of charity like this that the Charity Organization Society (COS) was established to combat. Founded in 1869, it sought to structure the way in which charities assessed and investigated those seeking aid and to coordinate the work of other charities. It encouraged local charities to interview applicants rigorously before offering assistance and to cooperate in establishing registers of the local poor, ideally in conjunction with the Poor Law authorities, to ensure that people were not claiming more than they were due. The rigorous methods and arguments of the COS had an impact on many Poor Law guardians in the late 19th century. According to its first secretary, Charles Loch, the Society was committed to the idea that 'to be beneficent, charity should assist adequately, i.e. so as to produce self-help in the recipient'. Unfortunately this message was widely misunderstood, and the Society soon acquired a reputation for pedantic meanness. Its critics, of whom there were many, claimed that its abbreviation stood for 'Cringe or Starve'.

The poor were able to use charities and the Poor Law as part of a survival strategy and it was not hard to work the system when charities and Poor Law authorities did not coordinate their efforts. Long-established charities run by the local church were often an easy touch, since they were not well organized. Speaking to a Poor Law conference in 1901, the Rev. L.R. Phelps, a guardian from Oxford, complained that:

> Charity people are the worst poachers in the world! This is brought home to me when I see them giving money and food to vagrants, encouraging loafers and beggars, relieving the people of the expense and care of their children... These are all, I venture to say, the proper objects of the attention of the guardians.

However easy it might have been, surprisingly few paupers seem to have taken advantage of the opportunities available to manipulate the system. Most were broken down people, struck by ill-health or ill-fortune, who were barely able to look after themselves, let alone mastermind any attempts at deception. In order to survive, they generally preferred to beg in the streets or turn to petty crime. The New Poor Law had truly established the workhouse as a place of last resort, fear of which spread far beyond those forced to experience life inside its walls. It was a reputation that guardians, for the most part, were happy to promote.

CHAPTER TWO

The Life Behind Doors

These prison or bastille sort of surroundings were organised for the purpose of making self-respecting, decent people endure any suffering rather than enter.

George Lansbury, My Life, 1931

WORKHOUSES, known sometimes as 'poorhouses' or 'houses of industry', were not a new concept, though early versions took a variety of forms. Linton in Cambridgeshire had established a 'taske house' as early as 1577, as well as a hospital which occupied part of the village's guild-hall. In 1582 nearby Cambridge proposed to build a 'house to set pore men on works in and of reformation for idle persons'. A few parishes also began to build cottages for the elderly and infirm or inherited them in return for caring for the friendless poor in their old age. In 1623 an Act was passed to encourage the 'erecting of hospitals and working-houses for the Poor' but there was no element of compulsion, let alone standardization, until 1834.

However, the workhouse movement spread during the 18th century, fostered in part by Sir Edward Knatchbull's Act of 1723. This allowed parishes to erect workhouses in which the poor were set to work and to which they were restricted except for Sundays; Knatchbull hoped that it would both reduce the rates and mould the demeanour of those relieved. Some 600 workhouses were established by 1750, most very small – the poor were often looked after in cottages converted for the purpose. At Ashwell in Hertfordshire, for example, the workhouse established as 'a house of good manners, piety, charity and industry' actually housed 12 people. Relief was to be denied to any destitute villager who refused to enter the 'house', while those who did were obliged to sign over their goods, to work and to attend religious services, while being forbidden to leave without the vestry's permission or, indeed, to gossip in the streets.

Gilbert's Act of 1782 (named after Thomas Gilbert, the MP who introduced it) encouraged parishes to unite to build and maintain workhouses to house the old, the sick and the infirm, and so share the cost of poor relief. Able-bodied paupers were explicitly excluded; instead, they were to be provided with either outdoor relief or employment near their own homes. In addition, farmers and other employers were permitted to receive allowances from the parish rates so they could bring wages up to subsistence levels. In many ways the Gilbert Unions, as they were called, were prototypes of the New Poor Law, so it is no surprise that they remained outside the 1834 legislation until 1868.

The spread of workhouses was patchy. In 1777 the county of Cheshire had 31 workhouses, 11 of which were in the vicinity of Macclesfield. At about the same time, the cities of London and Westminster and the county of Middlesex had 86 workhouses, which housed 15,000 paupers in total. St George Hanover Square alone had room for 700 paupers, while rural Hampton Wick looked after just half-a-dozen. Because of precarious finances and poor management many only lasted a few years. Others contracted out their management to private individuals. In 1759 Kingston's Churchwardens and Overseers of the Poor entered into an agreement with a merchant tailor of London, who undertook to provide food, fuel, clothes, medical care and other necessities to the inmates, to bury the dead and to provide food for poor apprentices. In return he was to receive £420 per year.

From almshouse to workhouse

In part, the Poor Law supplemented private provision made through almshouses, established through the wills of rich merchants and aristocrats to care for the elderly. In the Derbyshire village of Etwall, for example, Sir John Parr left money in 1577 for a hospital to care for the 'poor, needy and impotent' of the village. The earliest of these charitable institutions, such as the Great Hospital in Winchester, dated from the 11th century, and they continued to be founded up until the early 20th century. A few were large establishments, such as the Charterhouse in the City of London, which housed 80 'gentlemen', but most were small, looking after only a handful of men or women perceived to be of irreproachable character. Like work-houses, almshouses were scattered at random across the landscape. Some places, such as Richmond in Surrey, had half a dozen, while the neigh-bouring – and much more important – town of Kingston had only one almshouse. It was built in 1669, in memory of the merchant William Cleeve, for 'six poor men and six poor women of honest life and reputation'.

In all but the most affluent towns, however, the parochial poorhouse cared for the majority of parishioners who were unable to help themselves. The workhouse environment varied greatly. In well-run workhouses where there was no overcrowding, the elderly and the infirm must have been treated almost as if they were at home. In 1797 Frederick Eden found St Mary's Reading 'a comfortable and convenient lodging for the Poor, but not always sufficiently aired'. In most, however, living conditions were poor and there could be serious overcrowding, particularly in the years after the Napoleonic Wars. The workhouse at York, for example, was frequently con-demned as insanitary, with one inspection reporting 'a permanent reservoir of foul air, where idiots mix with children and with adults labouring with syphilis and gonorrhoea'. In 1787, at St Pancras, then on the northern edge of London, inmates slept five or six to a bed. In 1818 a survey by a Parliamentary select committee found that in Kettering:

> A considerable number of new beds are absolutely necessary – the total number is 48 and at present there are 95 persons in the house – a very great proportion of the beds are in a very poor state... The master ... has made a very proper division of the rooms for the separate accommodation of the men, women and children. The sleeping rooms of the latter are clean, wholesome and airy, but those of the men are confined close and exceedingly unwholesome.

Building the bastilles

By 1834, when the New Poor Law was introduced, many villages and towns had a workhouse. The Royal Commission on the Poor Law, which reported in 1834, was very hostile towards existing workhouses, describing them as places where:

The young are trained in idleness, ignorance and vice; the able-bodied maintained in sluggish, sensual indolence; the aged and more respectable exposed to all the misery that is incident to dwelling in such a society … and the whole body of inmates subsisted on food far exceeding … not merely the diet of the independent labourer, but that of the majority who contribute to their support.

In the eyes of the New Poor Law Commissioners, workhouses had three main objectives: to look after parishioners who could not look after themselves, that is the aged, the infirm and children; to act as a deterrent to those who would not work; and lastly, as always, to function as a means of reducing the poor rate by forcing the indigent into the workhouse. As their officials established the local boards of guardians, the Poor Law Commissioners generally insisted that existing workhouses be closed and that the guardians build new premises that conformed to current thinking. The design and layout of the workhouse made an important statement about the regime to be found inside, which was instantly recognized by pauper, ratepayer and guardian alike. Bare brick walls surrounded the buildings, which had little of the ornamentation given to other public buildings of the period. Sir Francis Head, Assistant Poor Law Commissioner for Kent, told a local magistrate who argued for the retention of the existing buildings:

The very sight of a well-built efficient establishment would give confidence to the Board of Guardians; the sight and weekly assemblage of all servants of the Union would make them proud of their office; the appointment of a chaplain would give dignity to the whole arrangement, while the pauper would feel it was utterly impossible to contend against it.

Naturally there were protests. Radicals railed against 'pauper bastilles' which would oppress the poor and destroy their ancient rights. Ratepayers and many guardians were concerned about the expense of the new buildings. And the poor themselves were fearful about the conditions found therein, their fears reinforced by some blood-curdling stories. In 1829 a pauper was sentenced to 21 days in gaol for spreading the rumour that the broth offered at Shadwell workhouse included human remains. And in 1839 Edward Tufnell reported to the Commissioners that in Kent it was rumoured 'that the children in the workhouse were killed to make pies with, while the old when dead were employed to manure the guardians' fields in order to save the expense of coffins'.

The erection of new workhouses was piecemeal. In areas where there had been considerable protests against the new legislation, particularly in the north of England and in Wales, they were only introduced slowly. Despite appalling conditions in the town workhouse (one of five maintained by the Union), Huddersfield in Yorkshire had to wait until 1862 for new premises at Deanhouse, which quickly proved unsatisfactory. In October 1866 Poor Law Inspector R.B. Cane regretted that 'so ill-arranged and incomplete a building was ever erected'. Another inspector later claimed that it had been built on the coldest and draughtiest spot in the Pennines. After many years of opposition Todmorden, Yorkshire, finally opened a workhouse as late as 1877, more than 40 years after the introduction of the New Poor Law.

By 1839, when there were 583 English and Welsh Unions in existence, 252 new and 175 old workhouses were in operation. A further 67 new workhouses were under construction, and nine old workhouses were undergoing renovation. Although geographically patchy – few new workhouses were initially built in London or the north – this was still the largest and most expensive State-run construction project witnessed in peacetime. There was no financial support from central government, and the Poor Law Commission's authorized spend of £2,000,000 had to be paid for either by local ratepayers or from the sale of the old workhouses. The new house at Bromsgrove, Worcestershire, for 300 paupers, for example, cost £5,150, plus another £440 to buy the three-acre plot of land. The contract was let in September 1836, and the premises opened during the spring of 1839.

In rural and semi-rural areas, workhouses were generally built on the outskirts of the central town or village in the Union. Bromsgrove's, for example, was on the main Birmingham road, about a mile from the centre of the town. In part this was because land was cheaper here, but the location also meant that paupers could come and go unseen. There was also, at least initially, little civic pride invested in them, so there was no desire to build workhouses in a prominent place, as might happen with a town hall. Nonetheless, a rural workhouse situated on the brow of a hill could dominate the countryside for miles around.

Industrial or urban workhouses, by contrast, were inevitably in the heart of the city, rubbing shoulders with the poor and looming over their lives. In 1844 Friedrich Engels described Manchester's workhouse as being 'like a citadel' that 'looks threateningly down from its high walls and parapets on the hilltop upon the working people's quarter below'.

The workhouses of the 1830s such as Southwell in Nottinghamshire and Bromsgrove were generally built to a pattern, with the central buildings surrounded by work and exercise yards. In some places, such as Blean, Kent, paupers' dormitories were ranged around the courtyard, which, as *The Times* pointed out, did not allow the inmates any view of the surrounding countryside: 'nothing is to be seen but dead walls'. Unsurprisingly, the most important rooms were naturally assigned to the master and matron; their quarters were often positioned in the centre of the workhouse complex, so that they could see at a glance what was going on. Most workhouses built in the 1820s and 1830s had this arrangement, and at Southwell it is still possible to see how it worked. Yet although this layout looked good on paper, the reality was different. Dr Edward Smith, the Poor Law Board's medical officer, inspected many workhouses in the southeast during the 1860s, and found that the rooms were very close in warm weather. He also argued that the master and matron were rarely in their rooms, and were constantly supervising the paupers in other ways.

Much more common were radial or windmill designs, where four three-storey buildings emanated from an octagonal hub (where the master and matron lived), set within a rectangle defined by a three-storey entrance block and single-storey outbuildings forming the perimeter of the workhouse, the whole complex surrounded by a wall. The basic design was not dissimilar to the prison 'panopticon', proposed by Jeremy Bentham to allow an observer to watch prisoners without the prisoners knowing, thus conveying a 'sentiment of an invisible omniscience'. The resulting geometrical conceit provided four exercise or work yards to be used by men, women, boys and girls, thus completing their segregation in the house. The basic design – by the young London architect Sampson Kempthorne – was for 300 paupers, but it could easily be scaled down or up to meet the requirements of the individual union.

A journalist from *Household Words* visited one such establishment in Hampshire in 1867:

Passing down Southampton-wards, the reader may remark a formal, gloomy building standing off the railway to the left. It has small narrow windows and high walls. Its shape is of the well-known windmill pattern, with the four wings for wards and the centre for the master's house. A younger brother of the Millbank Penitentiary, who has settled down to agricultural pursuits, with a surly regret for the turnkeys and warders, the handcuffs and punishment cells of the metropolitan head of the family, is what this building suggests most strongly as we pass it in the train.

The second major wave of building occurred from the mid-1860s onwards as the result of a damning series of reports by Dr Edward Smith and his Poor Law Inspector colleagues on infirmaries in both London and the provinces. At Worcester the inspector concluded that 'the provision for the sick is inconvenient and defective, especially that for males; the foul wards are confined in space and the medical officer considers that better fever wards are wanted'. And of St Saviour's workhouse in Southwark, London, Harry Farnall bluntly observed that: 'The workhouse does not meet the requirements of medical science, nor am I able to suggest any arrangements which would in the least enable it to do so.'

In addition, there was a growing realization that the workhouse had a purpose for which it was not designed. It was no longer solely a deterrent to the able-bodied; increasingly it comprised a hospital, an orphanage and a home for the elderly. Shortly after the Andover workhouse scandal, the *Illustrated London News* argued that the older designs were 'in fact tracings from designs for American prisons' and proposed a new generation of light and airy buildings from which inmates could see the open fields beyond. Inevitably, the first generation of workhouses soon came to be regarded as old-fashioned. Smith, writing in 1866, criticized their 'narrow rooms and inconvenient arrangement of the offices'. This was acknowledged by the Parliamentary Secretary to the Poor Law Board, George Sclater-Booth, in a speech to North-East Hants Agricultural Association in November 1867:

I think there can be no doubt that public opinion will require that the appliances and comforts bestowed upon these sick, aged and infirm shall be more in accordance with modern notions than was intended or expected 30 or 40 years ago when these workhouses were originally built

47

… we have no longer able-bodied paupers to be maintained in work-houses and that they are diverted from their original purposes and converted into receptacles for a different class of people altogether.

In the bigger workhouses, increasingly, there were usually separate build-ings for the infirmary and the casual wards, in order to prevent infection spreading and to separate troublesome vagrants from the more peaceable permanent inmates. Some 150 new workhouses were built between 1840 and 1875, largely in London, Lancashire and Yorkshire, where previously few houses had been built. As a sign that the workhouse no longer quite had the deterrent effect of old, the architects now adopted Italianate, medieval or Elizabethan styles; they fitted in well with contemporary fashion and looked less intimidating than those of the previous generation. A charming example, still surviving, is the gateway at Ripon, Yorkshire, which exhibits more than a hint of the medieval almshouse.

A clock tower over the entrance block or a decorated door entrance was common. Occasionally, the Poor Law Board felt compelled to inter-vene in order to curtail the ornamentation proposed by over-enthusiastic guardians. In 1870 they refused to sanction proposals for one workhouse which wanted 'to introduce encaustic tile paving in the entrance hall, moulded Portland stone stairs to the chapel, an elaborate coffered ceiling to the chapel, decorated ceilings to the committee rooms, Parian cement pilasters and other decorations in the covered way to the chapel, and Portland stone decorations to the front of the building'. But sometimes the improvements were realized, as at Prestwich near Manchester, where a new workhouse opened in March 1870. The *Manchester Guardian* eulogized the new buildings, which had cost £40,000 (including land) and housed 312 paupers in rooms which 'were well lighted, well ventilated, and airy, while every modern appliance had been taken advantage of which would add to the comfort of the inmates and conveniences of the officers of the union'.

The main features of the new generation of buildings such as the Prestwich workhouse were the long corridors with wards leading off them for men, women and children. This allowed greater ventilation, always a problem in earlier designs, and the inmates no longer felt that every aspect of their lives was under the gaze of the master or matron. Even so, the long walk down gloomy and dully painted corridors (brown or green and cream were favourite colour schemes) must have been depressing.

By 1870 fewer corridor workhouses were being built. Instead, buildings generically known as 'pavilions' were erected to house the various types of paupers, from children to the very old – recognition in bricks and mortar of the differences between paupers. The idea was to separate the buildings, so that it was difficult for disease to spread. The Manchester Union infirmary, which opened in 1878, had seven parallel three-storey pavilions, each with room for 31 beds, a day room, a nurse's kitchen and lavatories; all were separated from each other by airing yards about 80 feet apart.

The original 'pavilion' design was based on military hospitals built during and after the Crimean War, which provided light, airy and extremely well-ventilated wards for soldiers to recover in. Unsurprisingly Florence Nightingale, who had come to prominence during the War for introducing humane nursing and sensible sanitation, was an advocate of this new style of hospital. The largest of these (indeed the largest hospital ever built) was the Royal Victoria Hospital at Netley, which stretched a quarter of a mile along Southampton Water and provided 138 wards – which, ironically, turned out to be poorly ventilated. Workhouse pavilions proved to be usually less satisfactory than even the successful hospitals on which they were based. Inmates were allocated less space, as guardians argued that the wards would not be occupied during the day. Windows were smaller and the ventilation less effective.

Some 46 buildings in pavilion style were erected between 1870 and 1914, again largely in the north of England and on the outskirts of London (where a number of schools and infirmaries for inmates from several unions were built on greenfield sites). One of the first of the type was at Madeley in Shropshire, which opened in 1875. It replaced two smaller workhouses condemned by the Poor Law Board and consisted of a central single-storey block, containing a dining hall and kitchen, which was linked by covered walkways to two-storey accommodation blocks. Other separate blocks included an infirmary, isolation block, entrance block and workshops.

At Brentford, now the site of the West Middlesex Hospital, *The Builder* reported the opening of a new workhouse in the pavilion fashion in November 1902. It provided spacious modern accommodation for the inmates with facilities which would surely have drawn protests from guardians of an earlier generation that the paupers were being mollycoddled. However, the journal was keen to stress that 'the buildings are of plain design, no money being wasted in ornament'.

It would be easy to assume from the above that, over time, conditions for the paupers got better. Advances certainly occurred, though they were uneven; more took place in the larger urban workhouses where there was money and imagination enough to build, rebuild and invest in new facilities and better services. Life for a pauper here was much better in 1910 than it had been in, say, 1840. Nor were they the only beneficiaries. By the 1890s houses were occasionally built for the master and matron, and sometimes for other senior staff as well, in the workhouse grounds of the larger unions. In 1905, at Crumpsall in northern Manchester, the guardians built a large detached house for the new master, Captain Frank Cresswell, and his wife, showing the enhanced status of the master and the fact that he was not involved in the day-to-day supervision of the inmates. In contrast, the porter's lodge, where the porter and his wife lived, was still usually near the main gate so that the porter could be summoned whenever somebody desired entrance to the house. In the smaller workhouses, nurses had rooms near the wards, so that they, too, could easily be called in cases of emergency.

However, not every workhouse got better and most redevelopment was slow in coming. Most workhouses developed piecemeal as their function and organization evolved. New buildings were erected either when necessary or when forced by the authorities in Whitehall, and others were demolished or remodelled when circumstances changed. *The Times* in 1867 described the workhouse at Farnham, for example, as being an 'ugly ill-conditioned series of buildings... The infirmary buildings, workrooms, farm buildings, children's wards, as well as other wards, form three sides of a square in a hotchpotch building, if possible uglier and more inconvenient than the one in front, which completes the square.' Even after the damning public inquiry which exposed how bad conditions were inside, it was not demolished; instead new infirmary blocks were added in 1870 and 1900.

Conditions in small rural houses remained much as they always had been. When H. Rider Haggard visited Norfolk workhouses in the 1890s, he was shocked to come across 'poor girls with their illegitimate children, creeping dirty-faced across the floor', and 'the old, old women, lying in bed, too feeble to move'. And many of the casual wards described in 1929 by George Orwell in *Down and Out in Paris and London*, had clearly not changed much in sixty or more years.

All change at Marylebone

The Marylebone workhouse is in many ways typical of the changes that took place in workhouses across Britain during the period of the poor laws. The original workhouse there opened in 1752, but soon became over-crowded, as well as infested with rats from a nearby burial ground. A new workhouse was opened on the site in 1776 with room for 1,000 paupers, although initially it only housed 300. Despite outbreaks of fever which came from the burial ground, the original workhouse continued as an infirmary until 1791, when the authorities finally took notice after a fever had killed both the matron and the apothecary. A new and well-ventilated infirmary, with room for 300 paupers, was then built next to the new workhouse. The growing population of the parish meant that by the late 1790s the work-house was already overcrowded, although not as badly as the neighbouring ones. Further buildings were erected after the Napoleonic Wars to cope with the flood of people who arrived in London looking for work and failing, taking the capacity up to nearly 1,500, plus another 300 in the infirmary.

Although it was originally built in fields on the edge of the parish, the expanding metropolis increasingly surrounded it. In 1902 the journalist T.W. Wilkinson visited the new Marylebone workhouse for an article he was writing for *London Lives*, and noted that in a biblical simile that its location placed in stark proximity the 'front door of Dives' and 'the home of Lazarus'. The contrast between the two worlds was harsh. 'Plenty and poverty exist side by side. My lady's boudoir is on one hand; the pauper's dormitory on the other.'

In the mid-1830s the journalist James Grant found the building 'of very great size; it is not only the largest in the metropolis, but the largest in the United Kingdom... Of all the workhouses which I have seen, the arrange-ments in that of Marylebone seem to be better than in any other.' A decade later Marylebone, in common with workhouses across London, was over-whelmed by a flood of applicants fleeing the Great Famine in Ireland. The highest number accommodated on a single day in 1847 was 2,264 (there were beds for 1,500), when even the workshops were pressed into service as additional dormitories.

A recurring problem was how to deal with infants and small children; the guardians were severely criticized by the Poor Law Commissioners in 1843 for conditions in the infant wards. A particular problem was the provision of decent lavatories. The guardians themselves admitted, for example, that a 'proper urinal [should be erected] for the male children to prevent the clothes of the other children being wetted, which is frequently the case at present'. The problem was lack of space – there was nowhere to put new toilets, let alone make the other alterations which the Commissioners had recommended.

Slowly conditions began to improve as functions were transferred from the main site on the Euston Road. In 1860 children were finally moved to a new school about 10 miles distant in the countryside at Southall, but easily accessible by rail. In common with other workhouses, Marylebone was visited by Poor Law Inspectors at least once a year and generally more often. Their opinions on its effectiveness varied. Reports submitted between 1859 and 1866 by the Poor Law Inspector Harry Farnall emphasized that the premises were defective in size and internal arrangement, particularly the male able-bodied and convalescent wards. One of his colleagues, R.B. Crane, proved rather more sympathetic to the regime in 1863: 'The guardians seem to have used their best endeavours to obviate the defects in this establishment. The inmates appeared in a cleanly condition, well clothed and cared for, and apparently in a contented state. The workhouse, on the whole, was in as good order as I could expect to find it.'

By now most of the inmates were either elderly or infirm. In 1862 Farnall suggested that the guardians provide a warm shawl for each bedridden woman and a warm cape with sleeves for each man confined to bed. He also sought to have looking glasses provided 'so as to prevent the necessity of the inmates hoarding up, as they do now with so much care pieces of broken looking glass'.

Temporary casual wards opened in 1867 to cope with the needs of vagrants. Unusually, scriptural texts were painted in large red letters on a blue background on the walls. They exhorted vagrants to turn from their criminal and indolent ways – although it is debatable, of course, how many inmates could read them. The wards only lasted a decade before a new block, based on radically different and more secular principles, was opened in 1876.

'The Indoor Pauper', who was probably an inmate in the early 1880s, found it the harshest of all the casual wards he stayed at and describes the experience in unflattering terms:

> [Each casual] has four pounds of oakum to pick with not one of the usual aids. 'We do not allow you to beat the oakum here' remarked the taskmaster in truculent terms to myself. And every particular of the work has to be done before the casual is released… There is a metal pot, with a cover, in each cell; but the cover does not quite fit tight, and the pot, which serves as latrine, emits in consequence a most noisome smell. If ever the cholera visits London, I am quite sure it will make an early appearance in Marylebone workhouse and not spare the inmates.

During a smallpox epidemic at about the same time, a ward was created for victims from one of the men's workrooms. Nurses were strictly confined to the building and a man was posted at the yard gate to prevent communication with the rest of the workhouse; all food and stores were passed through him. The measures worked: out of 215 patients, only 22 died.

Also in 1867 part of the wall of the female infirm ward collapsed – fortunately killing nobody as all paupers were in bed at the time. It was clear that the main buildings, now almost a hundred years old, needed replacing. The infirmary moved west to Ladbroke Grove in 1881, although the confinement wards remained at the workhouse. The Architectural Association, which paid a visit before the infirmary opened, were impressed: 'The interior walls and tracery of the windows are very nicely executed in white Suffolk bricks. The chapel is warmed by means of one of Mr Saxon Snell's patent "Thermhydric" stoves, which are also used in the wards.'

The moving of the infirmary naturally freed up more space to accommodate the paupers, and numerous changes were made. During the 1880s, for example, a new block to house 240 able-bodied women was opened. However, conditions remained generally poor. In 1895 the Local Government Board approved a plan to rebuild the workhouse and demolish all pre-1867 buildings. This work was undertaken in two stages and cost in the region of £80,000. The foundation stone of the back block of buildings was laid in May 1897 by the Bishop of London in the presence of the boys' band from the school at Southall, and it opened exactly a year later. The front block, heralding the dawn of a new century, opened in March 1900, and it attracted attention and comment.

The journalist T.W. Wilkinson was particularly impressed by the size and the facilities of the new workhouse when he visited in 1902. The dining room had space for 1,200, and the kitchen was equipped with a mincing machine, used for 'artificially masticating the meat supplied to old and toothless paupers'.

Walls, wards and workrooms

There were plots of land around the buildings of both rural and suburban workhouses, where paupers, young and old, cultivated fruit and vegetables – although they did not necessarily get to eat the fruit of their labours (see p.110). In his manual for guardians of 1876, George Bartley recommended that workhouses keep pigs to eat any waste food, commenting that their meat 'makes a pleasant occasional change in the officers' diet', but he warned against keeping pigs too close to the house itself: 'I have seen a row of sties within a very short distance of the infirmary windows, and absolutely close to the work-sheds, used by all the old men for the greater part of the day. The smell was dreadful and must have been most injurious.'

Even in London some workhouses presented a bucolic appearance. At St Pancras in the 1850s Miss S.E. De Morgan found 'a flower garden which was cultivated by able-bodied paupers for the use of the master and matron'. The Rev. Osborne Jay hinted at darker reasons when, in 1891, he described one London workhouse in *Life in Darkest London*:

> A forecourt of neat flower beds, closely shaven grass plots, smooth paths, and trees which had been pruned until their branches had reached the legitimate amount of foliage. The Bastille stretched further than the eye could see, and seemed a standing rebuke to its poverty-stricken surroundings, for it was clean ... not a spot on it, not a stain, nothing to show a trace of sympathy for the misery and sin of the people who lived in the neighbourhood.

The workhouse would have been surrounded by walls designed to stress the separation of the paupers inside from the freedoms of the world outside. Many observers and critics of the new system, such as Miss De Morgan, thought that the 'high walls and bolted doors recalled the idea of a prison'.

In practice, the walls were not as secure as might be thought. It was not uncommon for outsiders to hoist over tobacco and alcohol for friends in the house. On occasion, inmates climbed the walls to make their escape. One of the witnesses in the trial for corruption of an Islington guardian in December 1889 was an inmate called French. According to a report in *The Times*, he was refused leave of absence over a bank holiday by the workhouse master, so he got out by climbing the wall and thus witnessed a cart from the workhouse carrying stolen items.

The walls could not prevent discharged paupers from talking about their experiences, so local people generally had a good idea of what it was like inside. These stories simply added to the bad reputation of the workhouse and acted as a further deterrent to anybody who might think about seeking admission. Andrew Doyle noted down one piece of doggerel he found in a casual ward in the mid-1860s:

> It's very unkind, nay, further, cruel
> To give here merely a drop of thin gruel
> But let them keep it, we can do without it –
> And I mean to let half the town know about it!

Contact with the outside world was further restricted by limited visiting hours. At Crumpsall workhouse in Manchester in 1879, visits to sick and infirm paupers could only take place on the first Saturday of the month between the hours of 2pm and 4.30pm (5pm in summer). Potential visitors were warned: 'No visit to exceed half-hour duration.' Paupers were also released from the workhouse for only a few short hours each month, although the Poor Law authorities were always keen to stress that paupers could discharge themselves at short notice.

Symbolically, there was only one entrance to the workhouse through which everybody had to enter and depart. Here paupers and visitors alike had to undergo interrogation by the porter as to the purpose of their visit.

Their reception was generally hostile. Miss De Morgan, who wished to visit inmates and was armed with a letter of introduction from Lord Torrington, later wrote: 'The porter at the outer door, who half opened it to ask what I wanted, shut it in my face, observing that he had something else to do than to take messages to the master and that they knew nothing about lords there.' George Lansbury had similarly negative impressions of his first visit to London's Poplar workhouse as a new guardian:

> Going down the narrow lane, ringing the bell, waiting while an official
> with a not too pleasant face looked through a grating to see who was
> there, and hearing his unpleasant voice – of course, he did not know me
> – made it easy for me to understand why the poor dreaded and hated
> these places, and made me in a flash realise how all these prison or
> bastille sort of surroundings were organised for the purpose of making
> self-respecting, decent people endure any suffering rather than enter.

Both the relieving rooms and casual wards were placed close to the entrance. The relieving rooms (wards) were where paupers stayed until they had been examined by the medical officer. Personal possessions were taken away and each new pauper was issued with an anonymous – and badly fitting – coarse blue uniform and a pair of slippers, boots or clogs. As T.W. Wilkinson perceptively noted, incomers lost some of their individuality as they passed through.

Often these rooms were in the worst condition of any in the workhouse. *The Times* described the relieving ward for women and children at Farnham in Surrey: '[It was] without ventilation, one person sleeping in it would make the atmosphere unwholesome in a very short time, if not actually poisonous, and yet several persons may have to sleep there, heaped round with stinking rags which in-coming paupers generally wear.'

Here families and couples were separated and placed into one of the categories laid down by Whitehall: male child under 14, able-bodied man between the ages of 14 and 60; old man over 60; female child under 14; able-bodied woman between the ages of 14 and 60; and old woman over 60. Infants under two were allowed to stay with their mothers. The paupers were then allocated to the appropriate ward in the house.

Some unions attempted to subdivide their paupers yet further. In the

1860s Mitford and Launditch had 20 categories for the 63 women in the workhouse at Gressinghall, including 'prostitutes', 'women incapable of getting their own living from syphilis' and 'idiotic or weak-minded women with one or more bastard children'. By the end of the 19th century the Local Government Board was encouraging workhouses to divide paupers, particularly the elderly, into 'deserving', who would be rewarded with better conditions, and 'non-deserving', who would not.

Personal possessions were taken away and stored until such time as the owners left, although many paupers tried to smuggle tobacco or other items in the crevices of their bodies, hoping that they would not be searched too thoroughly. In the Whitechapel casual ward in East London, Jack London was worried about being searched for tobacco. A fellow inmate told him, 'Oh no … this is the easiest spike (workhouse). Y'ought to see some of them search you to the skin.'

Sometimes there was a separate ward (the 'foul' or 'itch' ward) for applicants with skin diseases, where they might stay for a day or two before entering the workhouse proper. The authorities tried to guard against the itch (scabies), which was a condition suffered by many poor people and which could spread quickly through the house. Charles Dickens described the 'itch' ward at Wapping in south London, following a visit in 1850:

> in an old building squeezed away in a corner of a paved yard, quite
> detached from the more modern and spacious main body of the work-
> house. They were in a building most monstrously behind the time –
> a mere series of garrets or lofts … and only accessible by steep and narrow
> staircases, infamously ill-adapted for the passage up-stairs of the sick
> or down-stairs of the dead.

Also near the entrance were the casual or tramp wards housing the vagrants. Conditions in the casual wards were likely to be worse than in the rest of the house, because to provide a decent environment might attract hordes of vagrants. They were regarded, with some justification, as troublemakers who could be a bad influence on the rest of the paupers, so efforts were made to keep them away from the other inmates. They were also suspected of being disease-ridden. Jack London waited for admission to a workhouse with two men suffering from smallpox:

Whereat my flesh began to creep and crawl, and I asked them how long they had been out. One had been out two weeks, and the other three weeks. Their faces were badly pitted (though each assured the other that this was not so), and further, they showed me in their hands and under the nails, the smallpox 'seeds' still working out. Nay, one of them worked a seed out for my edification, and pop it went, right out of his flesh into the air. I tried to shrink up smaller inside my clothes, and I registered a fervent though silent hope that it had not popped on me.

In the main body of the workhouse, or in separate blocks or pavilions, were housed the various wards and other facilities, such as a chapel, schoolrooms, dining rooms and a laundry, as well as quarters for the master and matron and other members of staff. There were also exercise (often called airing) yards and work yards where able-bodied paupers were expected to contribute towards their keep by breaking stones or picking oakum. (Oakum consisted of the loose fibres obtained by unpicking old ropes and was sold on to shipbuilders; it was mixed with tar and used for caulking wooden ships.)

The exercise or airing yards were carefully separated by gender and category, and children might play there and adults talk or read. At Marylebone the airing yard was surrounded by beds of flowers which made it 'bright and cheerful, [with] seat after seat occupied by paupers reading in the sun'. However, 40 years previously Miss De Morgan had found at neighbouring St Pancras that, to approach the infirmary, the visitor had to pass through a yard where there were 'a number of idiotic epileptic and lunatic women and girls, all harmless but distressing objects, especially some of the girls who caught hold of the visitor's dress and clamoured, either for sweets or to be let out'.

Draughts of fresh air

At first, lighting would have been provided by candles, but these were soon replaced by gas. Bromsgrove, which was not the most progressive of unions, introduced gas lighting in 1851, when the local gas company had reduced its charges by half. Coal gas, however, was extremely smoky and produced layers of sticky soot which got everywhere and had to be thoroughly cleaned. Rooms also had to be well ventilated because gas depleted the oxygen in the air.

Ventilation was a constant problem. The wards were inevitably draughty either by accident or design, and paupers, particularly the old and the sick, must have felt the cold dreadfully. It is little surprise that they often resorted to stuffing airing bricks and windows with anything they could find, such as old rags or the pages from magazines, in order to keep in the heat. In many workhouses there was a constant battle between the staff, who tried to ensure proper ventilation and healthy blasts of fresh air, and the paupers trying to keep warm.

Each ward or day room had a separate fireplace or stove, but these were inadequate to heat the draughty rooms and posed a fire risk. In the 1890s, nurses at Crumpsall workhouse infirmary in Manchester wrapped lumps of coal in paper to avoid disturbing the patients when stoking the fires at night.

Other places had a system of central heating using hot water pipes, which threaded their way through the building and were supplied by a central coal-fired boiler. One of the first casual wards to include this form of heating was St Olave's workhouse in Rotherhithe, London, which opened in the early 1870s. It had 40 sleeping and working cells for men on the ground floor and 12 for women above, all of them supplied with hot water, heating and night commodes. At the fictional 'Romton' casual ward in the late 1920s George Orwell wrote: we had to 'roll up our coats and put them against the hot water pipes, and made ourselves as comfortable as we could. It grew foully stuffy, but it was not warm enough to allow us to put our blankets underneath so that we could use one to soften the floor.'

In larger workhouses the central coal- or gas-fired boiler might be maintained by employed boilermen, but in smaller institutions able-bodied paupers kept the systems going. This was a much sought-after job because, although the work was arduous, the boiler room was always warm – a rarity in the workhouse. Plentiful hot water was important in the kitchens and in the receiving and casual wards, where new inmates were bathed before their admission. It was not always achieved, however, and many grumbled that the water supplied was tepid.

Cleanliness, godliness and the daily routine

Keeping workhouses clean was always a battle. The older ones, in particular, were not designed with cleanliness in mind, as they had lots of small rooms and awkward corners, and domestic cleaning materials were not as effective as those in use today. Cleaning largely depended on the physical labour of the able-bodied women paupers, who washed, dusted, polished and scrubbed the floors. When Fred Copeman, who grew up in a workhouse before the First World War, came across his mother, she was always to be found on her knees scrubbing the floor. Such a situation was far from ideal, as the women were often physically weak (and on occasion mentally fragile) and certainly not motivated to work hard. As a result cleaning was often cursory and problems quickly built up through indifference and neglect. The pauper Mary Higgs, who stayed in a casual ward early in the 1900s, found that parcels of paupers' clothing had only been dusted on the front, and that nobody had bothered to open the parcels to tackle a moth infestation inside.

Both Higgs and her friend, who were fit and healthy, were at least required to clean the ward thoroughly before they left:

> My friend was told to stone [wash the floor and apply 'whitening' to give a sheen] the place completely through, including the three cells not used (which looked clean), to blacklead the hot-water pipes all down the passage, dust everywhere thoroughly, and clean the step. Meanwhile I had first to do some shelves, and then stone a spiral stair and floor of a small larder... I think, probably, the work we did would have taken the ordinary tramp a full day.

Such rigorous cleaning was valuable, but it was not always demanded. Many institutions managed without, such as the poorly-run Farnham, where one larder was described by *The Lancet* as resembling a 'stalactite cave of filth; there is no other image to adequately describe the foulness of these parts... A horrid smell used to issue from it into the kitchen which at times made [the cook] quite ill.'

Cleanliness and hygiene began to improve from the 1870s, largely because their importance increasingly was understood by doctors and nurses. Florence Nightingale, who was the leading campaigner for improved hospitals and workhouse infirmaries, emphasized in her *Notes for Nurses* that: 'The answer to hospital mortality is *neither prayer* nor *sacrifice* but *better ventilation, better drainage*, and a *higher standard of cleanliness*.' This emphasis coincided with the late Victorian obsession with the moral and physical virtues of cleanliness – it permeated respectable working-class households and was something that the Poor Law authorities were naturally keen to encourage. Nor were their concerns restricted to workhouse inmates. At Brixworth in Northamptonshire, and no doubt other unions as well, out-relief (that is, assistance outside the workhouse) could be denied to paupers who did not keep their houses neat and tidy.

Intimately connected with cleanliness was the laundry, although it was one of the least regarded parts of the workhouse. Each house got through vast amounts of linen, cotton and towelling, all of which needed washing and ironing, even if the result was often not much whiter than before. By the end of the 19th century most guardians had invested in steam laundries comprising vast tubs and huge spin dryers. You can see what one was like at the Norfolk Museum of Rural Life at Gressenhall workhouse which claims to have the only steam laundry still in working order.

As might be expected, the laundry was largely run by pauper women. In the 1860s Thomas Archer visited a workhouse on the eastern edge of London. He was one of the few visitors to inspect the laundry:

> A long outbuilding, almost open on one side, and furnished with sinks and troughs and coppers, which are fully sufficient to provide for the due cleanliness of all the apparel in the establishment... I am a little disappointed at the appearance of the women who are engaged in this part of the building ... they are amongst the least attractive females it has ever been my fortune to become acquainted with; and what personal advantages they may possess are not heightened by the flat-bordered workhouse cap, the blue check uniform covered with a coarse apron, and bare arms, the elbows of which resemble knobs carved out of some hard, but easily discolourable, substance.

On Merseyside, Nathaniel Hawthorne toured a laundry on wash day. He found 'the whole atmosphere ... hot and vaporous with the steam of wet garments and bedclothes. This atmosphere was the pauper-life of the past week or fortnight resolved into a gaseous state, and breathing it.'

Although the authorities liked to think that the chapel was the heart of the workhouse community, its real centre was the dining room. Often half-starved before they entered, and certainly not fattened on the diet provided by the guardians, most paupers spent a lot of time thinking about food. As the 'Indoor Pauper' noted, 'not a morsel more than is absolutely necessary to support life in a state of health is handed out to the cook'.

In larger workhouses there were separate dining rooms for men and women; otherwise they shared the same room but ate at different times to avoid contact between the sexes. The rule about eating together in a communal dining hall was sometimes ignored, especially in the older work-houses. At Pudsey near Leeds in the 1830s, one pauper remembered being served with 'large black bowls filled with oatmeal porridge and milk, and a big podgy person who figures as Master filling black earthenware mugs with a ladle and the poor, miserably clad people hobbling away with their meal to their room, which was not very tidy or over clean'.

The food was normally served up in the presence of the master or matron or another senior member of staff. In *Oliver Twist*, Dickens was fairly accurate in his description: 'The room in which the boys were fed, was a large stone hall, with a copper at one end: out of which the master, dressed in an apron for the purpose, and assisted by one or two women, ladled the gruel at meal-times.'

Dr Edward Smith, who prepared a report on dietaries for the Poor Law Board in 1866, described the process of serving food which seems to have been common in many workhouses. The paupers were allowed to have their meagre rations measured, and a notice to this effect was placed in the dining room.

> The soup, tea and other liquid foods are put into vessels of known capacity, and the pudding, meat, bread, butter and solid foods are weighed to each person. Relays of inmates are provided with trays to carry the food to the dining-rooms and the sick rooms. The process is effected with varying degrees of rapidity ... notwithstanding the exposure of the food to the cool air, it is for the most part still warm (sometimes hot) when the inmates eat it.

The eating utensils were normally made of battered tin – they would almost certainly have been stolen, had they been of any better quality. In most workhouses, meals were eaten off ceramic plates. In a few places, Smith

THE LIFE BEHIND DOORS

found that wooden trenchers were used, but they 'are very antiquated, require much labour in scouring to keep them clean, and keep up a daily distinction of inferiority between the table of the inmates of a workhouse and that of the poor living around them'.

The food was usually prepared in separate kitchens by paupers, under the supervision of a paid cook or, occasionally, the matron. The quality of the food offered was generally awful, because the skills of the kitchen staff were negligible (although Smith noted that their work was generally 'very fairly performed'), the quality of the provisions poor and the expectations of the inmates low. Food was usually boiled, although an increasing number of workhouses offered roast meat two or three times a week. Dr Smith found that the meat was 'almost universally salted in pickle' as a preservative – an important consideration when there was no refrigeration – which made it tough and probably less nourishing than it should have been.

The newer workhouses of the 1870s and later had better kitchens which could do more than just boil the food. The journalist T.W. Wilkinson was particularly impressed in 1902 by the kitchens in the new Marylebone workhouse:

> A large, lofty room, lined with white glazed bricks, and with a score of steam-jacketed coppers, tea coppers, roasting ovens, and the like, it seems to have been designed and fitted for a regiment of Brobdingnagians. Here they make sixty-gallon milk puddings, have three teapots of eighty gallons capacity each, cook a quarter of a ton of cabbage at an operation, and steam potatoes by the ton.

It was a principle of the Poor Law that inmates in the workhouse should contribute to their upkeep as far as possible. As well as reducing the burden on the ratepayers, this acted as a deterrent to any able-bodied pauper who might otherwise be tempted to enter instead of seeking gainful employment. Women cleaned, sewed and cooked, and men made goods for other paupers or for sale to the public. Miss De Morgan came across a group of aged women sewing a coarse stiff calico, which she was told was for shrouds: 'We've been at them all this week. There's many wanted now. We shall want them ourselves soon.'

Many of the tasks performed by the paupers, particularly the casuals and the male paupers, took place in work yards, which were open sheds or unheated rooms. At Whitechapel, in the 1880s, the author John Law found that:

> The workshops lay close together and in each of them men were redeeming the time by making something for the use of the workhouse. Tailors squatted on tables, boot-makers cobbled and patched, men plaited mats; each pauper had his task, and knew that the morrow would bring the same work, that as surely as the sun rises and sets, his task tomorrow would be the same as it was at the moment.

The paupers' labour provided a reasonable source of income for the guardians as their products were either sold or used in the house. In March 1908, Cheadle workhouse, for example, made a profit of £40 13s 3d on firewood and £8 12s 3d on broken stone (sold to the Highways Department to be used in surfacing roads), while £31 11s 2d worth of home-grown vegetables were consumed in the house.

Even the sick and infirm were expected to take a part. At Manchester, in 1882, the Local Government Board queried making patients in the surgical wards pick oakum. The chairman of the guardians defended this by arguing that 'the patients referred to were persons who were recovering but obliged to lie in bed and it was thought it would be more agreeable to them to find them something to do, than they should idle their time away'.

To outsiders and to the paupers themselves it often seemed that the workhouse remained unchanging, uncaring and unresponsive, yet this was untrue. Over the nearly hundred years of the New Poor Law they were built, rebuilt and demolished to meet changing demands. And conditions generally improved, except perhaps for the vagrants. But it was a depressingly dehumanising experience, particularly when new inmates entered the house. Stripped of their own clothing and possessions and separated from other family members, paupers faced the possibility that they would only see loved ones again if and when they left for the outside world.

ABOVE LEFT Will Crooks (1852–1921)
spent some time in London's Poplar
workhouse as a child. He later became
a trade union leader and politician, and
guardian at the Poplar Poor Law Union.
With his fellow Socialist guardian
George Lansbury, Crooks radically
improved conditions for the inmates
of the workhouse.

ABOVE RIGHT The son of a Suffolk
railwayman, George Lansbury
(1859–1940) was appalled by the
conditions he found in the East End.
Together with Will Crooks he made
major changes to the running of Poplar
workhouse, where he served as a
guardian for thirty years. He became
leader of the Labour Party in the early
1930s.

RIGHT Local guardians spent a lot of
time trying to keep vagrants away from
the workhouse. A popular way was to
have applicants vetted by the police on
the assumption that this would deter
known criminals. The Local Government Board encouraged London unions
to do this, although the duty was
disliked by the Metropolitan Police.

THE NEW WORKHOUSE PORTER.

MASTER PRIG. "BLEST IF THEY HASN'T PUT ON A BOBBY! PRETTY STATE WE'RE COMIN' TO, WITH
THEIR CENTRALISATION! LET'S CUT TO LAMBETH."

THE PAUPER'S FUNERAL AT TADCASTER.—TORCH-LIGHT PROCESSION.—During the past week the leading topic of conversation with every person in Tadcaster and the neighbourhood, has been the funeral of Elizabeth Daniel, the pauper whose death was reported in our last week's edition. Nothing could exceed the feeling of indignation expressed on every side, especially among the working classes, not only against the matron of the workhouse, but against the Board of Guardians, who are really the responsible party, for it appears from information we have received that the matron has been several times brought before them for misconduct, but they have invariably lent an unwilling ear to all complaints made against her. It appears, however, that action is about to be taken which will speedily elicit the truth or otherwise of the current reports of the treatment the inmates have for some time been subject to. The excitement caused by the proceedings in connection with the funeral reached its highest pitch when it was rumoured that it was intended to parade an effigy of the matron through the streets of the town, and then to burn it in front of the workhouse. Accordingly about eight o'clock in the evening of Friday, the 10th inst., a crowd of people, numbering 300 or 400, collected in the High-street, and then proceeded to the Market-place, headed by the Tadcaster drum and fife band, and a banner, on which was inscribed, "He that oppresseth the poor reproacheth his Maker." The people then sang "God Save the Queen" and "Rule Britannia," accompanied by the band, after which Mr. Edward Spink, the town bellman, got up and proclaimed the object of the meeting, which he stated was "to openly show their disapproval of the manner in which the matron of the Tadcaster Union Workhouse treated the inmates." He observed that "there could be no Christianity where there was an absence of common humanity," and concluded by stating that "he hoped every person would conduct himself in an orderly and decorous manner." Three cheers were then given for "common humanity," after which a procession was formed as follows : A sweep's donkey cart, containing a black coffin tied in with ropes, on the breastplate of which were the words, "In memory of a pauper, 1865," flanked by about a dozen men with lighted flambeaux. Next in order came a cart drawn by one horse, containing an effigy of a woman with a poker in her hand, striking a figure of a little boy. In this cart were half a dozen boys carrying lighted flambeaus. The drum and fife band and banner before mentioned brought up the rear. In this order the procession paraded from one end of the town to the other, accompanied by crowds of people, and proceeded to a field in front of the workhouse, occupied by Mr. Waterhouse, where the effigy was set on fire, and being stuffed with a "Jack in the box," and other fireworks, was soon consumed. The coffin was then set on fire, and some verses, composed for the occasion, were sung to the tune of "Auld Lang Syne." And then after singing "God Save the Queen," the crowd dispersed.

4 One of the press cuttings sent to the Local Government Board in Whitehall, following protests about the burial of Elizabeth Daniel in February 1865. Mrs Daniel, a pauper in Tadcaster workhouse in Yorkshire, had been mercilessly bullied by the matron Catherine Leivers. The matron was dismissed after a public inquiry (MH 12/15536).

5 ABOVE Unnamed inmates at Blofield workhouse in Norfolk, probably in the 1890s. By then the vast majority of residents in workhouses were either very old or very young. Unfortunately, it was increasingly clear that workhouses were suitable for neither.

6 BELOW The Poor Law system was all but destroyed by the scandal at Andover workhouse in Hampshire, when in 1845 *The Times* revealed that inmates were so hungry they were forced to eat the marrow from the bones they were made to crush. Remarkably, the Andover buildings survive and are now used as housing.

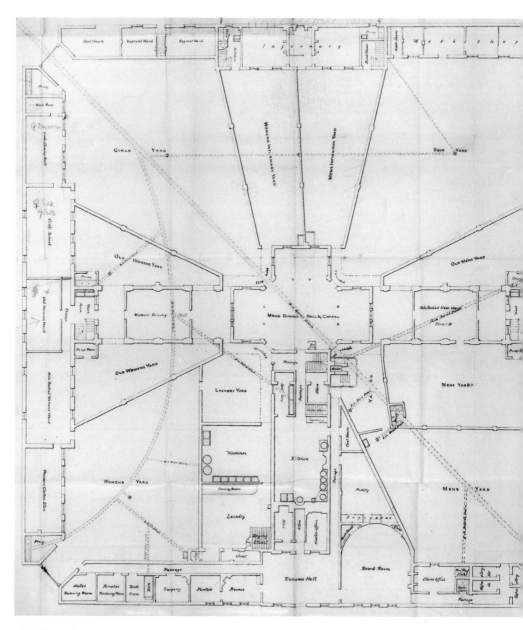

7 ABOVE Thame workhouse, Oxfordshire, which was built in the late 1830s, conformed to the cruciform pattern adopted by many workhouses of the period. At the centre was the master's quarters with separate yards for men, women, children and vagrants. Most of the buildings are still standing and are being redeveloped as housing, having previously been a technical college (MH 14/36).

8 LEFT A graffiti sundial carved in the brickwork at Southwell workhouse, Nottinghamshire. Graffiti was a way for bored paupers to while away a few hours. It might also provide information to vagrants about other workhouses in the area and allow the writer to vent feelings about the conditions in 'the house'.

9 ABOVE The infirmary at Marylebone workhouse as painted in 1803. It was built in 1792 with a capacity for 300 patients. The building was demolished in the 1880s when a new hospital was built in Ladbroke Grove.

10 MIDDLE The western end of Chapel Yard at Marylebone workhouse in London, as shown in a pencil drawing by a pauper in 1866. The artist was probably W.A. Delamotte, a member of a well known artistic family who had clearly fallen on hard times. The workhouse was built in the late 1770s and demolished in 1898.

11 LEFT The Abingdon workhouse, Oxfordshire, which opened in 1836, was typical of the period. Its design was influenced by contemporary prison design: this picture clearly shows how the sexes were kept apart. In addition children were separated from their parents. The building was demolished in the 1930s.

To the President and Lords Commissioners

of

The Poor Law Board

We the undersigned Ratepayers and Inhabitants of Tadcaster and Neighbourhood desire hereby to express to your Honourable Board the deep concern we feel for the Welfare of Paupers in general and especially those in our own parish whose misfortune it is to be dependent upon us for maintenance and support, and we are wishful that they should be kindly and humanely treated when alive and their remains decently interred when they die —

We have good reasons for thinking and verily believe that the Treatment of Paupers in the Tadcaster Union Workhouse by the Matron of that Establishment is unnecessarily harsh and cruel and as such merits our highest disapprobation

We also desire to express to your Honourable Board our disapproval of the manner in which the remains of Elizabeth Daniel late a pauper in the above named Workhouse were interred on the 2nd of February last in the Tadcaster Church Yard We consider the obsequies were of an unnecessarily degrading nature and contrary to the Custom of the Country —

We therefore pray that your Honorable Board will order an Investigation by one of your Inspectors to be made into the Conduct of the Matron of the Tadcaster Workhouse believing that her treatment of the Inmates of the Establishment is not only contrary to Law but very inhumane and we consider her quite unfit for the office she holds —

John England	Thomas Lofthouse	Chas. Shearon
Robert Jackman	Alfred Aspinall	Ben. Blaydes Thompson
Wm Michelson	John Allen	W Schofield
Wm Elsand	Chas B Dixon	Wm Lockwood
Turnbull	W Schofield	Joseph Fletcher

12 OPPOSITE The petition from concerned ratepayers of Tadcaster protesting to the Local Government Board in London about treatment of paupers in their local workhouse. It was submitted in February 1865 and caused Whitehall to send an inspector to investigate (MH 12/15536).

13 LEFT A feature of Southwell workhouse was the master's quarters on the first floor, designed so that he could keep an eye on the paupers wherever they were on the premises. However, where this was adopted in other workhouses the master and his family often found that they could better maintain discipline by being always among the paupers.

14 LEFT BELOW Senior staff at Gressenhall, Norfolk, in 1902. In the back row are Mr Whitby (assistant clerk) and his wife. In the middle row are Mr and Mrs Robert Neville (master and matron). Sitting on the ground are Robert Neville (junior) and the daughter of Mr and Mrs Whitby.

15 LEFT The master of Gressenhall workhouse, Robert Neville, in about 1903. In 1911 Neville would be sacked in a controversial manner for refusing to admit a sick pauper late at night.

16 BELOW Nursing staff at Doncaster's Springwell Lane Infirmary in Yorkshire, which admitted its first patients in 1900. When it opened it was one of the most modern in Britain and the chairman of the board of guardians boasted that Tsar Nicholas had asked for a set of plans so he could have a similar building constructed in Russia.

CHAPTER THREE

'Harnessed to the House'

The whole establishment – at least those who could leave their beds –
rose in open rebellion, and with old kettles, shovels, penny trumpets,
celebrated their departure from the premises.

Joseph Rogers, *Reminiscences of a Workhouse Medical Officer*, 1889

EVERY workhouse had a complement of full-time staff, sometimes referred to as the indoor staff, who generally lived in either the house itself or within the grounds. The numbers varied considerably, with the smallest rural houses possessing only a master, matron, porter and perhaps an assistant nurse. The largest workhouses in London and the major provincial cities, by contrast, may have employed several hundred men and women.

Firmly at the top of the workhouse hierarchy was the master (or governor) together with the matron; indeed, they were usually a married couple. In practice it was difficult for a man to advance through the Poor Law service unless he was married to a woman who had worked in the workhouse and thus could act as matron. An unmarried master put his case to the guardians at Bromley, Kent, in 1988: 'Being very anxious to obtain a joint appointment as Master & matron of a union workhouse and my greatest disadvantage being single, may I solicit the sanction of the Guardians to marry, my wife being outside the workhouse buildings.' Even though she had no connection with the Poor Law, the guardians did not object.

The master and matron had very clear duties based on the strict segregation of the paupers by gender and age. He was in charge of the house as a whole, as well as the men's side and casual wards, while the matron had responsibility for the women's wards and the infirmary. The porter, the medical officer and the labour or taskmasters reported to the master, while the matron managed the nurses and kitchen staff.

Often other members of his family might also have jobs in the house. Adult or teenage sons and daughters might teach the children or follow their parents into the business. For example, the sons of Daniel and Eleanor Pickett, master and matron at Stratford-upon-Avon, Warwickshire, between 1896 and 1927, themselves became masters of workhouses at Pontefract in Yorkshire and the Turnshurst Road Institute in Stoke-on-Trent. Younger children were more problematic. Guardians usually refused to employ couples with small children (euphemistically referred to as 'encumbrances' in job advertisements) and frowned upon those who had children while in post. Occasionally exceptions were made for suitable candidates, but in general it was thought that the workhouse and the company of paupers was no place for a small child. William and Mary Anne Bragger, who were master and matron at Wrexham, north Wales, in the early 1860s, exceptionally were allowed to have their two daughters with them, although an older son was boarded out.

Vera Littlewood's parents became master and matron of Ongar workhouse, Essex, in the early 1900s. She explained in her memoirs:

> The post was advertised for a married couple and they were told they must not have any children. I was later told how worried they were when first my sister Constance came along in 1905, [followed by] my arrival in 1911. However, they were not sacked, but I expect they were given dire warnings by the Board of Guardians.

The duties of workhouse staff were clearly laid down in a series of orders issued by the Poor Law Commission in London. The master was made responsible for the administration of the workhouse and the care and discipline of the paupers; in 1836 his tasks included reading 'prayers to the paupers before breakfast and after supper every day, or [to] cause them to be read' and paying visits to the wards at 11am every morning and 9pm each night. Staff duties remained largely unchanged during the whole period of the New Poor Law, although practitioners in the field interpreted the various orders in very different ways. In 1881 John Wyld, the master of Bishop Auckland in County Durham, told a Poor Law conference that the responsibilities of a workhouse master were:

> To evolve order; to arrange and classify [the paupers]; to listen to the various wants, troubles, complaints and wishes; to care for the suffering ones tenderly; and to rigidly exact from the able-bodied shirker his quota of labour to help to support the house that shelters him; to keep and preserve provisions, clothing and stock; to prevent waste; ... to keep his books and accounts; to exercise a gentle sway and controlling influence in harmonising any little differences that may ... arise between the other indoor officers.

The matron's role was also clearly delineated. She was responsible for the female inmates, as well as children under seven of both sexes, and the orders required her to 'see that the in-door work of the establishment is, as far as possible, performed by the female paupers maintained therein ... to pay particular attention to the moral conduct and orderly behaviour of the female paupers and children; to see that they are clean and decent in their dress and persons, and to train them up in such employments as will best fit them for service'. Practical housekeeping issues, such as ensuring that the bed linen was changed monthly, also fell into her domain.

In practice, the couple's work varied greatly depending on the size and importance of the workhouse. In the smallest rural houses, the matron may have actually nursed the sick inmates while the master dealt with male paupers and the tramps. In the larger urban workhouses, masters and matrons managed a large number of staff, such as nurses and porters, and must have rarely come in contact with individual paupers. It is perhaps no wonder that in his account of an inner London able-bodied ward 'the Indoor Pauper' mentions neither the master nor the matron – he probably never encountered them. For those trying to perform their duties conscientiously, these were demanding, often draining roles. The Royal Commission on the Poor Law in 1909 thought that masters and matrons had an almost impossible job managing schools, lunatic asylums, workshop and infirmaries, as well as running the workhouse itself.

The couple in charge

In general the guardians wished to appoint couples who could run the work-house at the minimum cost and maximum efficiency – for the lowest possible wages. Assistant Poor Law Commissioner Sir Francis Head advised Kentish guardians in 1835 that the master 'should be a person accustomed to the habits of your peasantry, acquainted with their character, of irreproachable moral conduct, with great firmness and mild temper'. Of the matron, the Commissioners in London required only that she should be comparable to a 'trustworthy female servant' and be paid at the same rate.

During the early years of the Poor Law, masters and matrons came from a variety of backgrounds. The first master and matron of Norfolk's Gressen-hall House of Industry in 1777 were James and Margaret Moore, an innkeeper and his wife from the nearby town of East Dereham. Many men had previously been non-commissioned officers (NCOs) in the army. There they had learnt how to instil discipline into unruly men and were suffi-ciently literate to deal with the paperwork required by the guardians and Whitehall. It was not always a guarantee of success, however. The notorious master of Andover workhouse in Hampshire, Colin McDougal, was a former sergeant-major in the Royal Artillery; he had had an exemplary career in the army before being discharged in 1836.

Nevertheless army backgrounds continued to find favour with those hiring workhouse masters. Between 1878 and 1904, for example, the master of Britain's largest workhouse at Crumpsall, north Manchester, was Frank Ballantine, who had risen through the ranks to become a Royal Artillery major. Another former NCO was Richard Cavendish, supposedly the illegitimate son of the king of Prussia. After seven years' exemplary service in the 4th Hussars (where he rose to the rank of sergeant), he became master of Langport workhouse in Somerset.

Others were promoted from within the workhouse themselves, partic-ularly porters and their female equivalents, 'porteresses'. In many smaller places, the porter was *de facto* the deputy master and thus in a good position to learn about the role's responsibilities. Porters learnt how to deal with all classes of paupers, for it was their duty to admit those who had a ticket from the relieving officer or a guardian as well as casual paupers, and to maintain discipline in the house. A porter was expected to search paupers 'or any other person whom he may suspect to have possession of any spirits or prohibited articles... To lock all outer doors and take the keys to the master at nine o'clock every night and to receive them again from him every morning at seven o'clock or such hours as shall be directed.'

Job advertisements give an idea of what the guardians were looking for. In *The Times* in August 1850, those in Amersham sought candidates who were 'man and wife without encumbrance, members of the Church of England, of good health and unquestionable character and the master must be a good penman and competent to keep the workhouse books and accounts and perform all the duties prescribed by the orders of the Poor Law Board'. On the same page, the guardians in Yeovil required that 'the master be a good accountant and write a fair hand, the matron a good needlewoman and understand cutting out garments'.

A career path soon began to emerge: ambitious men started as porters, or possibly schoolmasters, and then became the master at a small workhouse with the hope of crowning their careers by running one of the larger urban houses. Their wives may have been schoolmistresses or nurses, which gave them a useful knowledge of running the female side. In 1862 Poor Law Inspector John Lambert told a parliamentary inquiry that, since the introduction of the New Poor Law, 'there has been a great improvement in the kind of master who has grown up in the system; in my district there are several instances of workhouse masters who have been schoolmasters themselves, and they make some of the best workhouse masters'.

Whatever their background, they all had to be literate in order to deal with the mountain of paperwork required by the authorities in London and by the guardians themselves. The Poor Law Board believed that 'clear and accurate accounts must be kept, as well for the protection of the ratepayers and the poor, as of officers themselves'. But a committee that investigated the situation in 1903 found that all the witnesses they interviewed 'expressed the view that the forms of accounts were needlessly elaborate and entailed much useless labour upon workhouse masters'. The masters in rural unions, where there was no clerical help, had to devote so much time to book-keeping that 'they are often unable to pay sufficient attention to their other duties'.

The master and matron were at the centre of a three-way relationship with the guardians who employed them, the staff with whom they worked and lastly the paupers whom they oversaw. The most important of these was the relationship with the guardians. The master made regular reports to the weekly or fortnightly meetings of the guardians, describing what had happened in the house, briefing them on problems with the inmates and requesting permission to buy new stores. He also presented the many books he kept for their inspection, including the punishment book.

The reports that Alexander Chetham, the master of Spotland workhouse in Rochdale, Lancashire, made in the 1830s and 1840s are perhaps typical:

> 26 April 1837 Margret Lord was brought here in a chair Feby not expected to live long. On Monday morning she came into the kitchen and asked leave to go to Town. Mrs said she thought she had something about her that did not belong her. She said she might search her. She did so and delivered her of a gown she had round her body. She told her she had done rong in doing so. She imeadiately went up stairs brought her cloths and had them Examined and took herself off highly affronted.
>
> May 3 we have had two funerals since last Wedensday. James Crabtree upwards of 70 yr and Martha Cooper 69 years.
>
> May 10 Ann Clegg is yet very troublesome. We are in want of a Quantaty of knives.   [spellings as in the orginal]

Considering the responsibilities, wages were generally low, which must have deterred good candidates from applying and ensured that the most able and ambitious couples only spent a few months at a workhouse before seeking advancement. This was particularly true in the smaller rural unions. At Cleobury Mortimer in Herefordshire, 17 masters were appointed between 1854 and 1918; the average turnover in provincial unions during the same period was seven. There was no national pay scale, and the temptation for guardians was to keep the wages as low as possible. Herbert Preston-Thomas found that the practice of guardians in the West Country was to 'support the appointment of the person offering to do the work for the least salary, as otherwise their constituents would blame them for not being efficiently economical of the rates'.

Andover paid Mr and Mrs McDougal a joint salary of £80, plus board and lodging (referred to as 'rations'). This seems to have been about the average wage for the larger rural workhouses – Yeovil was also offering that in 1850. At the same time, Belford in Northumberland was paying £30 to Thomas and Mary Foster as master and matron, and even this low sum had had to be increased from £20 in order to attract the couple from neighbouring Alnwick, where they were already master and matron. Larger urban houses paid more. At Wrexham, with nearly 250 inmates, the master received £60 and the matron £40. At Liverpool, with 3,500 paupers, the master was paid £350 in 1869.

The low wages and generally poor conditions on offer caused difficulty in recruiting masters and matrons, particularly for the smaller rural workhouses. Despite the need for testimonials (Amersham required five) and the payment of sureties or bonds (Amersham wanted two bonds of £100 each), to be forfeited if service was unsatisfactory (p.77), it was all too easy to hire poor or inappropriate staff. Many of the couples employed at Belford, for example, proved unable to deal with the paperwork, instil discipline into the paupers or manage the house effectively. In a few cases they failed on all three accounts.

The shortage of qualified officers meant that it was relatively easy for inefficient staff, who had perhaps been sacked elsewhere, to find new positions. This could occur even in high-profile situations, where more care might have been expected. For example, the master appointed at Andover after McDougal's resignation in 1845, a Mr Price, had to resign after a few months when stories of overcrowding at Oxford workhouse, where he had previously been master, came to the public attention. He was succeeded by a Mr Brice, who was sacked after three years for taking liberties with female paupers. In London, the guardians at Lambeth workhouse employed George Catch, though they must have known of his reputation after he was sacked from the nearby Strand and Newington workhouses. This changed with the growth of a career path within the Poor Law from the 1870s onwards. Masters, matrons and their staff continued to be dismissed – usually for financial or sexual irregularities – but rarely for gross incompetence.

The opportunity for graft and petty corruption was rarely absent from the administration of the Poor Law. George Bartley acknowledged the problem in his guide for newly elected guardians published in 1876:

> If he is a good man and the Master of a Workhouse … he has enormous power for good or evil in his hands; underpaying him is very unjust and a great mistake; but if he is at all inclined to go wrong, underpaying him will certainly encourage him in doing so for he can easily make up his income in an improper manner.

Masters and matrons, if they were so inclined, could supplement their income by illegally selling the provisions or using them for their own families. (One of the reasons why the paupers starved at Andover was that Colin McDougal, the workhouse master, was stealing the rations to feed his own family.) Dr Joseph Rogers, who was a Poor Law medical officer in London between the 1860s and 1880s, wondered how it was possible that many 'masters of workhouses with limited incomes should succeed in leaving at their deaths so much money, as so many of them do'. He cited the example of Daniel Haybittle, the master of the Strand workhouse, one of the poorest and worst run workhouses in the Metropolis, who left £2,000 on his death.

Despite regular audits and the supervisory role of the guardians, it was not difficult to defraud the Poor Law Union and it was hard to prove that this was being done. The master at Gressenhall, Philip Reynolds, was accused on a number of occasions of feathering his nest, although nothing was ever proved and he remained in post for over 20 years. In 1871 John Webster, a pauper at Gressenhall, wrote to the Local Government Board alleging that Reynolds grew his own vegetables on the workhouse vegetable plot, appropriated materials to build himself a greenhouse, used firewood meant for the paupers and entertained visitors at the guardians' expense ('that you might as well be in Oxford Street, for the gigs rattling all night long'). When the inmates attempted to protest at these abuses, he had them locked up all night. The guardians investigated and dismissed the accusations. However, over the next few years there were a number of other small scandals, including complaints about the quality of workhouse food and a protracted affair in which Reynolds was forced to pay back £18 to cover the cost of coal that had mysteriously vanished from the workhouse stores.

In disputes and allegations at the workhouse, it was natural for the guardians to support their staff, particularly the master. At Marylebone in 1856 the master and two porters were accused of flogging two young women who had caused a disturbance in the refractory women's ward. A local magistrate brought the case to the notice of the guardians, who reprimanded the staff about the need to treat the inmates with kindness, 'considering the extreme provocation they had received', and warned them that they would be dismissed if behaviour like this happened again. Public pressure, however, forced the Poor Law Board to intervene; it demanded that the master, Richard Ryan, be sacked. Despite considerable protests from the guardians, he was forced to resign.

Public criticism of cruel or indifferent workhouse staff was severe, but it often took a tragedy to expose their behaviour. On 28 December 1872 *Punch* pilloried the superintendent of the casual ward of St Giles's workhouse in London 'who caused the death of a child by refusing to receive it, with its mother, on a vile night, and who stuck to his brutal lie that the mother was drunk'. The writer contrasts his cruelty with the charitable spirit of the season, noting that 'it is a Christmas thought to be heartily glad that George Cannon ... will spend his Christmas Day in gaol, and some three hundred and sixty days after in that edifice; at hard labour. And I hope the officials will take care that it *is* hard.'

At the Gressenhall workhouse, the guardians threatened to resign *en masse* when the Local Government Board peremptorily sacked the master without consulting them. Rudely awoken late one night in January 1911, Robert Neville refused to take in a man who had just tried to commit suicide. The rector of Whissonsett, from where the sick pauper came, complained to the Board in London, who sent an inspector to investigate. He concluded that Neville had been wrong not to admit the man. Unfortunately the guardians became annoyed when the inspector did not meet any of them to discuss the case, and they resented the superior tone adopted by the Board. Eventually the Board moderated their letters, and the guardians accepted Neville's dismissal, although they ensured that he received generous superannuation based on his long service in the Poor Law.

Often the guardians had no real interested in the paupers in the house and had minimal power over the master and his staff. The Poor Law

Inspector Herbert Preston-Thomas claimed that that the master could be a 'despot' because many of the guardians he knew exercised little control as they met infrequently and rarely visited the house. Before the scandal at Andover in 1846, for example, the guardians were generally apathetic, and the chairman of the board, the Rev. Christopher Dodson, had not visited the workhouse for five years.

Boards appointed visiting committees which, according to the Poor Law Board's medical officer Dr Edward Smith, visited 'too infrequently and in too great a hurry and are too much disinclined to recommend change'. It did not help that until 1893 guardians could only enter the workhouse with the permission of the master. Will Crooks' biographer noted that after this was changed 'there began, not only in Poplar, but all over the country, a marked improvement in the treatment of old people in the workhouse'.

On occasion the guardians or, in particular, the chairman would interfere too much in the workings of the workhouse. This was one of the charges made against the new generation of reforming guardians who were elected in the 1880s and 1890s. Will Crooks and George Lansbury, two working-class trade unionists elected to Poplar in London in 1893, found most of the officers very hostile. During a fire which broke out in the workhouse, one of the officers exclaimed: 'The only thing wanting is that Crooks and Lansbury should be put on top of it.'

The indoor staff

Each master and matron supervised a team of staff who ran the workhouse on a daily basis. Almost every workhouse had a porter and possibly his wife, a taskmaster to supervise the paupers' work, and a nurse or two to care for the elderly and infirm. Where there were children, there might be a schoolmaster and mistress. Poor Law Unions were also responsible for vaccinating children, so there would be a vaccinator (often the medical officer or doctor), and registering births, marriages and deaths (the registrar was often the clerk). On the professional side there was the clerk to the guardians (normally a solicitor), a medical officer and often a chaplain (usually a local curate). The admission of paupers to the house and the administration of out-relief was the responsibility of the relieving officer.

The smallest unions, such as Richmond in Yorkshire, were run by only a few staff. Here in 1849 the guardians employed just a clerk, a relieving officer and the workhouse master and matron. More typical, perhaps, was Richmond in Surrey which, at the same time, had 160 inmates and a staff of 18, comprising a clerk, treasurer, master and matron, workhouse porter, chaplain, two medical officers and vaccinators, two part-time vaccinators, a relieving officer, five assistant overseers and two registrars of births, marriages and deaths.

The largest workhouses, housing several thousand paupers, employed dozens of staff. Also in 1849, for example, Manchester employed 134 men and women, including two stokers and an assistant infant nurse at the industrial schools at Swinton, while in the main workhouse were found a barber, apothecary and clothing storekeeper. The workhouse at Whitechapel in East London, with nearly 200 staff, even employed a part-time fire-engine keeper, William Childe; he was paid £6 a year and combined this work with being a 'beadle and messenger for Trinity Square'.

Staff were recruited by various means. *The Lancet, Poor Law Journal* and other professional journals carried advertisements for medical officers and other specialist staff. Advertisements for other positions appeared in newspapers, for instance *The Times*, although few of its affluent readers would have desired the post of Assistant Porter at Bradfield, Berkshire, advertised on 9 June 1851 at a salary of £15 'with board, lodging, washing in the workhouse'. Other situations advertised that day were for a porter at East London, master and matron at Clifden (Bristol), a schoolmaster and mistress at Downham Market, Norfolk, and a parochial messenger 'of active habits' for St James's, Westminster.

Advertisements in *The Times* give an idea of the type of candidate the guardians were looking for. At Marylebone, in July 1848, the union was seeking to employ a porter and required:

> a married man, without encumbrance, between the ages of 30 and 50, of sober habits and good command of temper. He must be able to write a fair hand and keep plain accounts. Salary 14s per week with board, lodging and washing; his wife will be allowed to live at the lodge with him.

The successful candidate's wife would no doubt have been expected to supervise the female refractory ward or perhaps act as a seamstress. It would not have been an easy job for the couple to undertake – Marylebone workhouse at the time was grossly overcrowded with some 2,000 inmates, many of whom were destitute Irish who had fled the famine.

Attracting suitable staff was difficult because the wages were poor and the work irksome. There was a huge turnover of staff, particularly at the junior levels, such as porters and nurses; they often left within a few months for better paid jobs elsewhere or were sacked for misconduct. Between 1836 and 1899, for example, Bicester, Oxfordshire, employed 22 porters, each staying an average of just under three years each (although only three served between 1842 and 1860). One of them, Alfred John Payne, lasted only three months in 1876, resigning because he disliked the work. Another short-lived porter was John Bowley, previously been the porter at neighbouring Thame workhouse and appointed in May 1842. He was sacked six months later, in November, following complaints over his conduct.

The smaller workhouses generally preferred single men or widowers as porters, ideally with another useful trade. At Llanfyllin, in rural mid-Wales, for example, when a vacancy for porter became available in 1845 the successful candidate, John Griffiths, was offered a salary of '£18.4.0 per annum with an allowance of £3.3.0 a year in lieu of groceries together with the usual rations, apartments and washing in the workhouse'. Griffiths' job offer, however, was on condition that he learned how to make shoes. In the 1870s Congleton workhouse in Cheshire was looking for candidates who were bakers, in order that they could bake bread for the inmates. Such a provision also had the benefit of ensuring a certain level of intelligence and competence.

A few porters had recently been inmates or former paupers. They had the advantage of being cheap to employ, as well as knowing the workhouse and its secrets and perhaps being not overly worried about disciplining paupers. A good number seem to have been recruited by word of mouth or by notices placed on the workhouse door or in public places locally, particularly in rural areas. The porter often set the tone for the rest of the workhouse, for he was in many ways its public face. Porters dealt with the roughest and most abusive of the admissions, which may have coloured their generally abusive attitude to the inmates. In a Commons debate in 1891, an MP described how a vagrant was admitted into one workhouse 'in about the same tone in which a surly gamekeeper would address a half-broke retriever'.

The more important posts for masters, medical officers and porters were filled by interview with the guardians. Despite the low wages, on occasion the number of applicants for these posts could be surprisingly large, because there was a big pool of eager applicants from junior posts in the Poor Law service. Over 120 applications were received when the post of workhouse master and matron at the small Northumbrian workhouse at Belford was advertised in March 1902. The successful candidates were John and Leah Petrie, porter and 'porteress' at Sunderland, who were to be paid £35 and £15 respectively.

In some cases, details of the applicants were published in local newspapers. William Bragger's letter of application to become the workhouse master was printed, along with two others, in the *Wrexham Advertiser* in January 1857. The paper also printed an account of how he was elected to the post. First, Edgworth, the chairman of the guardians, read out all 22 letters of application and references to the assembled guardians. Then a shortlist of three candidates, Bragger, Roberts and Davies, was evidently prepared. At this stage, individual guardians who had been impressed by a particular applicant rose to make a speech of approbation. Mr Challoner rose to propose Bragger as master. He drew attention to his army credentials and his reference from Colonel Yorke, which was based on 20 years' acquaintance. Mr Dashwood Parry seconded the nomination, and this was enough to secure Bragger's selection.

Applicants were asked to bring testimonials from previous employers and to provide a guarantee bond to indemnify the guardians in case of financial fraud or personal bankruptcy. This was a common requirement in the public sector; even teachers at board (local authority) schools had to provide such bonds, and there were a number of companies whose business was providing them. It was a good business to be in, because they were rarely invoked. At Southwell in Nottinghamshire, the successful applicant for the post of master had to provide two sureties of £50 each.

Then, as now, references might not always mean very much, particularly if the guardians were keen to see the back of a member of staff. James Kilner, the clerk of the Strand Union and a friend of the brutal workhouse master George Catch, recommended Catch and his wife Selina for the post of master and matron at Newington with the comment that 'their general conduct ... has been characterised by honesty, integrity and sobriety, and that they discharged the duties of master and matron with firmness and efficiency'.

Each group of guardians decided how much they could afford to pay based on local circumstances and the nature of the people they employed. Ever conscious of the ratepayers who elected them, the guardians were notoriously reluctant to pay more than the bare minimum, although they would often increase the rate paid in order to keep good staff or to reward good performance, such as helping out in a particular emergency or saving the ratepayers' money through cutting expenditure. The Petries, at Belford, were paid an additional £5 each in 1903 after having been in post for a year. Eventually they left in 1908 to go to better paid positions at Barton Regis on the outskirts of Bristol.

Discontent among workhouse officials and their staff was endemic. George Bartley warned new guardians that they should expect to be regularly approached by the officers:

> In one year I noted that almost every person except the master of the workhouse, who perhaps deserved it most, came up with the same application, namely for an increase in pay... The truth was that in our union the rate of pay was pitched so low that even with the increase, everybody was dissatisfied and only looked forward to sufficient time elapsing when they would be able with decency and some chance of success, once more to apply for a repetition of the increase.

He thought that there should be annual incremental increases based on performance, but this sensible course was not adopted until the 1930s.

The low wages were compensated for, to an extent, by the fact that board and lodging were included, and there were pauper servants to cook and clean. From the guardians' viewpoint this meant that the indoor staff were always on the premises and always on duty. The 'rations' provided to the staff were much the same as those given to the paupers, although rather more generous. In the larger workhouses, the master, matron and their senior staff at least could live very comfortably.

The master and matron received six times the rations given to the paupers. In 1865 Catherine Leivers, matron of the small Tadcaster workhouse and the centre of a national scandal in 1865 (p.85), was entitled to the following rations per week: '1lb flour; 1/2lb sugar; 1/4lb butter; 1/4lb bacon; 1/4lb cheese; 1/4lb coffee; 3oz tea; 12 pints ale at 1s 6d per gallon; 6lbs fish or 4lb meat; 4 eggs'. Other staff members were less generously treated and the levels of rations were often a matter of dispute with the guardians. The Poor Law Inspector Baldwyn Fleming told a parliamentary inquiry in 1902 of the case of a nurse whose ration of bacon was reduced from cured bacon at 7d a pound to the cheaper green bacon at 4d.

> One of the guardians said, 'I have to eat green bacon and I do not see why officers at the workhouse should eat better bacon than I get', quite overlooking the fact that the appetite of a man who lived the greater part of the day in the open air on a farm was quite a different thing to the appetite of a nurse, who spends her time in the vitiated atmosphere of the sick wards. The nurse left, and I believe myself that this was the straw which broke the camel's back.

In most small and middle-sized unions, salary rates hardly increased during the 19th century. At Bicester, for example, the amount paid to the porter (£20) remained unchanged between 1836 and 1899, while the master's salary actually fell from £70 in 1836 to £50 at the end of the century. This may seem strange, but the Victorian period suffered little inflation. Indeed, during the last two decades of the 19th century the cost of living fell by about a fifth, largely as a result of the import of cheap food and manufactured goods, so even the poorest workhouse officials would have found themselves better off.

However, expenditure on wages rose from about 12 per cent of the national expenditure in the Poor Law in the early 1870s to 18 per cent 30 years later. Much of the increase was attributable to the greater numbers of nursing and ancillary staff taken on to run workhouse infirmaries, together with contributions to the new superannuation scheme introduced in 1896.

It was not until 1884 that the National Association of Poor Law Officers was set up to represent men and women employed in workhouses, although less than ten per cent of officers were members in 1893 and under a third in 1898, at the height of its power. The Association had little influence in negotiating pay rises; its greatest achievement was to campaign for a super-annuation scheme based on contributions from guardians and the officers themselves according to length of service. It also offered guarantee bonds for members at a cheaper rate than that provided by commercial insurance companies.

Because the staff were relatively isolated, they created their own small social world in which friendships – and sometimes romances – developed as well as rivalries and squabbles. Staff communities were roughly similar to those formed by the servants in the great houses of the period, although they were markedly less rigid because the turnover of staff was much greater and they were not trying to ape their betters. Instead they were trying to overawe their social inferiors.

The social status of workhouse staff was an enduring concern, of great significance to themselves and their employers. The social reformer and Poor Law guardian Louisa Twining noted that masters and matrons were all of the 'low and uneducated middle-classes', but in fact their status was perhaps closer to that of headmasters and mistresses in state or 'board' schools – firmly within the respectable lower middle classes. However, the National Association of Poor Law Officials, who negotiated with the Local Govern-ment Board on the issue, argued that workhouse staff should be compared to the rather better paid prison governors and governesses.

In the less happy houses social differences, real and perceived, often led to friction between the officers. At Blean, Kent, the master wrote to the guardians in 1854: 'I do not wish to disparage the porter – but I do dis-tinctly say, if we have the porter forced upon us to take his meals, it will (in the eyes of the inmates) very much lessen the position we have held as master and matron of this Union.' The fact that the porter had formerly been a pauper probably had something to do with the protest. When the master and matron were allowed to have their meals separately, however, the schoolmistress began to object to the eating habits of the schoolmaster and porter. It did not help that because the workhouse was isolated, it was difficult for the staff to escape one another. The porter at Blean soon resigned, 'being unable to give satisfaction and quite tired of this secluded way of living'.

There were nevertheless paradoxes within the system. Within the workhouse itself, for example, the master was generally inferior in social class to the guardians, chaplains and medical officers. This sometimes caused tension, although possibly less often than class-conscious commentators observed. One example was George Catch, who brutally ran several central London workhouses in the 1850s and 1860s (p.84). Semi-literate, he had a huge inferiority complex when dealing with university-educated medical officers in particular, and spent a lot of time obstructing their work as a result. 'You are worth no more than this doorpost,' he repeatedly told one doctor at Newington workhouse in south London.

Arguing for the appointment of well-born and educated medical officers to serve in the workhouse itself, *The Times* observed in January 1845:

> There ought to be a gentleman in or about an establishment containing 400 or 500 persons… You cannot make the establishment *go*, that is to go regularly and correctly of itself. Your bluff governor, ex-constable, sergeant, ex-gardener won't do… Why, what is a gentleman made for – what is the use of that expensive personage at all in the social institutions of this country – if you can keep 500 paupers decent and clean, and sweet and comfortable without one?

There was some concern that middle-class officers would be directed by their social inferiors or have to endure conditions to which their station had not accustomed them. Poor Law Inspector Baldwyn Fleming was concerned about the quality of the eating utensils that middle-class nurses might have to use: 'In many places they are rough and not at all what the nurse is accustomed to. They may have to eat with a steel fork and a pewter spoon, and things of that kind; that is a matter of very small outlay, which the Guardians could meet without any trouble.'

The frustrations of the work, boredom and the fact that the staff were almost always on duty meant that it was easy for employees to rub each other up the wrong way. As many workhouses were situated on the edge of towns or in villages, and holidays were either short or non-existent, it was difficult for the staff to escape even for a few hours. In consequence, a constant stream of complaints about conditions and the behaviour of the master and his staff was sent either to the authorities in London or, more often, to the guardians. They usually concerned sexual improprieties supposedly involving female paupers, petty corruption or irresolvable disputes between workhouse staff.

Yet conversely many workhouses seem to have been happy places to work in, judging by the surviving photographs of Christmas dinners and fancy dress dances. This seems to have particularly been the case from the 1890s onwards when workhouses largely became refuges for the aged and the sick, where there were sufficient properly trained staff, better conditions and the strict discipline over staff and paupers had been gently relaxed.

The good, the bad and the ugly

The level of care offered to the inmates varied tremendously between workhouses and even within a workhouse. To a certain extent, it depended on the facilities provided by the guardians, the attitudes of the master, matron and senior staff, and the physical layout of the building. Abuses were certainly more common in the older and smaller workhouses than in the newer ones built in the 1870s and later.

Such scandals were the exception. Many masters and matrons attempted to maintain decent conditions and an effective administration for their inmates. The Poor Law reformer Louisa Twining paid tribute to these men and women: 'They are generally a most respectable and deserving class of persons, discharging very onerous and disagreeable duties with zeal, kindness and fairness.' Caring, well-organized and motivated individuals could make a great deal of difference to how a pauper was treated. James Greenwood was impressed by the seemingly unflappable and sympathetic 'Daddy' who supervised the wards at Lambeth. Indeed, for a short while 'Daddy' became a minor celebrity on the music hall stage as a result of the popularity of a song based on the articles Greenwood wrote for the *Pall Mall Gazette*.

At Wrexham, William Bragger was a generous and imaginative workhouse master, rarely using the punishment book and dressing the paupers in different clothes to give them a sense of individuality and lessen the stigma of being in the house. In his obituary, in the *Wrexham Telegraph* in July 1863, it was noted that the master 'seldom' returned from the market without gifts in the form of tobacco and snuff for male inmates and toys and cakes for the children, and he was in the habit of paying the debts of certain inmates in dire financial straits. And during 1862 the guardians were surprised that Bragger had not entered 'the nature and length' of punishments to inmates in his log book, only to be told that the former sergeant-major avoided inflicting punishments on the poor if he could help it, preferring to govern the house without such sanctions.

Nearly a century later the obituary of Daniel Pickett in the *Stratford Herald* in 1934 stated that:

> Mr. Pickett will be remembered by many residents as the large-hearted Master for 33 years of the Stratford-on-Avon workhouse. The thousands of men who came under his care, representing the flotsam and jetsam of humanity, had a very warm regard for the 'Guvnor' who, with his great capacity for friendship, his rare sympathy and kindly nature was always ready to do his best for the travellers who came his way. During the tenure of his office at 50 Arden Street, Mr. Pickett witnessed many improvements in Poor Law administration and the local institute was brought up to date by the erection of the women's infirmary, the new tramp wards and laundry.

This generosity was relatively rare. In most workhouses the inmates were not cruelly treated, but they were institutionalized and neglected, and their complaints and concerns were largely ignored. Will Crooks found that in the Poplar workhouse:

> The inmates had not sufficient clothes and many were without boots to their feet. The food was so bad that the wash-tubs overflowed with what the poor people could not eat. It was almost heart-breaking to go round the place and hear the complaints and see the tears of the aged men and women. 'Poverty's no crime, but here it is treated like crime,' they used to say.

The problem was not just a lack of resources, although penny-pinching by the guardians was often a factor; usually the staff just did not care. Masters and matrons, in particular, normally accepted conditions as they were and proved unwilling or unable to improve matters. Joseph Rogers described one master at the Strand: 'he had lived long enough in the service of the Poor Law … to be fully aware that no good would accrue to him or his by too much zeal in the performance of his duty.' The other officers would have followed the master's lead – there was little incentive for them to do otherwise, as there was no financial reward, scant chance of advancement, and eager novices were soon discouraged by the old hands.

A determined master and matron could run the workhouse more or less as they liked, with little interference from the guardians, let alone the Poor Law Inspectors or, provided all the paperwork was completed satisfactorily, the authorities in Whitehall. The master's word was law and both staff and inmates could suffer if the master (or indeed matron) took against them.

In the absence of effective supervision, a number of workhouse masters and matrons were cruel in the extreme. The scandal at Andover is the best-known example, but mid-Victorian newspapers and the correspondence with the authorities in London are littered with other cases. One of the most unpleasant of workhouse masters was George Catch. He had begun his career as a policeman but, on the election of a friend of his as chairman of the Strand board of guardians, he became the workhouse porter. On the retirement of the workhouse master and matron, he and his wife, 'being equally unsuitable' in the eyes of Dr Joseph Rogers, the Union medical officer, took over their positions.

Rogers eventually exposed Catch before the guardians for the mistreatment of a woman in the lying-in ward. Despite the woman's extreme pain, Catch had delayed calling the doctor in until nine days after the birth of her child, so that Rogers did not qualify for a fee for being present at childbirth. Subsequently, Mr and Mrs Catch got another appointment at Newington workhouse in south London. In his autobiography Rogers noted: 'So intensely tyrannical and cruel had been the rule of this man, that the day that he resigned the keys and was leaving the House, the whole establishment – at least those who could leave their beds – rose in open rebellion, and with old kettles, shovels, penny trumpets, celebrated their departure from the premises.'

At Newington, Catch's treatment of the inmates did not improve. He once deprived a crippled pauper of his crutches and again fell out with the medical officer, whom he accused of sleeping with a nurse. Forewarned by Joseph Rogers, the medical officer produced a certificate, signed by the chief gynaecologist at Guy's Hospital, testifying to the girl's virginity. The parliamentary inquiry into George Catch's behaviour at Newington showed how much day-to-day power masters had. Catch was accused of 'refusing to appoint special advisers for insane patients … in transferring sick people from the body of the house to the infirmaries without instructions from the medical officer, and in opposition to his wishes … in refusing to admit Margaret Dillon into the workhouse at night, although she had an order of admission from the relieving officer, on the plea that she was intoxicated, but without seeing her, in consequence of which she remained all night at the workhouse gate'.

Assisted by friends on the Strand board of guardians, Catch ended up at Lambeth workhouse, where his behaviour became worse. He harassed a young woman, who ran away. Catch, thinking she was hiding up a chimney in one of the female infirm wards, tried to smoke her out by pouring hydrochloric acid onto some substance and directing the fumes up the chimney. Had the girl been in the chimney, she would have suffocated, but the only effect was that the old women in the ward started sneezing and coughing. This was reported to the Poor Law Board, where Henry Fleming, Poor Law Inspector for London, minuted: 'If Mr Catch had been an old & faithful officer, with an excellent general character, I think this act of his might have passed with a severe reprimand. But considering his previous history, the odium of which his apt [appointment] has brought upon the P.L.B.', there was no course but dismissal.

Supported by many of the guardians, Catch declined to go. Instead, he took action against the solicitor, Samuel Shaen, who had circulated a pamphlet exposing Catch's misdeeds. Although Catch won the case, he was nonetheless dismissed, and was described in the 1871 census for Kensington as a 'poor law official (out of employ)'. Without much sympathy, Rogers noted that, in his final years, 'he drifted downwards until ultimately, being without means and having tired out all his friends, he in a fit of despair threw himself in front of a Great Western train and was cut to pieces'.

The case of Catherine Leivers is less well known. She was matron of the small Tadcaster workhouse, where she was the sole paid employee, a most unusual situation by the 1860s. In February 1865 her brutal regime was exposed as a result of a public protest against the way in which one of her victims, Elizabeth Daniel, had been buried. There followed a torch-lit demonstration in which an effigy of the matron was paraded and eventually burned in front of the workhouse. According to a local newspaper:

> A crowd of people numbering 300 or 400 collected in the High Street and then proceeded to the Market Place, headed by the Tadcaster drum and fife band and a banner on which it was inscribed 'He that oppresseth the poor oppresseth his maker'… Mr Edward Spink the town bellman got up and proclaimed the object of the meeting, which he stated was 'to openly show their disapproval of the manner in which the matron of Tadcaster Union Workhouse treated the inmates'.

A petition was sent to the Poor Law Board in London, which requested that an inspector be sent to investigate the matron's bad behaviour. The local inspector Andrew Doyle was sent to investigate. He interviewed a number of witnesses who revealed Leivers' sadistic behaviour, not just towards the women but also towards the young children. One witness was Bridget McCormick, who had been inside the house for two months. She said:

> I saw Mrs Leivers strike Elizabeth Daniel with the poker on the head and cut a great gash in it. Also she hit her with the coal rake and cut her arm. She also struck repeatedly with the rolling pin. During the two months I was in the workhouse, Mrs Leivers beat Elizabeth Daniel three or four times a day… I saw her beat Charley Townend and Willy Townend on their bare backs with a thick stick until they were black and blue, for taking a drink of water. She also beat them with the rolling pin.

The guardians were naturally very defensive about the accusations. John Bromet, the clerk, wrote to London:

> The board wish to remark that almost from the very day the matron came to the workhouse and introduced the system prescribed by your Board a prejudice has existed against her in the town and has gradually increased up to the present time. To this they attribute the circulation and the consequent exaggeration of many false reports with reference to the treatment of paupers in the workhouse… Any complaints by the paupers have been very rare indeed… The house itself, the linen etc are always remarkably clean.

The public inquiry did not last long, however. As the first witnesses began to give their damning evidence, the guardians dramatically left the hall with Mrs Leivers and demanded her resignation, thus forcing the abandonment of the inquiry. We do not know what happened to Mrs Leivers – she may well have been employed again elsewhere.

Certainly most scandals were the result of weak or ineffectual guardians who failed to control inappropriate behaviour by workhouse staff. Even a conscientious and experienced guardian such as George Bartley offers no advice in his guide for dealing with the master and his staff or visiting the house.

As a consequence, not a few unions were effectively run by their officers rather than by the guardians. At Great Yarmouth, in the 1880s and 1890s, the union was dominated by a local solicitor, Frederick Palmer, clerk to the board of guardians. When Ethel Leach was elected to the board in 1895, she found that there were no agendas for meetings of the board, let alone minutes or accounts. When she asked to see the minutes of the assessment committee (which administered the collection of the rates), she was forbidden to look at them in his office and had to read them on the quay. Eventually Palmer overstepped the mark; the Local Government Board insisted on his dismissal after he circulated a salacious cartoon at a meeting of the guardians.

It is perhaps in workhouses infirmaries that some of the most shocking abuses emerged. At Rotherhithe in southeast London, for example, an inquiry into the infirmary castigated the master and matron for laziness in 1866. Among the claims that Matilda Beeton, a nurse at the infirmary, made to the Poor Law Board was that she had complained 'to the master and matron ... both of the conduct of the pauper nurses and the condition of the patients; but the matron had told her that she (Miss Beeton) "must get used to all that, as workhouses were not like hospitals"'.

Such a view was all too common. Another nurse, Jane Bateman, told the Poor Law Inspector about the death of a Mrs Ward at another London workhouse, this time in Paddington:

When I went around the ward where she was one afternoon, I observed her pillow had been taken away, and she looked very ghastly, and asked

Vernum [an elderly pauper nurse] where the pillow was, and she said 'She's nearly gone and I always take the pillows away to make them go quicker, and I have taken her pillow away.' I had the pillow put back immediately, but Ward died half an hour later.

The general attitude can perhaps best be summed up by Matilda Beeton, the nurse who summarized conditions at Rotherhithe: 'On the whole it did not seem to me that a pauper's life was regarded in any other light than the sooner they were dead the better.'

Where the workhouse was well managed by the master and the matron, and the staff worked in good conditions with appropriate levels of pay, the lot of the pauper inmates was much improved. Too often, however, the guardians were only interested in keeping the rates low, with the result that the workforce were meanly paid and indifferently managed, while poor conditions fostered friction between colleagues and a high turnover of staff. Matters did improve, however, particularly from the 1880s when better trained and more professional medical staff began to be appointed. Yet even they could often do little to improve the lives of the paupers, allowing an apathetic and uncaring attitude to the inmates inevitably to set in. The system tainted all those who worked in it. As the 1909 Royal Commission found: 'The men and women we harnessed to the service of the workhouse invariably develop an all-embracing indifference to the suffering they cannot alleviate, the insane they cannot enliven, to the virtuous they cannot give courage, to the indolent they cannot correct, and to the vice they cannot punish.'

CHAPTER FOUR

'Fit for Purpose': the Able-bodied Poor

All paupers ... shall rise, be set to work, leave of work and to bed at
the appropriate times... They shall be allowed intervals for meals which
will be announced by the ringing of a bell.

Poor Law Commissioners, 1835

A T the heart of the workhouse were the able-bodied paupers – men and women deemed capable of working by the authorities but who, for one reason or another, 'sought the house'. The Poor Law regime was specifically designed to discourage the entry of such people by making conditions worse than they might expect outside and offering a variety of further petty humiliations, from uncomfortable uniforms and dull food to tedious, unending tasks. In reality, many of those considered able-bodied had some form of physical or mental disability that made them difficult to employ, but taking the guardians' hospitality was designed to be a degrading process that none but the desperate would undergo. In this regard the Poor Law system proved successful – within a decade or so relatively few able-bodied men and women were to be found inside the house, except perhaps at times of economic depression when thousands were thrown out of work with nothing to fall back on. Even so, despite the abundant evidence, the concern remained that to make the workhouse more welcoming would attract the shirker and the lay-about.

Forced into the 'house

The Old Poor Law was on the verge of collapse in the early 1830s because of the large number of rural unemployed or, more often, underemployed men and women seeking relief, which led to a spiralling rise in the rates. The Poor Law (Amendment) Act of 1834 cut poor rates at a stroke by insisting that the able-bodied only receive relief within workhouses with worse living conditions than in the paupers' own homes ('the workhouse test'). In theory, out-relief (small weekly allowances or pensions to the sick and elderly) was banned, although it continued to an extent in many places despite the efforts of the government in Whitehall. Every so often instructions would be issued demanding an end to out-relief, but it was not until the 1870s that the numbers in receipt of assistance really began to fall – largely because the central authorities became more rigorous in enforcing the rules (see p.211).

In most of the cases that came before the relieving officers or the guardians, the granting of a few shillings out-relief would have proved considerably cheaper for ratepayers and better for applicants. However, this was not how the guardians saw it. Those seeking relief were to be offered the workhouse and nothing else.

The Bethnal Green Standard for March 1866 reported the case of the wife of a wine porter who was in Guy's Hospital, London, with a poisoned hand. His wife applied to the relieving officer for temporary relief during her husband's absence:

> She told him that she had one day's work every week, and that altogether she could earn about 1s 6d per week, that she was unwilling to break up her home, and that moreover she had friends who would assist her if the parish would do something for her. He ordered her the workhouse, and gave her an order to attend the Board [of Guardians]. She did so, and says that she was not asked a question, and was stopped when about to speak… She then went to one of the clergy, who gave her 2s 6d, and ordered her to make a fresh application, making use of his name, and saying that he would be willing to increase the stipend of the parish, if one were granted. The relieving officer called at her house, and said that nothing more could be done.

George Bartley's manual for Poor Law Guardians of 1876 largely consists of warnings to new members of boards about not paying out unnecessary relief. If in doubt, he suggests that applicants be 'offered the House', instead of out-relief – a decision which, as he acknowledged, often met resistance. In most cases he found that 'when the House is offered, an exhibition of temper is common and cases of great insolence are not unheard of. Many, however, particularly the old hands, prefer the more dignified way of retiring with a toss of the head, saying but too plainly "thank you, sir, I am above that".'

In the early days of the New Poor Law, the clerk to the Bicester Union, Oxfordshire, told the Poor Law Commissioners of the case of a tailor who had come before his guardians: 'On the relieving officer giving his order [to the workhouse] he was rather abusive at first, but said he would rather be tied to the top of the highest tree in the parish than go there, and he has never applied for relief since.'

Sometimes there was no alternative to the workhouse, and when applicants accepted that they had no choice, it could be traumatic. The journalist James Grant noted the wretchedness of applicants to London workhouses in the late 1830s: 'There are many who, in being compelled to seek an asylum in one of these places, resign themselves to utter despair. They regard themselves as entirely out of the world, and as placed beyond the pale of society as well as beyond the reach of sympathy.' And Lucy Luck, the daughter of a pauper, wrote in her old age that, before her family entered the Tring workhouse in Hertfordshire in 1851, they stopped nearby: 'My mother sat down with one [child] on each side of her and one in her arms, crying bitterly over us before she took us into the union.'

The nature of the applicants inevitably changed over the 90 years of the New Poor Law. The number of young and middle-aged men and women 'applying for the house' fell dramatically, as they either obtained work in the booming Victorian economy or found alternatives to the workhouse and its petty humiliations. In 1844, for example, just over half of those admitted to the workhouse in Richmond, Surrey, were recorded as being unemployed or destitute, a quarter were ill or infirm and a fifth were children under the age of fourteen. Twenty years later, the numbers of unemployed or destitute had fallen to 40 per cent and the proportion of ill or infirm had risen to just over a third of all applications. By the end of the century, the number of those admitted who were unemployed or destitute had fallen to less than a fifth.

In some places the New Poor Law proved almost too successful in reducing the number of able-bodied paupers, whose cheap labour was needed to keep the workhouses running at the lowest possible cost to the ratepayers. In the 1840s rural workhouses were already reporting that they did not have enough able-bodied paupers to undertake all the work which needed to be done. As early as June 1846 the guardians at Caersws in mid Wales were considering hiring labourers to perform some of the heavier tasks. And in rural Norfolk a shortage of female able-bodied paupers meant that local women had to be employed to help clean and cook in the workhouse.

With the exception of the workhouses in London and the largest provincial towns, most workhouses were housing only the incapable, elderly and sick by the late 1840s. In 1852 Robert Pashley noted that 'each building which we absurdly call a workhouse is in truth a general hospital, an almshouse, an idiot house, a blind asylum, a deaf and dumb asylum … and a workhouse. But this last part of the establishment omits to find work even for the able-bodied.' Pashley and his fellow commentators had failed to notice that the able-bodied paupers, for whom the system had been designed, were disappearing rapidly, leaving only the unemployable. Even in Stepney, in the heart of London's depressed East End, Charles Booth found by 1889 that most able-bodied paupers were in the house because of sickness or decripitude. A decade later in York the other great social investigator of the period, Seebohm Rowntree, described the residents of the workhouse as follows: 'although not imbecile or infirm, [they] nevertheless belong to the class of the "unfit". Some are feeble-minded and dull-witted, others have some physical defect which puts them at a disadvantage in the industrial struggle.'

However, contemporary observers, such as 'the Indoor Pauper' and Charles Booth clung to old preconceptions, tending to cite the weakness of a pauper's character as the reason for his or her plight. 'The Indoor Pauper' wrote: 'I question if five in a hundred will ever be found to owe their degradation to anything save their own misdeeds… The truth is, the general run of indoor paupers deserve their fate, and a great many seem to like it better than any other.' Charles Booth shared this view, giving examples of men and women at St Pancras workhouse in London such as: 'Single man. Labourer. Age 38. Chargeable many years; could get his own living, but too lazy to work; nothing at all the matter with him.' Many of the cases Booth describes had either grown up in the house or come from broken homes, for example:

> Youth. Aged 18. His father was a labourer, a total abstainer and a respectable hard-working man who died some years ago. His mother was a chronic drunkard, and immediately after her husband's death the whole family had to go in. The boy has been prosecuted for throwing up situations. Refused to work except 'when he liked'.

Few applicants to the workhouse had ever earned enough to save for the periods of hardship – or if they had, it now lay in pawnbrokers' shop windows or in the hands of pub landlords. Because they rarely had permanent employment, they could not join a friendly society, which entitled other workers to benefits to help with illness or unemployment.

The complex reactions of Booth, Rowntree and others to workhouses and their inmates were characteristic of the age. Most Victorians had two contradictory views of the pauper. The first, deep-rooted notion was that paupers were a plague and had to be prevented from succumbing to this condition by whatever means possible. It was argued that such people were naturally lazy, only too willing to take everything offered by society and then grumble that it was not enough. Their lives had been corrupted by indolence and vice, particularly drink and, in the case of women, immorality. To provide anything more than the bare minimum would encourage an increase in their numbers because it was natural to them to live off the ratepayers rather than do a day's honest toil.

The second attitude adopted by contemporaries was much more sympathetic, particularly towards the elderly and children. The authorities and the middle classes had an increasingly rosy view of the elderly couples worn out by years of honest toil, who they felt should be encouraged to spend their declining years at leisure in the house. Children, too, were seen as being innocent victims of the Poor Law, who should be trained so that they would not become a burden on the poor-ratepayers in later life. However, the unimaginative and penny-pinching ways in which most workhouses were run frustrated attempts to improve conditions until the late-Victorian period.

The system's deficiencies were occasionally viewed with sense as well as sentiment, with some observers also noting the effect of the workhouse on paupers. The institution often proved a quagmire from which, once drawn in, a man or woman found it increasingly difficult to escape, except perhaps in fantasy. Fred Copeman, who grew up in Wangford workhouse in Suffolk during the First World War, remembered his mother, who was also in the house, 'always seemed to be discussing what she would do when her ship came home. All the inmates had this habit and talked constantly of what they would do when they got out. Very few of them ever left, however.'

One unfortunate inmate who seems to have struggled to cope outside was Elizabeth Sexton, admitted nine times to Smallburgh workhouse, Norfolk, between 1839 and 1844. On her first visit she was accompanied by her husband and five dependent children. A year later, in April 1840, pregnant and deserted, she entered the house again with her children. Here her daughter Louisa was born and died, and she also lost a son before she was discharged in September 1841. She was back in the house a week later and stayed until March 1842; she was readmitted ten days later. Three months later, in June, she was discharged, but was readmitted the same day. By this time she was pregnant, claiming that the father was the workhouse master, although this could not be proved; a son, Richard, was duly born in October. In May 1843 the entire family was discharged but was readmitted the same day; they were next discharged in July and readmitted in August. The family spent the winter as indoor paupers and were discharged in April 1844. A month later the younger children were readmitted, having been abandoned at the workhouse gates by their grandmother. In July their mother and the two older children were readmitted. Two days later they discharged themselves, but were readmitted the following day and remained for a fortnight. Thereafter, Mrs Sexton and her family seem to have left the area, but it is likely that the children spent much of their upbringing in other workhouses.

Fallen women

If workhouse children excited pity, the worst form of condemnation was heaped on the mothers of illegitimate children – arguably even vagrants received better treatment. Many large towns had lying-in hospitals, paid for by voluntary donations, where poor women could be delivered of their babies, but many refused to admit single women. Such prohibitions were a moral issue: society had long condemned the bearing of children out of wedlock. But there was an additional problem for the Poor Law authorities, as an illegitimate child could end up being the responsibility of the parish until he or she had reached the age of ten. This was particularly a problem before 1834.

Under the Old Poor Law great efforts were made to track down the fathers and make them either pay for the upkeep of the child or marry the woman. Illegitimate children could be quite a burden on the ratepayers, so it was in the interest of the authorities to minimize the expense where possible, either through compelling the woman to marry or by passing the responsibility on to another parish. This often involved forcing the woman back to the parish of her birth, so that the authorities there had to take responsibility for her and, more importantly, her bastard child – a third of the women who were removed from parishes in Cambridgeshire between 1660 and 1834, for example, were expectant mothers.

In theory, marriage provided authorities with the most acceptable solution to a woman's predicament, even if the union was not entirely a voluntary one. It was not unknown, however, for the man who had married a woman in a 'knobstick wedding' (as the phrase was), and enjoyed a wedding feast at the expense of the parish, to disappear without trace, thus leaving the authorities to bear the costs of the wedding and raising the child. In 1793 Esther Herbert, from Fulham, London, became pregnant with the child of Samuel Gillingham, a local ne'er-do-well. The overseers made the couple marry and, in a calculated fit of generosity, the parish paid for a marriage licence and a celebratory dinner. Having had his fill of roast beef and ale, however, Gillingham fled immediately after the proceedings, never to return.

Despite the authorities' best efforts, women still entered workhouses to have their children. Elizabeth Bennett, a widow with four children, was delivered of an illegitimate child at Andover in June 1845. She was alarmed when the chaplain 'spoke to her about adultery and false oaths' and then prayed with her. She admitted adultery to the inquiry ('it was bad, but not very bad') – but denied she was a common prostitute. She said that when she found she was pregnant the guardians had taken away the out-relief provided to her children.

The authorities despaired when women came to have several illegitimate children, often by different fathers. One such case was Eliza Wright at Maidstone, Kent, in the 1850s; her husband had died, leaving her with a toddler. Thereafter, in the workhouse, she had four children, presumably by separate fathers because their names are not shown on the birth certificates. Eventually, she settled down with John Bright, a labourer at a local paper mill, and it is possible that her last son, John, was his.

A study of St Martin's workhouse in central London in 1817 and 1818 suggests that a third of the women between the ages of 16 and 44 who entered the house did so to have children, and another 11 had been returned from other parishes to have their babies. After 1834 the pointless and cruel removal of pregnant women declined, although it did not cease altogether and the legislation was not finally repealed until the 1946. But that was the best that could be said for the New Poor Law. Strenuous efforts were still made to discourage mothers from having bastard children, and the illegitimacy rate did fall dramatically during the 19th century. Nevertheless, in 1880 five per cent of births were still out of wedlock and likely to take place in the workhouse.

Neither mother nor child was entitled to outdoor relief, so the woman was automatically forced into the workhouse if she was unable to support her child at home. Depending upon her circumstances, her children could be taken and raised in the workhouse until she was able to care for them. Inside the workhouse these mothers endured an unenviable existence, subject to petty humiliations to remind them of their shame. On appearing before the guardians before admission, they were likely to encounter sniggers and knowing winks. In a few places they were made to wear a yellow top (which earned them the name 'jacket women') instead of the blue one worn by other paupers. This practice was forbidden in 1844, although some unions, such as the one at Gressenhall, continued to issue the jackets for at least another 20 years.

Lying-in women in general received a poor diet as they recovered from the birth of their children. In some workhouses mothers were given a diet of fluids until the seventh day after the birth of their children and then returned to the general food regime or dietary, without any supplements or special treatment. In 1866 Edward Smith, the medical officer to the Poor Law

Board, found that 'the diversity in the amount of food obtained by lying-in women is very remarkable; and the feeble gait and pale spiritless aspect are proof that the quantity of food allowed is deficient for some'. Other workhouses were better – Smith found some in which nursing mothers were placed on a diet of meat, sometimes with the addition of butter, tea or perhaps beer.

However, it was not uncommon for mothers of illegitimate children to be further discriminated against. At Andover in Hampshire, for example, any additional items allowed for new mothers, such as tea and sugar or toast and water, were not given to those who had had illegitimate children. Mrs Bennett told the assistant commissioner investigating conditions at the workhouse in the 1840s that it was not until five weeks after her confinement that she was allowed anything nourishing, that is 'between a quarter and half of a pint of beer, a little tea in the morning, and a piece of bread with a little dripping on it' – and even that was not always provided. Initially she was offered cheese but could not eat it, receiving instead mouldy bacon and beef 'which had been boiled to a rag' and toast and water, although the bread 'was sometimes burnt up into a coal'. Bennett pleaded with the matron, Mrs McDougal: 'Will you allow me a bit of something extra otherwise I'll never get out of this bed. I get so weak; I keep giving the child the breast, but I have nothing to eat. I am very hungry in the night.' She was reluctantly given a little beer.

The child itself suffered: 'Poor dear goose. It was pretty near starved to death; pretty near. The mistress said nothing would be allowed for it until it was a month old. Some cold water was given to it. The doctor afterwards ordered some arrowroot, but it was almost a week before I got it.' Indeed, Bennett was still so weak that she collapsed during the cross-examination and had to finish giving her evidence from a bed brought into the town hall. It is difficult to know whether her treatment reflected that offered to all mothers in the workhouse at the time of their confinement, or whether Mrs Bennett was treated more severely because her child was illegitimate. A further factor was her general misfortunate to end up at the Andover workhouse, where conditions were particularly poor.

The situation improved from the 1880s onwards with the arrival of women guardians, who combined the censorious attitudes of the period with a desire to improve the lot of single mothers and their children. The Workhouse Girls Aid Society was founded by a group of London guardians to find foster parents for the babies and suitable work for the mothers, in the hope that they might re-enter respectable life. The Society even accepted that 'a girl gets more than one chance before we give up trying to help her', although women guardians were noticeably harder on those who had more than one illegitimate child.

Keeping body and soul together

Nothing summed up the penny-pinching nature of the Poor Law in the minds of the general public better than the dull and mean food and drink provided to the paupers. It is something which surfaces time and again in literature of the period, beginning, of course, with *Oliver Twist*. Most dramatic were the horrific revelations about conditions in the Andover Union workhouse, where starving inmates were forced to eat the marrow from rotting bones to survive and children lived on scraps thrown to the chickens.

For most paupers and for the staff the most important room in the workhouse was the dining area. Here men, women and children ate their dull meals in separate rooms so that there could be no communication between them. In fact, there should have been no noise at all, for the Workhouse Orders and Regulations laid down by the Poor Law Commissioners in 1836 stated that 'silence, order and decorum should be maintained'.

Further orders were given about mealtimes. Breakfast took place at 6am in summer (7.30am in winter), dinner was at 12 noon, and supper was at 6pm. Meals were to be eaten in a dining hall or day room under strict supervision. No food was to be taken away uneaten, although it was not uncommon for paupers to smuggle out pieces of bread to be swapped or sold for tobacco. Samuel Green, one of the starving paupers at Andover during the scandal of 1846, told MPs: 'Most of the people who take 'bacco sell their bread. 'Bacco is a very wholesome thing especially in the workhouse.'

Will Crooks' father, who with his family had entered London's Poplar workhouse in the late 1860s, was disciplined for providing his son with food saved from his rations:

Somehow his father, away in the men's ward, got to know that young
Will ... was not able to eat the fare provided in the workhouse. The
men occasionally had suet pudding and one dinner-time the old man
secretly smuggled his portion into his pocket. In the afternoon he
made over to the children's quarters, hoping to hand it to Will. The
pudding was produced, the lad's hungry eyes lighted up, when, behold!
It was snatched away, almost from his vary grasp. The burly figure of
the labour master interposed between father and son. This was a breach
of discipline not to be tolerated in the workhouse. 'But the boy's hungry,
and this is what I've saved from my own dinner,' argued the father
(all in vain).

It was difficult to compare what was provided in the workhouse with the
diet of the average labourer, although many observers thought that it was
better than that available to the poorest labourers outside the house. For
example, in 1852 one critic, Alexander Somerville, claimed that the 'workhouse diet in this county, low as it is, is better than half the Wiltshire workers
get at home'. Such was not the intention, however. The Workhouse Orders
and Regulations of 1836 clearly stated that 'the diet of the paupers shall be
so regulated as in no case to exceed, in quantity of food the ordinary diet
of any class of able-bodied labourers within the same district'. To provide
too much might excite complaints from aggrieved ratepayers and even
encourage the poor to enter the workhouse. To provide too little would
provoke scandal, as the Andover workhouse and *Oliver Twist* showed. In
general, the authorities erred on the side of caution. Paupers had to be fed at
the lowest possible cost on a diet which was no better than that available to
the poor outside the workhouse.

Sixty years after Somerville, Seebohm Rowntree's survey of poverty in
York found that the dietary laid down by the Local Government Board was
more generous than that enjoyed by families in the city living below what he
called the poverty line. In the case of one family, he remarked that although
the wife was 'an exceptionally clever and economical housekeeper', the
family budget was '4s 5d per week below the sum required to provide such
a family with the diet supplied to the able-bodied poor in the York
workhouse'.

Most observers did agree that the prison diet was an improvement on that available at the workhouse – and this fact provoked angry comments. To loud cheers, Lord Carnarvon told a meeting of the Hampshire Quarter Sessions in 1868:

> I must say that when a poor man without a blot on his reputation, who has perhaps lived a long life without the slightest shadow of suspicion attached to him, is at last obliged through misfortune or through old age to resort to the workhouse and receives hardly sufficient to keep body and soul together, while the sturdy felon, who has been committed and recommitted over and over again, is well fed and comfortably cared for, it is dealing with guilt and innocence in a most unsatisfactory manner.

The daily bread

Ever fearful of the charge of luxury, the Commission and its successors kept strict control over meals served in the workhouse. At the heart of the system was the dietary, or menu, that laid down what was to be offered to the paupers at every meal, together with the weight or volume of the food to be provided.

Until 1848 workhouses had to use one of six dietaries, that is a weekly rota of meals laid down by Whitehall. These were no means arbitrary: government officials took a great deal of care in preparing dietaries that were as nutritional as possible according to the knowledge of the time. As early as 1846 Dr Lyon Playfair devised a scientific scale listing the weights of food provided in the workhouse rations in terms of nitrogen and carbon, in an attempt more accurately to meet the inmates' nutritional needs.

The dietaries also specified the exact amounts of food to be offered to the various types of pauper. The foods specified were bread, gruel, meat, broth, cheese, potatoes and rice or suet pudding. Some regional differences were allowed for so that on the coast, for example, fish was often provided in place of meat. Special dietaries were provided for women, new mothers, children and the aged. In general, they were a scaled-down proportion of that offered to able-bodied males. For adult women (who generally received 80 per cent of the male diet) and the old, this may not have mattered much, but for babies and young children the dietary was at best poor.

The scandal at Andover led to this strict control over menus being relaxed, partly because during the inquiries it was revealed that a Poor

Law Commission clerk had made a mistake when he sent instructions to the guardians about the dietary, which was consequently flawed. Thereafter unions could choose their own dietary, but it, and all minor changes to it, had to be agreed in London. Improvements appear to have been marginal. In the 1860s Dr Edward Smith conducted an investigation into the effectiveness of the regimes for the Poor Law Board. He noted that:

> The general effect of the dietaries in use is upon the whole to maintain a fair degree of health and strength; but they do not gratify the taste or meet with the cordial approbation of the inmates. The aspect of the inmates is not commonly that of robust health, neither is there any marked accumulation of flesh; but the aspect is not generally unhealthy, and the appetite, spirits and general strength are fair.

Despite the relaxation of the rules, it was common for the Poor Law Board to object to items or meals proposed by the guardians. Even simple things such as an allowance of sugar for tea or treacle for gruel could be struck out. The Wharfedale Union in Yorkshire, for example, wanted to introduce a new dietary in 1869, but it was told that milk porridge should replace tea on Tuesdays and the quantity of pudding should be increased from 12 to 14 ounces for adults. The Board also indicated that it was 'unusual to allow beer and also undesirable to allow tea for the aged', although this was left to the guardians to make a decision.

In 1901 workhouses returned to dietaries laid down by Whitehall, although unions now had a wider choice of dishes they could serve. A lot of the petty regulations requiring the approval of any changes to menus were abolished. The intention was to allow paupers, especially children, to eat as much as they liked of the cheaper carbohydrates, particularly bread, in order to fill them up. Unfortunately, the guardians and their officers did not always understand the new rules, and this led to problems. The *Congleton Chronicle*, for example, reported that one guardian claimed that the bread ration was more than he could eat, while another joked that they should print up menu cards for the workhouse.

Many paupers were also unhappy with the changes. In Ripon, Yorkshire, the Visiting Committee noted that: 'There were complaints that the new diet list did not include meat and potato pie which had proved to be the most popular dinner.' Further south in Bradford, paupers decided to take matters into their own hands. In March 1901 the *Manchester Guardian* reported:

At the Bradford Workhouse yesterday the new dietary of the Local Government Board came into operation, when served with gruel instead of tea, according to the order, the women rose in a body and left the room. Three women who were ringleaders were yesterday brought before the Stipendiary Magistrate. These women, with others, had refused to work on the food, and had also behaved in a rowdy manner to the Work-house Master… Each defendant was sent to prison for a week.

Generally the food on offer was just plain and unexciting, in part because the hot dishes were almost always boiled. Edward Smith found that 'the cooking of the food is a very simple process and consists of boiling almost exclusively'. Suet pudding was also typical of the dull fare offered, although it could be improved with a savoury sauce or gravy. The medical officer at Belford Union, Dr Cunningham, was moved to write to the guardians about the pudding in 1877:

The inmates complain they cannot eat it… I consider it a very indigestible meal for old people and especially for the women – they never taste it. I would submit for your approval that a dinner of rice and milk be substituted. It would have the advantage of being digestible, nutritious, one that the inmates desire and at the same time it would cost no more than the meal they get at present.

However, his request was not acted upon.

In some places the food served to paupers was on occasion unfit for human consumption. At the Marland Infirmary in Rochdale, near Man-chester, which housed the sick and the insane, an investigation by the Poor Law Board found that Saturday was special pudding day with suet and currants 'as firm as a rock'. Monday was 'lobby' day, that is, 'mutton and potatoes, frequently sour'. The 'lobby' was retrieved from Thursday's weekly meat dinner, after Friday's pie had been made from it. Potatoes were the only vegetable used in the workhouse and all the food was steamed. The piggery stood next to the children's yard. The pigs were fed on what the inmates could not eat and were said to be in 'superb condition'.

In the late 1880s a guardian of Camberwell workhouse in southeast London, Miss Augusta Brown, tried to improve the soup served there, which was made of water, onions and grease. She took a bowl of it to the board meeting, but her fellow guardians refused to touch it. As the soup had already been rejected by her cat and dog, she thought that wise. Indeed, few guardians were prepared to taste the food served in their name.

Some dishes were better than others, and occasionally the inmates enjoyed a particular meal. Edward Smith noted that dishes with some residual flavour were the most popular: 'Meat and potatoes, meat and potato pie, and Irish stew are the most generally liked. Pea soup is less generally disliked by the adults and the aged than I had expected to find, but disliked by boys and girls.' Amazingly, the popular Liverpudlian dish of lobscouse, or scouse, made from meat, hardtack [dry] biscuit and vegetable stew, may itself have originated in the workhouse. The first recorded use of the term was in 1837 by the cost-conscious medical officer of the Liverpool workhouse; he reported to the Poor Law Commission on the successful application of the 'evaporating process' to 'Meat Scouse', leaving 'a solid mass of nutritious food'. Despite its continued association with pauperism, scouse became a popular local dish. It was always eaten with red cabbage pickled in vinegar; the presence of meat depended on economic circumstances, with 'blind scouse' (that is, without meat) an option in hard times.

One reason why the food improved was because of an increased interest taken in it by a new generation of women and working-class guardians in the 1880s and 1890's. Guardians such as Charlotte Despard in Lambeth, south London, instituted simple changes such as providing sliced bread for the elderly and children, who had difficulty cutting loaves or gnawing chunks.

Others found more fundamental faults. On his election as a guardian in Poplar in 1893, George Lansbury visited the workhouse, where he viewed the supper of oatmeal porridge with concern:

> On this occasion the food was served up with pieces of black stuff floating around. On examination, we discovered it to be rat and mice manure. I called for the chief officer, who immediately argued against me, saying the porridge was good and wholesome. 'Very good, madam,'

said I, taking up a basinful and spoon, 'here you are, eat one mouthful and I will acknowledge I am wrong.' 'Oh, dear no,' said the fine lady, 'the food is not for me, and is good and wholesome enough for those who want it.' I stamped and shouted around till both doctor and master arrived, both of whom pleaded it was all a mistake, and promptly served cocoa and bread and margarine.

Only the larger workhouses employed a cook. Food in the smaller estab-lishments was generally prepared by the workhouse matron, who had no training in catering, assisted by able-bodied paupers of varying degrees of competence. As a result, elementary mistakes were made. One visitor described the Huddersfield workhouse as follows:

> They had two coppers so set that their tops were separated only by a space of three inches. When I was there they were boiling clothes in one and soup in the other; and there were no lids on them. When the soup boiled over into the clothes I raised no objection, but when the clothes boiled over into the soup, I said I would not stay to dinner.

Another guardian, Louisa Twining, found tea and cabbage boiled in the same cauldron at Tunbridge Wells workhouse in Kent.

The whole system for the provision of food was open to abuse. Most guardians were either oblivious to the abuses or connived at them. In many workhouses, perhaps the majority, contractors supplied inferior products, short measures were given to the paupers, and goods were stolen from the stores. The 'Indoor Pauper' pointed out that 'in many workhouses [the paupers] are half starved or a little more, just that a few may make illicit gains, while a few more gorge inordinately'. There was a general belief that there was collusion between tradesmen and the master of the workhouse. Occasionally this sparked off public protests. In 1852 there was a riot in Ripon when the workhouse matron was accused of boiling 19 lbs of meat in a copper from which only 15lb of meat was produced. The Poor Law Board was called in to investigate.

As a deterrent to short measures, printed copies of the dietary were prominently displayed in workhouse dining rooms, although (at least in the early years) relatively few paupers could read them. In addition, food was measured in front of the inmates, though few dared to complain to the master, let alone the guardians, if the food provided was short measure or unsatisfactory. In one provincial workhouse kitchen, the journalist Thomas Archer found that 'every pauper can demand to see his rations weighed; and some newcomers exercise this privilege with a morose disbelief in the probability of their obtaining their just due – a disbelief for which their previous experiences may perhaps have given some grounds'.

The only time the dullness of the diet was varied was at Christmas or the occasional royal celebration, such as a coronation or jubilee. Then a special meal was laid on, invariably with a centrepiece of roast beef, although for the coronation of Edward VII in 1902 residents at Congleton Union in Cheshire were offered a meat tea. Officially this was frowned on by the authorities. Guardians who sought permission to organize such events were told that the funds had to come out of their own pockets. In replying to such requests, the Poor Law Commissioners usually said: 'The commissioners feel as usual that the guardians will perceive the propriety by a degree, even in deference to so joyful occasion, the burden of those who contribute to the rates. Many of whom by the most strenuous exertion and rigid economy can only just help themselves above parish relief.'

In Nottinghamshire, to mark the young queen's coronation in June 1838, Southwell guardians collected money from local well-wishers. They provided workhouse inmates with roast beef and plum pudding for dinner, plum cake and tea for supper 'with one pint of ale for the old men each'.

A badge of shame

On their admission to the workhouse, paupers were placed in the receiving ward and awaited inspection by the medical officer. Here they would be searched, undressed, washed and provided with workhouse clothes. Objects such as cards, dice, 'spirituous liquors' and matches were confiscated. At Belford, in 1864, Catherine Rogers, in response to an inquiry, described her admission: 'I was put into the receiving ward and got washed – I was then given two petticoats, a gown and an apron – a pair of stocking legs without feet – a pair of carpet shoes down at heel and one old shift.' It was a traumatic experience, vividly recounted by George Lansbury when, on his election as a guardian in Poplar in 1893, he paid a surprise visit to the workhouse. Thirty years later he could still remember it:

It was not necessary to write up the words 'Abandon hope all ye who enter here'. Officials, receiving ward, hard forms, whitewashed walls, keys dangling at the waist of those who spoke to you, huge books for name, history, etc, searching and then being stripped and bathed in a communal tub, and the final crowning indignity of being dressed in clothes which had been worn by lots of other people, hideous to look at, ill fitting and coarse – everything possible was done to inflict mental and moral degradation. The place was clean: brass knobs and floors were polished, but of goodwill, kindliness there was none.

It was all too easy to rob the innocent newcomer. 'The Indoor Pauper' described how, on arrival at his anonymous London workhouse he had enjoyed the luxury of a dip in clean warm water and was then supplied with a flannel singlet. The pauper issuing the clothes assured him that

> this was a very great favour indeed, and therefore well worth a bit of tobacco or a copper. And he got a penny – my last… But the old fellow lied in every particular. The singlet, as it turned out, was a portion of the ordinary workhouse dress, while the clothes were so bad that the taskmaster ordered them to be exchanged for better ones a few days later. Thus my first experience of the place was to be victimised.

Clothes and other objects were taken away and cleaned (often literally fumigated in a stove to kill the vermin) and then ticketed with their owner's details, ready to be returned on departure. Their condition was seldom improved, despite the fumigation. In a Lancashire workhouse early in the 1900s, the pauper Mary Higgs was set to sort out the storeroom full of paupers' belongings. She discovered that many were 'unparcelled, and some dirty and foul-smelling'. The heat provided in the workhouse was often very dry, and this could lead to infestations of moths. Her closer inspection of the clothing revealed that 'most all the bundles which were not tightly tied were more or less moth-eaten. It made my heart ache to see these clothes in such a state, remembering that they were all that poor people possessed.'

The new inmate was given a distinctive, coarse and usually ill-fitting blue uniform to wear. This helped identify paupers should they abscond from the workhouse, and perhaps more importantly was intended to reinforce the idea that they had lost all identity on admission. In Poplar, George Lansbury found that there was 'plenty of corduroy and blue cloth. No undergarments of any kind for either men or women, no sanitary clothes of any sort or kind for women of any age, boots were worn until they fell off.' In Norfolk workhouses women were issued with stays, a flannel or linsey petticoat, a striped serge or grosgrain or union chambray gown, camblet jacket or shawl, checked neckerchief, slate-coloured hose, ankle shoes and a white calico cap or cambric hat.

Workhouse uniforms were extremely unpopular and it was not uncommon for their wearers to try to destroy them. Vagrants, in particular, often tore up their clothes in the hope that they might receive new ones. So common was this practice that in some workhouses cheap canvas trousers were provided to those who had done so.

Until it was forbidden by the Poor Law Commissioners in 1844, Camberwell Union in south London gave casuals jackets imprinted in large letters with the messages 'Camberwell Parish' and 'Stop it'. They provoked curiosity and ribald remarks on local streets. One vagrant, Thomas King, was given three shillings by sympathetic bystanders when wearing such a jacket, before he was arrested and taken before Lambeth magistrates for begging on the public highway.

Not all workhouses had uniforms, however. Smaller ones saw no point in issuing them; at Belford, for example, the guardians explained in 1851 that 'persons who come into the workhouse who are likely to be permanent paupers are allowed to wear out their own clothes and are from time to time afterwards supplied with such clothing as they require'.

Divide and rule

Once admitted, men, women and children were placed in separate wards and families were split up. They ate in separate dining rooms and exercised and worked in separate yards. This rule was another deterrent, perhaps the most effective of them all, designed to discourage poor families from 'seeking the house', and workhouses built after 1836 were rigidly divided in this way. A newspaper report on the opening of the new Lambeth workhouse in 1874 noted:

Each class has its own and distinct day-rooms, dormitories, staircases, lavatories, waterclosets, airing-grounds, and workrooms; the only common-place of meeting being the chapel and dining-room, where conversational intercourse is forbidden. The several classes in each sex are for aged, able-bodied of good character, and two subdivisions of able-bodied of bad character, together with accommodation for a limited number of boys and girls. There is a dining-hall for each sex leading direct from the kitchen.

Some workhouses also placed 'females of loose character' in a special ward, in part because the Victorians feared that they might spread the contagion of immorality to the respectable poor, but more often because they were notoriously difficult to control. However, as 'the Indoor Pauper' pointed out, communication was often possible. Able-bodied women paupers were always around cleaning, while men might be engaged in doing odd jobs. He describes the flirtations, even the romances, which went on behind the master's or overseer's back: 'More progress in an intrigue is made in five minutes, by a pair of indoor paupers when they happen to meet, than is made in as many weeks by persons more fortunately placed.'

The workhouse operated to a strict, almost monastic, timetable, set down by the Poor Law Commissioners in London, and generally implemented with little variation by the guardians:

All paupers except the sick, the aged or infirm, and the young children shall rise, be set to work, leave of work and to bed at the appropriate times: rise 5am (summer) and 6am (winter); work 7am or 8am to 12 noon, dinner until 1pm; work 1pm to 6pm (all year) and bed 8pm (all year). They shall be allowed intervals for meals which will be announced by the ringing of a bell.

In theory the paupers were fully occupied, either locked in their dormitories or in the workshops, with short periods in the dining room, but of course they could not always be under the eye of the master or his staff. In particular, they were left very much to their own devices after lights out, even though each dormitory had a wardsman responsible for discipline and also for nursing any sick paupers to be found there. Most wardsmen, however, wanted a quiet life or were quite incapable of maintaining order. If 'the

Indoor Pauper' is to be believed, Saturday nights were lively ones in the wards. He described quite a music hall atmosphere, with songs and stories aplenty to while the hours away. Each person was expected to contribute a song or a recitation, and those that did not, joined in the choruses.

Perhaps the worst aspect about the workhouse was the almost unrelieved boredom that all but the dullest inmate endured. Even in the best-run workhouse, the routine and the conditions encouraged inmates to become indolent and apathetic. Sunday was the worst day of the week, when there was no work and almost nothing to stimulate the inmates. 'The Indoor Pauper' criticized the way in which the days were conducted:

> A hardening and deteriorating process is always going among them [the indoor paupers], and most rapidly when they are most unemployed, that is on Sundays ... the listless and lazy become more so; the filthier grow filthier still; while those who heretofore possessed merely a lurking and uncertain inclination towards certain vices have it strengthened and confirmed here.

Apart from the chance to go to church (the larger workhouses had their own chapels), there was absolutely nothing to do and nothing to read except religious tracts or perhaps a tattered 'penny dreadful', an old newspaper or a cheap novel. Some men took the opportunity to write letters, although there were rarely enough pens, paper and ink to go round; most just lounged around, waiting for lunch or dinner. Sunday was perhaps worst of all for children. Will Crooks remembered: '[I] thought that time could not be more terrible anywhere. They had dinner at twelve and supper at six, confined during the yawning interval in the adult day room with nothing to do but look at the clock, look out of the window and then back to the clock again.'

Earning their keep

Provided they were not bedridden or elderly, paupers were expected to contribute to the costs of their upkeep by undertaking work as directed by the master or the taskmaster. Women were expected to clean, cook and help in the sick wards. Men helped to maintain the buildings and garden.

Most rural and suburban workhouses had a large garden or even a farm, as at Southwell and Gressinghall. At Caersws workhouse, the guardians' minutes for September 1844 noted that in the previous quarter five hundredweight of early potatoes and sundry vegetables had been grown. Often the vegetables were sold to help pay for the workhouse. An elderly agricultural labourer in the Richmond workhouse wrote to the Poor Law Board lamenting the fact that the inmates' efforts did not result in their ever having fresh vegetables.

Occasionally there were complaints that pauper labour undercut commercial producers outside. In 1888 the Firewood Cutters Protection Association protested that their desperately poor members' livelihoods were being taken away as a result of cheap firewood being sold by unions in the East End. Whitechapel offered a robust response, arguing that it was not prepared to admit 'that the fact of a man being employed in the workhouse deprives him of the right to contribute to the labour of the country the produce of which he is a consumer'.

The most prized jobs were within the house itself. First of all, paupers could be paid a small gratuity. At Marylebone in 1846 one shilling a week was given to the 53 pauper women who acted as nurses, 20 laundrywomen, two blind men who taught the school children singing, one driver and horse-keeper, one cutter-out (of cloth for uniforms), three assistants to the master and clerk, four pauper bearers and two chairmen (to carry the sick inmates). Two shillings a week were paid to the cook and barber, and 1s 6d was received by a pauper who taught handwriting in the school and the woman who laid out the dead.

Kitchen work was particularly prized for the extra food it offered and the opportunity for graft. Fred Copeman was befriended by Maggie, a cook in the master's kitchen. Unlike the other paupers, she

> was round and fat with a perpetual smile. One of my jobs was to turn the butter churn in the dairy, and as this was attached to the Master's kitchen and pantry, Maggie would leave me something nice to eat, hidden behind the churn – an apple, a handful of raisins or some other luxury, which the inmates never saw in the main hall.

It was also possible to steal goods and sell them either to fellow paupers or outside the house. 'The Indoor Pauper' complained about a meal he had just had: 'The soup too was about as poor as soup could be; and yet immediately after dinner the pantry-men were selling basins, full to the brim, and anything rather than thin, to those who could afford to buy. It was shameful. But I regret to say such things are the rule.'

But most men and women were engaged in menial and dreary tasks, such as picking oakum, performed with a large metal nail known as a spike (which may be where casual wards and flophouses got their nicknames) and very hard on the fingers. Paupers were supposed to pick three pounds of oakum a day, but few achieved that target. A petition to the Poor Law Board from James Shrimpton and other paupers at Stepney in 1850 complained that 'we are kept locked in the cell yard to break stones and kept on bread and water every other 24 hours because we cannot break 5 bushels of stone per day, being mechanics and never broke any before'.

The work was often done badly or very slowly to eek out the time available, on the assumption that the authorities would not try to hard to make the paupers meet their quota. Margaret Harkness, who described London's Whitechapel workhouse in her novel *Captain Lobe*, said:

> The Whitechapel Union allows no man to remain idle from the time he gets up until he goes to bed again. A sodden look has settled on the faces of the older men and they apparently thought little of what they were doing … not a voice was to be heard in the workshops, the men did not whistle or sing; they looked like schoolboys in disgrace rather than free-born Englishmen.

The tasks they had to perform (in theory at least) to earn their keep were generally pointless. An alternative to picking oakum was removing hemp from telegraph wires, a task given to the 'Indoor Pauper' and performed in desultory fashion:

> There was no hurry over the work – very much to the contrary – but plenty of chatter and larking when the taskmaster was out of sight… Skulking … I found was common all over the place, most of the inmates vying with one another, as to which should do the least possible work, and with much success I must confess.

Other workhouse tasks, such as nursing the sick, were often beyond the inmates' capabilities – though many were assigned to them nonetheless.

The ones who got away

Few able-bodied paupers held down any sort of permanent work – if they had, they would not have been in the position they were. Or if they had in the past, it was now beyond them. The exception was during times of economic slump, particularly during the 1830s and 1840s, when unemployment drove many into the house. Most men were casual labourers in the fields and factories, in the docks and building sites, or just hung around the streets hoping to earn a few pence for holding a horse, carrying bags or taking messages. Women were domestic servants and labourers, no doubt in many cases combined with prostitution. Many were admitted because they had been deserted by husbands or lovers and left with small children they could not feed.

These employment patterns were reflected in the fluctuating numbers admitted to the workhouse. The winter months were almost always busier, largely because more casual work was available in the summer. Periods of cold or wet made work difficult for those employed outdoors in agriculture or in casual labouring in the cities, while a prolonged cold snap could force thousands of poor people into the workhouse. In London, and to a lesser extent in other fashionable centres, trades were often subject to the vagaries of the Season – the weeks between March and the end of July when the wealthy came to the metropolis. This created an increased demand for servants, builders, dressmakers and workers in various luxury trades.

George Bartley noted that workhouses emptied out during the summer, as the harvest and market gardens demanded labour: 'Old women are very much on the move at these times of year. Many want to go weeding in the market gardens, where they can pick up a few pence a day even when quite infirm.' 'The Indoor Pauper' said that during the hopping season in August and September many people left the workhouses in London. He found that, despite a strict ban on the sexes mixing with each other: 'Each man must have a female companion – "a hopping wife" as she is termed – selected from the females on the other side. As I write (middle of August), not less than a dozen negotiations tending in this direction are in progress, literally within earshot.'

These particularly troublesome paupers were universally referred to as the 'ins and outs' because they were constantly discharging themselves and seeking readmission, either on the same day or a short time after. The authorities had no real redress, for inmates had the right to be discharged at will – it was one of the few differences between the workhouse and a prison.

One man at St George Hanover Square in London discharged himself 93 times in 1889, almost always being readmitted on the same night. His only lengthy absence from the house was when he was in prison for 21 days. Robert Hedley, the Poor Law Inspector for London, thought this case was 'an abuse of Poor Law Relief'.

'The Indoor Pauper' explained that:

> some of these fellows go out on a job, keep at it as long as it lasts, lay in good stores of tobacco at the end, and then spend every farthing left of their earnings in a 'topping spree', lasting one to three days, according to the amount received. Then hey for the workhouse, or 'spike' once again! Here the blackguards recover from their debauch, and drown away the days, until they are ripe for another job and another 'topping spree'.

Among the 'in and outs' were beggars and professional thieves: 'These are fellows at the bottom of the professions, as a rule,' wrote the 'Indoor Pauper', 'low footpads who waylay children, and rob them of their school pence – who snatch articles from passing carts or who stole from street-stalls or on the displays in front of shops.'

Any pauper could discharge him or herself at any time provided he or she gave reasonable notice. This was generally accepted to be three hours. If they had brought their family into the house, they were discharged as well in order to prevent parents from abandoning their children. Sometimes men and women discharged themselves for very short periods, just because they wanted a breath of fresh air and a change of scene. Charlie Chaplin, who was briefly a child pauper at Lambeth and then sent to the Central London School at Hanwell, Middlesex, recalled in his autobiography that, after two months at the school, he and his half-brother were returned unexpectedly to Lambeth. Here they were met at the gate by his mother Hannah, dressed in her own clothes. Desperate to see them, she had discharged herself from the workhouse, along with the children. After a day spent playing in Kennington Park and visiting a coffee shop, they returned to the workhouse where they were readmitted.

Many of the more respectable men and women, whom fortune had forced into pauperism, left determined never to return. It was often possible for the more deserving to persuade the guardians to give a small grant of money or clothes when they left the workhouse, in the hope that this would be enough for them to find a job and so not remain a burden on the poor rate. George Bartley said that, at his board of guardians, the workhouse master announced all those who were leaving the house, 'and they generally appear before the board hoping to get "a trifle to leave the house". If they have behaved well this request is granted, and a shilling or two and some loaves, according to the family, are given to them.'

Occasionally, a pauper was more generously treated. One was Thomas James, who impressed the guardians at Caersws. The minutes for November 1846 note that he 'has not only made himself useful in the gardens and stables of the workhouse but has on a number of occasions been entrusted with and carried out the duties of porter when the post was vacant, be allowed £2 and clothes suitable for an independent labourer as he intends to take his discharge'.

Although it was possible for the guardians to discharge inmates if they considered that they were capable of supporting themselves, it was unusual. A former naval pensioner, John Thomas Wimble, was discharged by Hackney guardians in 1896 and complained bitterly to the Local Government Board: 'As a consequence I walked about destitute for two days.' The guardians claimed that Wimble had been ordered to go to the Hadleigh Farm work colony in Essex, where he would be taught a new trade. The Board admonished the guardians saying that 'they would not be justified in adopting this course unless they had satisfied themselves that the able-bodied person is not destitute or has been offered work and declined it'.

Occasionally the master or guardians would attempt to dissuade a pauper who was in no fit state to leave. In 1856 *The Times* reported the suicide of Elizabeth Mann and the deaths of four of her children. Mrs Mann was clearly very mentally disturbed and had been in Marylebone workhouse several times and repeatedly sought her discharge. On the last occasion, one of the guardians, Mr Potter, spent a quarter of an hour trying to persuade her to stay but without success.

Many cases cited by Charles Booth involved generations of the same family. Perhaps the most extreme example was the family of Martin Rooney (not his real name) who, Booth suggests, were 'prolific paupers'. The relieving officer said that he did not know a more drunken, disreputable family than that of the Rooneys. In 1889 Rooney had been resident in Bromley by Bow workhouse since 1878 and was aged 86 and blind. At the same time his wife, Eliza King, was also an inmate; the relieving officer said that he had seen her 'beastly drunk' at all times of the day. She occasionally left the house, working sometimes at the lead works and sleeping either with her sons or rough.

The couple had three children. The eldest son, Patrick, had been a Royal Marine. but was discharged in 1885 for striking a petty officer. He had then become a stevedore and received several short prison sentences for stealing from the docks, but at the time of writing was in Poplar workhouse, suffering from a bad leg. James, the other son, did not trouble the authorities. The daughter, Bridget, had married a bricklayer's labourer, John Murdock, and borne him four boys. Murdock had deserted her on several occasions and been sent to prison. She in turn had left him for another man. As a result, he had spent some time at Bromley with the children. The two eldest children 'were emigrated to Canada'. Murdock's brother, George, lived with a prostitute, Anna Peel, whose parents were at that time in West Ham workhouse. She had been admitted to Bromley suffering from syphilis in 1885.

Rooney's sister-in-law Mary had also been admitted to the house after desertion by her husband in 1867; she had been in and out of the workhouse ever since. Her married daughter, Mrs Wilson, and grandson, Michael, had also received support over the years.

Eliza King's sister Jane was very familiar to the relieving officers. She married Thomas Milward, who died in 1879, and was noted as being a 'notorious drunkard'. By 1882 she was living with a carpenter, Robert Belton, who had been in the workhouse in 1879 with a bad leg and later died in the sick asylum in 1885. Having sold up Belton's home and spent the money on drink, she was admitted to Poplar workhouse in 1887. Since then she had been in and out several times, as had all her adult children.

The punishment books

There is no doubt that discipline was strict, with a long list of offences ranging from swearing and smuggling food out of the dining room to breaking windows and assaults on workhouse staff. Particularly in the early years of the New Poor Law, when buildings were overcrowded and the conditions were appalling, many masters and their staff experienced difficulties in maintaining order. The problem was greatest in the large metropolitan workhouses, where conditions were worst. In January 1846 alone *The Times* reported that at least 57 paupers from several workhouses had been prosecuted for various misdemeanours, including 27 casuals who had been involved in a riot at Christchurch workhouse in London's East End.

Young women could be particularly troublesome. At Holborn, for example, in the early 1840s, a gang of four or five girls caused mayhem. Their leaders, Margaret Callaghan and Elizabeth Burgess, came and went from the workhouse at will and, when refused readmission, broke windows, scaled the walls and generally misbehaved. In March 1841 Hannah Foley, Mary Curran and Elizabeth Allen were sentenced to 14 days for fighting and disorderly conduct and later that year were convicted of stealing another inmate's shawl.

In *The Uncommercial Traveller* Charles Dickens recalls being shown around Wapping workhouse in southeast London by the matron. During the tour, they came across a group of refractory (difficult) girls who were picking oakum:

> They sat in line on a form, with their backs to a window; before them,
> a table, and their work. The oldest Refractory was, say twenty; youngest
> Refractory, say sixteen…
>
> 'A pretty ouse this is, matron, ain't it?' said Refractory Two,
> 'where a pleeseman's called in, if a gal says a word!' 'And wen you're
> sent to prison for nothink or less!' said the Chief, tugging at her oakum
> as if it were the matron's hair. 'But any place is better than this; that's
> one thing, and be thankful!"
>
> A laugh of Refractories led by Oakum Head with folded arms – who
> originated nothing, but who was in command of the skirmishers outside
> the conversation. 'If any place is better than this,' said my brisk guide, in
> the calmest manner, 'it is a pity you left a good place when you had one.'

Because of their sex, women were likely to be more gently treated, particularly by the magistrates, and there was legislation which forbade the corporal chastisement of women in workhouses. Despite this, in 1850 the Poor Law Board had to remind unions that they could not discipline nursing mothers in the same way as other inmates.

Refractory paupers could depend on a certain amount of public support from the press (particularly *The Times*) and the magistrates, many of whom were unsympathetic to the meanness of Poor Law officials. And although it is possible to make too much of it, they often had the support of local people; many of the poor would have had direct or indirect experience of the house, and the more affluent would have been sympathetic to the plight of paupers. The ill treatment meted out to Ann Dowling and her 10-year-old daughter Jane Kingston by the master at Bethnal Green in 1844 led to letters in *The Times*, a public meeting attended by 200 people and a collection in order to pay the cost of prosecuting the guardians.

Initial punishment was usually a reduced diet, such as bread and water, rather than the usual dietary. However, if an inmate repeatedly offended or damaged the building, the guardians could order them to be put in solitary confinement for a few hours.

In more severe cases, usually relating to the theft of workhouse property or an assault on another inmate, paupers could be taken before the magistrates and sentenced to a term in prison. Between 1837 and 1842 there were over 10,500 committals for breaches of workhouse discipline, nearly a fifth of which had occurred in London. And as late as 1873 some 1,200 paupers were still being sent to prison each year. Even in peaceful rural areas there could be trouble. In March 1888 the *Belford Advertiser* reported that 'Robert Rogers, a deformed pauper, was sent to prison for 14 days ... for wilfully breaking four panes of glass in the Receiving Ward the previous evening'.

The punishments meted out by the master and his staff were recorded in punishment books, which were regularly presented to the guardians for their inspection. The surviving volume for Southwell for 1864 gives an idea of the offences and how they were punished. On 1 February Mary Anne Cox was taken before magistrates for 'striking the inmates'; on 14 May Ann Morrison and Sarah Slater were found fighting ('Morrison had 2 very bad black eyes') and taken before the board; on 9 October Hannah Hickling spent five hours in the refractory cell for 'using obscene and profane language and annoying the other inmates'; on 14 November John Fox and William Crooks had their 'meat stopped at dinner' for fighting; and finally, on 19 November, Sarah Watkins and Ann Morrison also had their meat stopped at dinner for 'quarrelling and persisting in making a great noise when ordered to be silent by the Master'. He added that they 'are two very disagreeable women'.

The best masters and their staffs avoided punishing the paupers unless absolutely necessary. Daniel Pickett, who was master at Stratford-upon-Avon workhouse for 32 years, told a newspaper reporter on his retirement:

> 'Really, I don't think I have punished half-a-dozen people, or taken more than two before the guardians, during my 40 years in poor law service. I don't believe in too much power being allotted to one man. I'll show you my punishment book.' He did – it took ten minutes to find it. When he did produce the book, it was covered with dust, so rarely was it used! 'To go to bed after tea each day for a week' was the harshest chastisement that the pressman noticed.

The paupers' views

The opinions of the paupers themselves are hard to determine, since most of what we know about them has come to us through the Poor Law authorities. The paupers are, as the historian David Englander suggests, 'ephemeral figures' in their history, as very few left memoirs or wrote letters; for the most part, they were incapable of doing so.

A major source for the paupers' views is the numerous letters of complaint from inmates that were addressed to the authorities in London. Some were naturally deranged and pathetic, but others make some serious points about the organization and conduct of the workhouse. A group of Spitalfield silk weavers, for example, petitioned the Poor Law Commissioners in the mid-1840s about having to break stones, which would wreck their sensitive hands and thus prevent them from getting weaving jobs again. Surprisingly, the letters to the authorities in Whitehall were often taken seriously and led to investigations into the behaviour of staff and conditions in the wards.

However, it was hard for inmates to complain about conditions within the workhouse itself. Few had the necessary intelligence, confidence or social skills, and neither the master nor the guardians were much disposed to listen. And although they grumbled, not many were prepared to do anything more.

Mary Windser, a pauper nurse and laundrywoman at Paddington workhouse, told a parliamentary investigation into conditions at the infirmary that the guardians regularly visited the wards and spoke to the inmates, usually without the workhouse master being present:

> I never heard of any of the patients complain to the guardians, but
> they would talk as soon as the guardians were gone; they would say what
> they might have told the guardians, but did not; I used to say 'Why did
> you not?', but they used to turn it off; sometimes they complained to
> me, but I did not tell the guardians.

Even at Andover, where paupers lived close to starvation in desperate conditions, there is just one solitary entry in the guardian's minute book: 'A complaint by William Brown, an inmate of the Union House, was heard as to not having sufficient food and wishing to leave the house and says he might as well live out with little food as in.'

There were a small number of paupers who knew enough about the law and their rights to cause trouble or to put their complaints in a cogent way. They wrote letters to the authorities in London or gathered petitions from their fellow inmates about unfair or pointless regulations or how they were treated by particular members of staff. The residents of Stepney workhouse submitted a petition in 1850 complaining about the drunkenness and brutality of the taskmaster. They were probably used to this from their experiences in the building yards and docks of the East End, but they particularly resented the lack of respect they were shown and the fact that they were constantly being called 'old buggers' and 'old sods'.

Some complainants were largely harmless, such as the gentleman met by Charles Dickens: "'Sir, I have a complaint to make against the master." "I have no power here, I assure you. And if I had –" "But, allow me, sir, to mention it, as between yourself and a man who has seen better days, sir. The master and myself are both masons, sir, and I make him the sign continually; but, because I am in this unfortunate position, sir, he won't give me the countersign!'" Others were more problematic. In 1844 the schoolmaster Thomas King submitted a number of detailed complaints to the Poor Law Commissioners about conditions at Woodbridge workhouse near Ipswich in Suffolk. He alleged that, as a patient in one of the sick wards, he had 'witnessed the most heart-rending acts of cruelty, oppression and neglect towards the sick and other inmates of that establishment, whereby the poor were left to die in the darkness of the night'. King further alleged that he had witnesses who would attest to 'the disgusting conduct of the matron whilst in a state of drunkenness, furiously driving through the streets and in some instances vomiting over the side of the cart'.

The Commissioners were concerned enough to send Sir John Walsham, Poor Law Inspector for East Anglia, to investigate; he later published his findings in a parliamentary paper. Although Sir John found some minor infractions, they were nothing as great as had been alleged by King – who, in turn, was systematically exposed as a natural troublemaker. At Barham, Suffolk, he had been dismissed from his post as the union schoolmaster 'for having been guilty of very improper conduct in interfering with the duties of the governor and setting forth various falsehoods'. A witness who knew him there described King as being a 'gross and shameless liar'. Even a fellow pauper, Mary Harvey, remembered that 'he was the most disagreeable man on the sick ward, and that neither she nor her husband could bear him, because he was always a breeding of mischief and lies'.

The most difficult pauper of all was probably Daniel Thompson. Over a 20-year period between the 1850s and 1870s, he bombarded the Home Secretary, the Poor Law Commissioners, the Lord Mayor of London and others with complaints about his treatment in the City of London workhouse. Taking into account his time in gaol, by his own reckoning he had been in and out of the workhouse at least three hundred times. He appeared regularly before the courts and was quite capable of conducting his own defence. In 1857 he called the workhouse master and porter before the Guildhall magistrates for confiscating his papers and refusing relief. In his defence, the master said that Thompson was exceptionally trouble-some and had already been committed on at least 21 occasions for being refractory. More importantly, by reading newspapers aloud and encouraging his fellow paupers to send petitions to the Commissioners, Thompson had managed to 'render the paupers dissatisfied and to create a great deal of insubordination'.

Thompson also objected to work and, in 1863, he was prosecuted for refusing to pick oakum. He argued in his defence that he 'objected to the tyranny and oppression of the menials in the Union House, as a violation of the rights and liberties of a British subject. He protested against being compelled to pick oakum. It was felon's work, and had so been described by Mr Selfe before a committee of the House of Commons.' He lost his case and was sentenced to 21 days in prison, but this did not diminish his ardour. In 1868 he was again prosecuted for refusal to work – the fiftieth time that he had been charged with refractory conduct – and in the following year appeared in court for a similar offence.

On a number of occasions grumbling led to riots, particularly when there was overcrowding or a sudden worsening of conditions. The most serious disturbances seem to have occurred when discipline collapsed because the workhouse master was either too severe or unable to impose his will on a gang of unruly paupers. Urban workhouses, with their wards of semi-brutalized young women from the streets, seem to have been particularly prone to trouble. It is sometimes easy to read too much into this. For the most part, paupers were apathetic recipients of what was on offer. The conditions at the Andover workhouse, for example, were not exposed as a result of protests by the inmates (they were either too cowed or too enfeebled), but by *The Times*.

The world beyond the walls

Long-term paupers were entitled to the occasional period outside the house, normally one half day a month. The elderly in particular looked forward to this break in the tedium. Margaret Harkness described how in the Whitechapel workhouse in east London the younger paupers were not allowed out at all, while 'the old ones only get one holiday in the month. Then the aged paupers may be seen skipping like lambkins outside the doors of the Bastile, while they jabber to their friends and relations.'

On a visit to an old persons' ward at Whitechapel, Dickens met one 'hoarse old man in a flannel gown' who told him:

'I am greatly better in my health, sir; but what I want, to get me quite round,' with his hand on his throat, 'is a little fresh air, sir. It has always done my complaint so much good, sir. The regular leave for going out, comes round so seldom, that if the gentlemen, next Friday, would give me leave to go out walking, now and then – for only an hour or so, sir!'

Who could wonder, looking through those weary vistas of bed and infirmity, that it should do him good to meet with some other scenes, and assure himself that there was something else on earth? Who could help wondering why the old men lived on as they did; what grasp they had on life; what crumbs of interest or occupation they could pick up from its bare board.

Guardians also regularly granted leave to inmates to visit children or look for work. This privilege could be stopped if it was abused, and the minute books are full of examples where the guardians' trust was not repaid. At Richmond, for example, the volume for 1851 noted that 'Elizabeth Taylor having been allowed to go to the school to see her child and having drink on the way home, she returned to the house drunk – that she be imprisoned for four hours each day with spare diet'.

Visitors were also permitted at certain times of the month. At Congleton workhouse the published hours in 1858 were between 2pm and 4pm on Tuesdays and Fridays. People were forbidden to bring in provisions or articles of any kind for the use of the inmates. Their visits were much welcomed, nonetheless, particularly by the elderly.

In large unions there were also more formal visits from groups of women workhouse visitors. They brought flowers and improving books to brighten up the wards of the young and the elderly, and also kept an eye on the sick. Initially these visits were arranged by Louisa Twining through her Workhouse Visiting Society, established in 1858. Within a few years the Society had 340 women members who regularly visited workhouses. Unsurprisingly, the reaction of guardians to such activity was generally hostile, at least initially. In Richmond, for example, a concerted campaign by women and the local churches was needed to persuade the guardians to change their minds.

It took workhouse visitors, usually middle-class ladies, and then, from the 1880s, the election of women and working-class guardians to introduce a more human face. Initially, visitors provided flowers and books, but it was the rising generation of guardians who made more fundamental improvements to conditions, from painting rooms in bright colours to introducing diets which could be eaten by old people lacking teeth.

Although able-bodied paupers of either sex soon became relatively uncommon, the Poor Law system remained largely focused on them. Living conditions were designed to deter their admission in the first place, and then to make life highly uncomfortable for those who did go into the house. Once inside, paupers were confronted with dull and meagre food, demeaning uniforms and shameful or difficult tasks. Workhouses were often unfavourably compared with prisons – although in theory inmates of the former could at least discharge themselves at will, in practice many of the destitute preferred to commit petty crimes rather than enter the workhouse. Most destructive of all was the faceless institutionalism in which individual identities were lost. The notorious photograph of the dining room at Marylebone, showing row upon row of men sitting with no spark about them, reflects the degradation imposed by a system that haunted people across generations. Small wonder that those who could turned their backs on the house, preferring to endure great hardship before entering its doors.

CHAPTER FIVE

Suffer the Children...

We take everything that is right and good away from them;
we take fatherhood and motherhood away.

Mrs Henry Kingsley, Richmond guardian, 1887

IT was only children growing up in the workhouse who inspired universal sympathy among the Victorians, although many a hypocritical tear was shed over the very old. It was not without reason that Charles Dickens chose to condemn the New Poor Law through the figure of Oliver Twist – an innocent victim to be pitied rather than condemned. Here also was a child who, like so many others, was at the mercy of an uncaring bureaucracy.

At the time that *Oliver Twist* was written in 1837 there were large numbers of children in workhouses – about a third of the total number of indoor paupers in 1839. Many were illegitimate, and such children posed a real problem for the Poor Law authorities, particularly before 1834, as they could become the responsibility of the parish or Poor Law Union until the age of ten. Outdoor relief was not given to women with illegitimate children, nor did the child receive any, so mothers were forced to enter the workhouse if they were unable to support the child. Other children could also be taken into the workhouse, depending on the mother's circumstances; they would be raised there until she could take care of them at home.

However, the numbers decreased as the century advanced. In the 1870s roughly 55,000 children were in the charge of workhouse guardians; about 40 per cent of these were in permanent care, having either been orphaned or deserted by their parents. Another 15 per cent were children who had one or both parents also living in the workhouse, or were the sons and daughters of widows or prisoners. The rest were the offspring of vagrants, tramps and the 'ins and outs' who were always coming and going from the house.

Sometimes children were brought into the workhouse because their parents had simply run out of alternatives. In 1860 at Poplar, East London, Will Crooks' mother had a small grant of three shillings and a couple of loaves of bread a week from the guardians, which was just enough to survive on, because her husband had been crippled by a work accident. In his biography of Crooks, George Haw recalled how the family were summoned to see the guardians:

> The chairman singled out Will, then eight years of age, and pointing his finger at him, remarked solemnly: 'It's time that boy was getting his own living.' 'He is at work, sir,' was the mother's timid apology. 'He gets up at quarter to five every morning and goes around with the milkman for sixpence a week.' 'Well can't he earn more than that?' 'Well, sir, the milkman says he's a very willing boy and always punctual, but he's so little that he doesn't think he can pay him more than sixpence yet.'

Convinced that the young Will could earn more, the guardians declined to continue the out-relief, instead offering the family the house: 'The mother said "no" at first, marching them all bravely home again. Stern want forced her to yield at last. The day came when she saw her five youngest, including Will, taken from home to the big poorhouse down by the Millwall Docks in East London. The crippled father was admitted into the House at the same time.'

The reluctance of Crooks' mother was understandable: life for a pauper child was bleak and hard. The workhouse and its routines were not designed for children and their needs, schooling was often harsh, and there was at best erratic training for the world outside the workhouse. Even so, it was probably better than living – and possibly dying – on the streets of London or Manchester, or working for a labour-master in the fields.

The autobiographies of workhouse children contain none of the fond memories that appear in the memoirs of those who went to public schools. Allowing for a layer of Victorian and Edwardian sentiment, they are all fairly brutal accounts of loneliness, pointlessness and violence. And the workhouse boys who wrote them (I have been unable to find an account by a girl) were the children who were intelligent enough to overcome their upbringing: Charles Chaplin, later the greatest of all silent film comedians; Henry Morton Stanley (John Rowlands as he was christened), a great journalist and explorer; Will Crooks, a prominent trade unionist and labour leader. Other accounts include those of Charles Shaw (in adult life a North Staffordshire potter) and an extremely honest one by an anonymous young man identified only as 'W.H.R.', which was published in the Local Government Board's annual report for 1874. All except Chaplin experienced workhouses in the 20-year period after about 1842; Chaplin was first a pauper child at Lambeth workhouse, then attended the Central London School at Hanwell in Middlesex in the late 1890s.

These children arrived for different reasons, none unusual among their contemporaries. Chaplin and 'W.H.R' entered the house with siblings because their parents could no longer look after them; Rowlands had been abandoned by his family; and unemployment forced Crooks and Shaw into the house with their parents. The shock of the transition from life outside was severe. Before 'W.H.R' entered, for example, he describes himself as a street urchin 'without shoes or a cap... [I] knew all the public houses round about ... [and had] never been inside a church or school.' Aged about eight (his sister was six), the children were taken to the Woolwich guardians by an uncle; eventually they ended up at a 'union workhouse on the west side of London'. His first experience there was being made to take a hot bath: 'I never was so afraid in my life; I thought they were going to kill me.' Chaplin was aged six when, together with his older brother Sydney, he was transferred across London from Lambeth workhouse to Hanwell in 1895. 'The first few days I was lost and miserable, for at the workhouse I always felt that mother was nearby, which was comforting.' Initially, he was in the 'infant department' and remembered being bathed by the older girls: 'having to submit to the ignominy of a young girl of fourteen manipulating a face cloth all over my person was my first conscious embarrassment'.

Charles Shaw's first memory of Chell workhouse in the Potteries was that it was all 'so unusual and strange, and so unhomelike'. He was taken into the schoolroom, where he found 'hungry-looking lads, with furtive glances, searching everything and everybody, and speaking in subdued whispers'. Hunger was to dominate his experience of life there. At Chell, Charles Shaw found the skilly (gruel) served for supper, with its 'mustiness and fustiness ... most revolting to any healthy taste. It might have been boiled in old clothes, which had been worn upon sweating bodies for three-score years and ten.'

Charles Dickens was right in *Oliver Twist* to comment on the food, and the lack of it, served to the pauper children. 'W.H.R' also complained of the small rations: 'Four ounces of sop bread [scraps of bread mixed with milk and water] for breakfast, four ounces of bread and butter for supper and dinner in proportion is not enough... [It was] a scanty ration... Nearly every boy fortunate enough to have a halfpenny or penny would directly after breakfast nag about the stairs leading to the bed-rooms to catch the old women who used to make the beds, and ask if they had an allowance of bread for sale.' Little changed in subsequent years, although more food was provided. Sydney Chaplin, who worked in the kitchen, would occasionally pass over a sliced bread roll with a big lump of butter, which would be shared with another boy, 'not that we were hungry but the generous lump of butter was an exceptional luxury'.

Night-time could also be traumatic. Charles Shaw slept in a long dormitory with beds 'hard enough for athletic discipline', where the 'boys there as cruel as neglect and badness could make them' tormented the younger or more nervous children with blood-curdling tales of ghosts and murders and practical jokes. In Will Crooks' dormitory (which he shared with his young brother) there was 'an idiot boy, who used to ramble in his talk all through the night, keeping the others awake'. 'W.H.R' was very homesick and particularly missed his sister: 'I remember putting my head right under the bed-clothes and having a quiet cry. Night after night I did this.'

Inside the workhouse, children were physically separated from their parents and from adults as a whole, although the older boys might share wards with adult males. On Sunday afternoon Charles Shaw and the other children who had parents in the house were allowed to see them, which was 'an hour of unspeakable joy ... a reminder of home and humanities outside'. Chaplin's mother occasionally travelled from South London to visit her children. Once, after he had had his head shaved and covered in iodine because of ringworm, his mother visited:

Her presence was like a bouquet of flowers; she looked so fresh and lively that I felt ashamed of my unkempt appearance and my shaved iodined head… Mother laughed, and how well I remember her endearing words as she laughed and kissed me 'With all thy dirt I love thee still'.

John Rowlands (Stanley) was less lucky. His own mother, Elizabeth Parry, who had been admitted to the workhouse with her step-children, was once pointed out to him: 'I had expected to feel a gush of tenderness towards her, but her expression was so chilling that the valves of my heart closed as with a snap.'

Eventually they all left. Charles Shaw was at Chell for just over a month; his father managed to find work as a painter and gilder in a local toy factory and he escaped with a feeling of 'exultant joy… All seemed sunshine and gladness.' As Will Crooks left: 'The boys crowded round him, wishing they were in his place. Poor miserable lads, he parted from them with feelings of the deepest pity.' Because of their mother's mental illness, Charles and Sydney Chaplin were discharged to the care of their father, whom Charlie had met only once. And according to his autobiography, Rowlands (Stanley) fled the workhouse with a friend at the age of 15, after a blazing row with James Francis in which he knocked the master unconscious. 'We climbed over the garden wall and dropped in Conway's field and thence hastened through the high corn in the Bodfari direction, as though pursued by blood-hounds.' Unfortunately, the workhouse records make no mention of this dramatic incident, and it seems that he was discharged in the normal way. Rowlands concluded that his treatment in the workhouse was 'ferocious and stupid', citing the tasks that he and his fellow inmates had to under-take, 'such as sweeping the playground with brooms more suited to giants than little children, the washing of the slated floors when one was stiff from a caning'.

Admittedly conditions for workhouse children could be bad, but it was not all brutality and boredom. There were special meals at Christmas time and to celebrate royal events or perhaps the wedding of a prominent guardian. Visitors often brought toys, and ladies of the town, or the guardians them-selves, organized treats or presents for the children. The master of Ripon work-house in Yorkshire, for example, noted in the official report for 24 June 1884 that:

Miss Beckersdeth kindly sent a large quantity of toys for the children last Saturday. I made to say how much the children appreciated the thoughtful kindness of Miss Beckersdeth. I ought to have reported two or three weeks ago that Lady Ingham on visiting the house brought the nursery children toys and the aged inmates a quantity of plum cake.

The cases of bright workhouse children were sometimes taken up by local people, who would raise money to help them in their careers. Occasionally mistakes were made. At Battle in Sussex, in the mid-1840s, James Joseph Crouch showed a lively intelligence and local do-gooders encouraged him to enter the Catholic priesthood – but after three years in a seminary in Rome he was expelled for vicious behaviour. However, his training did come in handy in later life; as an imposter and conman in England, America and Australia (where he embezzled goldminers' funds), he invariably posed as a clerical figure.

Preparing for the future

The policy of separating children from their parents and most adults was partly to deter families from entering the workhouse if at all possible, but it was also rooted in concerns for the children's moral welfare. Particular care was taken to keep girls away from young women, because it was feared that the latter would spread the contagion of pauperism and immorality through their irresponsible behaviour. It proved difficult to achieve in practice, however; in 1850 a Poor Law Inspector wrote that it was a 'hopeless task to raise [children] from a state of pauperism, dependence and crime to one of honest independence and correct moral conduct in the present [work-house] as the children were continually in contact with the adult inmates, who were generally of depraved habits'. Nearly 40 years later, in 1887, Mrs Henry Kingsley, a guardian from Richmond, Surrey, told the Central Poor Law Conference that, despite the kindness of the staff and guardians, if she had her way not a single child would be placed in the house: 'We take everything that is right and good away from them; we take fatherhood and motherhood away. We certainly feed and clothe them, but that is not all. We want something higher and better if we want to raise the tone of the whole of the coming nation.'

It was certainly true that all too often children were let down by their upbringing, both before they arrived at the workhouse and during their time there. This made it hard for many children to make the best of their chances – and until the 1880s and 1890s there were no agencies they could turn to for help. Young girls found it particularly difficult to adjust to life on the outside (p.142). Inevitably, a certain number kept returning to the workhouse throughout their adult life.

Until the late 1840s in many unions, particularly urban ones, the guardians farmed out children to separate institutions, often run by private contractors to save money. It was also an easy way to resolve the serious problem of the large numbers of orphaned and abandoned children who were entering the house. Under the Old Poor Law, children had been sent from London workhouses to contractors, who were paid a few shillings each week to look after them. The unfortunate children were 'educated' and put to work by the contractors, who profited from their labour – a practice that continued well after 1834. By the 1840s there was so much demand for these services from the guardians that contractors such as Peter Drouet at Tooting, London (once described by Dickens as 'vile, vicious and cruel') and Frederick Aubin at Norwood, Surrey, built large schools capable of housing hundreds of children. It was an extremely profitable business; they received 4s 6d a week per child and had almost a free hand to do as they wished with them.

The guardians and their staff occasionally gave these places a cursory inspection. Mr Eaton, master of London's St Pancras workhouse, thought Drouet's 'altogether a well conducted institution ... [and] saw nothing at all objectionable with regard to the place'. He visited Tooting repeatedly, he said, not by order of the Board but 'from his anxiety to see that the children were properly treated'. However, the system came crashing down after a cholera outbreak at Drouet's killed 180 children out of nearly 2,000 inmates. The resulting investigation revealed horrific mistreatment of the children. One boy, Thomas Leach from Kensington, said that:

> in one of the rooms in which he slept on the ground-floor there were five beds, and in each bed six boys slept, three at the top and three at the bottom of the bed. They had only a straw mattress to sleep on, which was covered by a sheet. The floor of the room was a stone one.

Legislation was quickly passed which outlawed baby-farming – the practice of paying foster parents in the country to look after small children often in appalling conditions – and Whitehall encouraged unions to combine in establishing large district schools (sometimes referred to as 'industrial', 'monster' or 'barrack' schools). Mr Aubin's establishment at Norwood was bought by the new Central London School District. Others were built in the outer suburbs at Upper Norwood and Sutton in Surrey, in Hanwell, Middlesex, and Forest Gate in Essex. Outside London, similar schools were established in Manchester (at Swinton) and Liverpool (Kirkdale), but otherwise few were built – perhaps because they were soon criticised as being nothing but over-large regimented 'barracks'. A few unions also built schools at some distance away; London's Marylebone, for example, which housed the children ten miles away in rural Southall. It was hoped that the district schools would give children a real chance in the outside world, through the provision of decent facilities, child-centred education and healthy surroundings, and sometimes the principles seem to have come close to working. A reporter for *Household Words* was impressed by his visit to Swinton in July 1850. He found a happy and disciplined place:

> The children obeyed the summons to school with pleasing alacrity.
> This is owing partly to the agreeable mode of tuition adopted, and in
> some measure to the fact that the lessons are not allowed to become
> tedious and oppressive. As soon as any parties give unequivocal signs of
> weariness, either there is some playful relaxation introduced, or such
> children are sent into the play-ground. On the present occasion, as soon
> as the master applied his mouth to a whistle, away trouped the
> children in glad groups to an ante-room.

And pupils also found the district schools better, at least in comparison with the workhouse schools they had come from. In the early 1860s 'W.H.R.' had been dreadfully mistreated by a Mr Saltley, who taught tailoring at Woolwich District School in the early 1860s. Saltley once beat the boy insensible; 'W.H.R.' later wrote that the 'blood spurted from my ears. I have never thoroughly got over it … there is never a winter goes by when I do not feel much pain in the ears and head generally'. The boy thought himself fortunate when he was transferred from Woolwich in the mid-1860s to the

131

South Metropolitan District School at Sutton. Impressed on arrival by the size of the place, he saw it as a chance for a new start: 'It did certainly look a magnificent place, and as I got up nearer to it … I admired it the more and resolved to do the best I could do there.' 'W.H.R.' ended his time there as a pupil teacher.

Reading, writing and 'rithmetic

The schooling of children varied greatly between unions. The difference was particularly marked between the large urban unions, which educated hundreds of children in district schools, and the small rural unions, where a single schoolmistress might look after all the children or, increasingly, where the workhouse children attended local schools. The choice of approach largely depended on the guardians and their attitude to education. The Newcastle Commission on Education, which reported in 1861, commented that in all but the largest towns the guardians were 'taken from a class generally indifferent to education, often hostile to it'.

Not every guardian, therefore, could be convinced of the need for education, particularly the teaching of reading and writing, which some thought would lead to freethinking and questioning by children of their place in society. In Pershore, Worcestershire, in 1839, the guardians decided that it was 'quite unnecessary to teach the children in the union workhouse the accomplishment of writing' and objected to a proposal to buy pens and paper for the schoolroom.

At the same time, neighbouring Martley attracted national attention for refusing to teach their children at all. The Commissioners forced the guardians there to appoint a schoolmistress, although a subsequent inspector found that she had made little headway. In the workhouse he came across a 'nice-looking and intelligent' 16-year-old girl, an inmate for nearly seven years, who 'did not know how to write a word nor does she know the use of a single figure'.

Many rural unions provided three hours' teaching every morning, apart from Sunday, followed by a few hours' work for the older boys in the fields and vegetable patches surrounding the workhouse. The infamous James Francis at St Asaph, north Wales, was an advocate of this, arguing that it kept the children out of mischief, that it would improve their health and 'besides that it would learn them to use their limbs and to be useful when they left the workhouse'. Before Francis arrived, all the boys did in the afternoon was pick oakum, while the older boys worked with the tailor. 'All the exercise they had was going out walking along the road for half an hour or so.'

In the cities, school could last most of the day, leaving little time for play. At Marylebone in the 1850s, school for children between the ages of seven and sixteen lasted from 9am to 5pm, with two hours for lunch. In the morning, boys would be taught historical reading, general and mental arithmetic, and grammar 'parsing and dictation', and the girls were taught reading, spelling, tables and arithmetic, and writing in copy books. After dinner, the boys also wrote in copy books, read and learnt about geography 'with maps', while their sisters would be taught 'needlework, knitting, learning the time of day and domestic employment'. The infants (aged between two and seven) were expected to spend two or three hours a day in reading, spelling and learning their tables. Wednesday afternoon was a half-holiday, when on fine days the children would be taken into nearby Regent's Park.

Education of workhouse children was the responsibility of the chaplain – who with few exceptions had no educational qualifications nor any interest in teaching children. Yet the chaplain was often the best paid of all workhouse staff, combining his duties in the workhouse with his position as curate in a local Anglican parish. His contribution was perhaps to give a weekly lesson on religious instruction using totally unsuitable religious books as textbooks, and to stock the workhouse library. 'The Indoor Pauper' said that the religious tracts produced every Sabbath and the Bible that lay on one of the window sills were generally ignored unless a 'hypocrite of a certain class' picked them up and appeared to study them 'in order to make an impression on somebody and to secure a selfish end'. The staunchly Methodist Charles Shaw remembered the Anglican chaplain visiting Chell to say grace over Sunday lunch; it went on and on:

> as long as the sermon he had said in church... We were told ... of the great mercies we enjoyed, the good food provided, of the comfortable clothing we had, and how we were cared for by those all around us. All this was said, while before us on the table lay a small hunk of bread, a small plate with a small slice of very thin cheese and some jugs of water.

Far more important for real education were the schoolmasters and mistresses. In all but the smallest places, workhouses were required to appoint a least a schoolmistress. In some houses they might be the son, daughter or relative of the master and matron, but generally they were recruited from young men and women of a reasonable education, but few prospects. In July 1848 Ludlow Union placed an advertisement in *The Times* for a schoolmistress at £20 per annum. She was required to instruct the children in reading, writing and arithmetic, 'the principles of Christian religion, as well as training them in habits of usefulness and industry'. Candidates were requested to supply their application in their own handwriting, stating 'residence and occupation in previous life', as well as testimonials.

Most schoolmasters and mistresses came from lower middle-class backgrounds. It was one of the very few career opportunities open to young women, and for intelligent girls it was almost the only alternative to domestic service. Some had been former pupil teachers (sometimes known as monitors), that is bright pupils who were used to teach the younger children, such as 'W.H.R' did at Sutton. William Rush, aged 13, had taken over teaching his fellow pupils at Gressenhall in Norfolk when the schoolmaster was taken ill. When the school inspector James Kay visited in 1837, he was impressed to find 'the whole discipline and routine of the garden workshop and class instruction went on unbroken'. At Swinton, *Household Words* found the monitor system in operation:

> It was a pleasing sight to see half-a-dozen children seated or kneeling in a circle round the same book, their heads almost meeting in the centre, in their earnestness to see and hear, while the monitor pointed quickly with the finger to the word which each in succession was to pronounce. All seemed alert, and the eyes of the monitors kindled with intelligence.

Few schoolmistresses and masters, at least initially, had any formal training, although there was a short-lived training college for workhouse teachers at Kneller Hall in Twickenham in the 1840s and 1850s. An alternative was one of the religious-based training colleges which came into existence in the 1840s and 1850s.

Schoolmasters and mistresses had one of the most difficult jobs in the workhouse, which may explain why they rarely lasted for more than a few months. They were woefully underpaid and very overworked, teaching large classes of unruly boys and girls who were often uninterested in learning (or unable to) and subject to the petty interference of the guardians over what and how they taught. The rapid turnover of staff inevitably had an effect on the children, particularly in smaller rural unions, where there might be a gap of several months between the departure of one teacher and the arrival of a successor.

Other factors also encouraged swift departures. A number of schoolmasters were dismissed for having affairs with the older female pupils or other pauper women in the house, while schoolmistresses were all too often tempted by the male staff. The teachers could themselves be troublesome; many of the disputes and much of the fractiousness that often disturbed the atmosphere at workhouses involved the teaching staff in some way.

However, a small number made a career of teaching. Robert Bradfield at Gressenhall retired in 1874 after 34 years' service. On his retirement, the guardians minuted that he had 'conducted himself in a manner most satisfactory ... while his general character and conduct has been unimpeachable', despite having been accused, on at least one occasion, of fathering a baby by a pauper woman in the workhouse. Others transferred to better-paid teaching posts at larger schools or found other jobs elsewhere in the Poor Law service. Teachers could also rise within the system. Several of the workhouse masters at Belford, Northumberland, such as Samuel Rose and Robert Guthrie, had been schoolmasters, while the schoolmaster and mistress at Gressenhall, Frank Roach and Elizabeth Skinner, were successful in their joint application to run Fakenham workhouse, Norfolk, in 1879.

Before the introduction of a nationwide system in the 1870s, the education provided by the workhouse could be better than that offered to working-class children elsewhere. At Atcham, in Shropshire, Andrew Doyle was able to boast in 1850 that the children there received 'an education beyond all comparison better than is within the reach of the labourers in any part of the county'. Indeed, legislation in 1845 insisted that pauper apprentices be able to read their indenture documents and to write their signature on it. This requirement was used by Whitehall to force recalcitrant unions to provide at least a basic level of education. In 1846 Rev. H. Mozely, an inspector of workhouse schools, found that workhouse children were better at reading, writing and arithmetic than pupils in the national schools (the Anglican parish schools), while those in the national schools were better at grammar, geography and history.

Unfortunately, the tuition was desperately dull, even by the low standards of the day. When HM Inspector of Schools Henry Bowyer visited schools in the Midlands in the mid-1840s, he found a shortage of secular reading books, maps and blackboards. Instead, children were expected to learn to read using the Bible and other holy works, whose language even then was archaic and bore little connection to their own lives and experiences. One old boy at least was thankful for this; the explorer Henry Stanley wrote that 'without this teaching I should have been little superior to the African savage'. But for the majority such reading material must have been almost meaningless. Too often the lessons were unimaginative, and classes were taught by rote or by copying words into copy books. When the HM Inspectors of Schools asked pupils questions, they found that the children did not understand what they were being taught. At Stourbridge in the Black Country in 1864 the students were said to 'read too slowly and monotonously ... [and they] do not understand the words in their books that they are in the habit of using themselves and hearing'.

Inadequate supplies of books and other equipment was a common problem. Although the Poor Law Board allowed unions to buy textbooks at a substantial discount, few unions took up this offer. Among the titles available were *The Child's First Reader* (price halfpenny), *Singing Tables for Elementary Schools*, and *Reading Disentangled*.

All the children endured discipline, which meant beatings, whether in the schoolroom or elsewhere at St Asaph. It took Henry Stanley (John Rowlands) time to learn the unimportance of tears, as he and his fellows endured sadistic treatment from the

> heavy masterful hand of James Francis ... soured by misfortune, brutal of temper and callous of heart... The ready back-slap in the face, the stunning clout over the ear, the strong blow with the open palm on alternate cheeks, which knocked our senses into confusion, were so frequent that it is a marvel we ever recovered from them.

The quality of instruction was poor, and teachers were generally known for their brutality rather than their pedagogical skills. Charles Shaw felt that 'hardly a boy escaped some form of it, and it was usually a merciless form'. At Hanwell, punishments were meted out, military style, in the gymnasium on Friday mornings, when the children were lined up to witness them. They were administered with a cane by Captain Hindrum, a retired naval officer: 'Slowly and dramatically he would lift it high and with a swish bring it down across the boy's bottom. The spectacle was terrifying and invariably a boy would fall out of rank in a faint.'

'W.H.R.' was a rebel but, as he later admitted, more out of loneliness and fear than as a result of innate badness. When first he had his hand caned by a master, 'I yelled and flew at him and, before he was aware, had given him one or two good kicks.' He was rarely out of trouble with his teachers and regularly received beatings. Once he settled down, he began to progress academically, but by then it was too late, so far as the Woolwich District School was concerned. 'W.H.R.' was regularly thrashed for no reason by Mr Allen, the tailor, so 'it was quite a common thing for the boys to examine the marks about my body every Saturday when we went to the bath'. In later life he recognized that, for all the brutality, the workhouse school had given him some prospects. When he went to the South Metropolitan District School at Sutton, aged 13, 'W.H.R' 'knew how to read, write and calculate pretty fairly, [and] had learned that God's name was sometimes mentioned without an oath'.

Even the brutal school at St Asaph had its supporters. Andrew Doyle, who inspected the institution in 1850 while Stanley was a young pupil there, noted that the 'boys' school was one of the best managed in the district. The children are remarkably intelligent.' Many children left workhouse schools able to read and write (at least after a fashion) and do simple arithmetic; and perhaps most important of all, so far as the guardians were concerned, they were aware of the fundamental aspects of the Christian faith. Underlying all this was the intention to inculcate habits of industry and docility and, in various ways (deliberate as well as innocent), a hatred of the workhouse and the Poor Law system.

Yet officials were also aware of the limitations of the schooling provided for the children in their care. In 1873 the Local Government Board commissioned Jane Nassau Senior (the first woman Poor Law Inspector) to report on the suitability of metropolitan workhouse education for girls. Her findings were damning. She found that formal educational standards were higher than those which prevailed at board (local authority) schools, but in almost every other way the district schools were as damaging as the workhouse itself, producing 'a type of character peculiarly hard, helpless and apathetic, incapable of adapting itself to persons and circumstances, and presenting a remarkable degree of stubbornness and violence in a large number of instances'. She talked of the 'most absolute monotony, both of sight and sound – only it is called order and regularity – and there is intense dullness under the name of method and discipline. White walls, dull rooms, the same dinner (and the same quantity to eat) on a given day of the week.' Mrs Nassau Senior called for them to be closed down and replaced by smaller workhouse or 'separate' schools; but she really wanted the schools to be abolished. Instead, the children could be 'boarded out' – fostered, with working-class families where they could have a reasonably normal upbringing.

Improvements were made to the industrial schools, but they were too useful (and economic) to abandon altogether. In the late 1890s, while attending the Central London School at Hanwell, Charles Chaplin noted that: 'Although ... we were well looked after, it was a forlorn existence. Sadness was in the air.' A Select Committee on Pauper Education of 1896 unanimously condemned industrial schools, both on account of the dangers of disease, especially eye and skin infections, which were common when so many children were crowded together, and because of the emotional damage resulting from isolating children from the community and depriving them of individual care and affection.

In East London both Will Crooks and George Lansbury did their best to improve the Forest Gate District School in east London, where pauper children from Poplar and the local unions were sent. In his memoirs Lansbury wrote of his first visit in 1894:

long dormitories for scores of children to sleep in, very little accommodation for recreation, and at the time I first saw it the children were dressed in the old, hideous Poor Law garb, corduroy and hard blue serge, and the girls with their hair almost shaved off, with nothing at all to make them look attractive in any sort of way. The food was quite coarse and I should think at times insufficient. It was apparent that the place was organised and controlled as a barracks. I daresay the superintendent, who had been a military man, was, according to his light, quite a decent person, but then his light was deficient.

Improvements began to be discernible in the new century. Within a decade an inspector of schools felt able to report that there 'is very little (if any) of the institution mark among the children' and said the teaching and conditions compared favourably with the best elementary schools.

In 1907 the Forest Gate school moved to a former farm at Shenfield in rural Essex where children were housed in cottages with a dining hall, laundry (for the girls), swimming pool and an assembly hall. The move was strongly encouraged by George Lansbury, who became a much-loved figure among the children there. The story is told that when Queen Mary visited the school with Lansbury in 1919, the children forgot all their lessons, broke rank and surged forward, shrilly crying, 'Good old George! Good old George!'

Alternatives to the industrial school were also increasingly becoming available. The boarding-out system, whereby children were fostered with working-class families, had proved very popular in Scotland, where 90 per cent of pauper children were cared for in this way. It was much less common in England, where guardians found it hard to find suitable couples who would do it for love rather than the money. In a speech in 1903 Will Crooks argued that 'in some villages I found "boarding-out" a staple industry. Boarding-out is all right in good homes; the difficulty is to find good homes.' Nonetheless, by 1914 some 12,000 children were cared for in this way.

From the 1870s the more enlightened urban unions (such as Bolton in Lancashire, Dewsbury in Yorkshire, Wolverhampton in the West Midlands and West Ham in East London) chose to place their children in cottage homes. Under this system, groups of about 30 boys and girls lived with a house parent or a couple, although it was sometimes difficult to find house parents. Those that were found could prove inappropriate. Nine of the first 23 in Sheffield, for example, were sacked, in some cases because they were suspected of being involved in prostitution. Often the houses were sited around a green, with boys' houses on one side and the girls' on the other. The Kensington and Chelsea School District, which erected homes at Banstead between 1878 and 1880, gave the impression of being a 'well-designed model village'.

A variant was the scattered home, whereby small groups of children lived in homes on residential streets; this enabled them to become part of the local community and attend local schools. In 1893 Sheffield bought a number of such houses and filled them with groups of boys and girls of mixed ages, carefully separating Catholics from Protestants. Bath and other unions soon followed suit, and by 1903 Camberwell in south London owned no fewer than 18 separate homes in the area. In many ways this was a good solution; the children liked them and they were easy to manage, as well as being relatively inexpensive.

With the establishment of local elementary (board) schools after 1870, many smaller unions stopped employing schoolmasters and mistresses and sent children to these schools instead. This had the added advantage of allowing pauper children to mix with other boys and girls of the same age, something that the government in Whitehall was increasingly keen on. Occasionally disputes broke out between the school authorities and the guardians – usually over the fees paid to educate the workhouse children – and the students would be returned to be educated in the workhouse again.

Attending the village school could be traumatic for children who had known only the strange world of the workhouse. On his first day at the school in Wangford in Suffolk, Fred Copeman was greeted with a roar of laughter from his fellow pupils and burst into tears. He ran away, but was eventually forced back. There he found out the reason for their reaction: 'I was the only boy in the school with long trousers and his hair shaved off. I must have looked to them like a funny old man.' He found it difficult to make friends with his classmates; only a little girl called Mary took pity on him.

Because of their upbringing, workhouse children could be a disruptive influence on village schools, and many were sometimes made scapegoats for the misbehaviour of a few. In 1887 the Gressenhall guardians were advised to take all the workhouse children out of the village school because the bad behaviour of two brothers, William and George Farrer, had severely provoked the schoolmaster.

Learning for life

Boys and girls were often given training for industry and agriculture within the Poor Law system, in the hope that the skills that they learned would be of use to future employers. Those workhouses that ran their own schools often provided basic tuition for the older boys and girls in work-related trades. At Maidstone, Kent, in the early 1860s, Mr Pigott, a Poor Law Inspector, reported that the 'Guardians have taken pains to have the pupils industrially trained. A number of boys are taught shoemaking. Girls are taught housework and laundry work.' In many rural workhouses, the boys were set to work in the fields, learning the skills that they would need when they left the house. The income from the crops they produced was also a useful addition to the workhouse budget.

In 1850 the children at Atcham in Shropshire learned a variety of tasks, including knitting, netting and plaiting straw. Thomas Everett, clerk to the union, reported that 'it became a natural habit in the children to be doing something that was useful, so that when fatigued with heavier toils the child sat down to rest, it was ... an instinctive feeling that led him to take his straws or needles in his hand'. Everett recommended that boys between the ages of nine and fourteen be allowed two acres of clear ground to be exclusively theirs. In 1850 they grew potatoes, turnips, carrots, parsnips, cabbage, beans and onions, which were sold to local traders for £61 12s 6d.

Also in Shropshire, the Quatt school at Bridgnorth provided training for boys and girls from various unions in the county. In the morning they were taught the three Rs and the principles of the Christian religion. Boys spent the rest of the day 'employed in the cultivation of four acres and a half of good turnip and barley land, and in the management of cows and pigs', while the girls were 'instructed in house and dairy work, baking, washing, ironing and in sewing'.

It was difficult for many smaller unions to provide any real form of industrial training, partly because they did not have the resources, but also because there were very few child inmates. In some places, staff (usually the porter) were required to have skills such as cobbling to impart to the few children in the workhouse. By contrast, in the industrial schools a tailor might have to teach a class of a hundred or more. It is little wonder that when, in 1867, Poor Law Inspector T.B. Browne asked a tailor whether he would take a boy who had received some training in preference to one who had none, the answer he received was that he preferred an apprentice whom he could instruct himself.

Because of the nature of Victorian society, it was easier to train boys for the variety of trades and occupations which they could adopt. The choices for girls were much more limited – the overwhelming majority ended up as domestic servants, for which they received little formal training. It is hardly surprising that about a quarter of girls ended up back at the workhouse, either through misconduct (in other words, prostitution) or other causes (generally pregnancy), while the proportion for boys was lower, at 15 per cent.

It is safe to say that the vast majority of girls who entered service were totally unsuited to – and almost untrained for – the work. William Lancey, a former butler, wrote in his memoirs: 'I never knew a servant from an orphanage or institution shine in my time.' Their experience in the workhouse was totally different from the routines found in a middle-class home. Much of their previous work consisted of the never-ending scrubbing of dormitory floors, the preparation of vast amounts of vegetables and mending hundreds of clothes. Henrietta Synnot made this point when describing dinner at a district school in the 1860s:

> A large hall capable of holding 1,500 children. A smell as of laundry
> and kitchen combined, and a great deal of steam. Enter four men bearing
> two enormous wooden washing tubs, containing a stew of Australian
> meat. Then it is ladled out into small basins, and placed by boys on the
> tables. The sound of martial music is heard in the distance and presently
> a thousand little paupers, headed by the brass band, file in and take their
> places. After singing a grace they fall to… When the girl who has
> assisted at this meal goes to service, she has not, as far as I know, to serve
> out soup from a washing tub, or to sing a grace, or not to throw away
> what she sees on the plates … nearly everything which a girl sees and
> does at school is absolutely opposed to what she sees and does at service.

A few boards were aware of the problem and a training school was established in Norwich, but this closed in 1874. The guardians at Shepton Mallet, Somerset, opened a kitchen in 1880 for the purpose of teaching the older girls. Unfortunately, only two girls could use it at a time.

At worst, there is a suspicion that in some places the available training amounted to little more than using the girls to clean the house and help cook the inmates' food. In one unidentified workhouse, the matron had formed groups of girls over 14, 'whom she instructs thoroughly in all branches of domestic service, and by them, and them alone, the whole of the cooking, washing, and ironing of the Union is carried out'. They also waited upon the master and matron, 'laying their table and washing their china'.

There were a number of reported cases of cruelty to young pauper servants. Jane Wilbred, a 14-year-old orphan, had been placed out to a Mr and Mrs Sloane by the West London Union in 1849. At first she was well treated, but the situation changed when Mrs Sloane's pet bird died and Jane was accused of frightening it to death. From then on she was subjected to a regime of starvation and beating, and her condition seemed visibly worse to neighbours. She was eventually rescued in November 1850, debilitated and marked from the beatings. The Sloanes were tried and sentenced to two years in prison. The trial caused a sensation and led to a change in the law, forcing guardians and relieving officers to monitor children until they were 16 years old.

Of the 51 girls who left London district schools in 1868 and who were traced by Mrs Nassau Senior five years later, only 18 were 'doing well or fairly well' and another seven had 'dropped out of sight, of whom last tidings were satisfactory'. The rest had had unsatisfactory reports or, for one reason or another, were no longer servants. In 26 cases complaints had been made about the girls' bad temper, 21 were in bad health, and nine 'were beset by bad relations'. So the girls went from position to position and, without good references, many inevitably ended up on the streets. Henry Mayhew claimed that in the 1850s half of the girls from Marylebone workhouse who had been placed in service ended up as prostitutes.

From the 1880s, however, two charities – the Girls Friendly Society and the Metropolitan Association for Befriending Young Servants (MABYS) – began to help young women find decent situations, and provided training as well as safe and clean hostels. By 1898 there were over 200 training homes in England and Wales to which girls from workhouses and orphanages could turn. Through their efforts, workhouse girls gradually became sought after as servants.

In the early years of the New Poor Law, many boys (but fewer girls) were indentured or apprenticed to a master in order to learn a trade. By the 1850s apprenticeships had rapidly fallen away, because of the decline in traditional craft occupations, such as shoe- and boot-making, as a result of the arrival of mass-produced goods and clothing. In 1845 the Leicester guardians resolved not to send any more boys to be apprenticed as frame-work knitters, 'as the trade is so over-handed already that it is only apprenticing a boy to learn pauperism under another name'.

Apprenticeships were first introduced under the Old Poor Law. Many local charities were also established to apprentice children in what were known as 'proper trades'. In 1719, for example, money was left in the will of William Harding, a wealthy local farmer in Aylesbury, Buckinghamshire, to establish such a charity. Although children supported by charities were generally apprenticed to respectable masters and learned a good trade, workhouse children rarely had these opportunities. In urban areas they were often dispatched at a very young age to work in factories or up chimneys. Chimney sweeps, in particular, were always looking for thin young boys to climb up awkward chimneys and clean them. One such figure of dread appears in *Oliver Twist*: 'Mr Gamfield [a sweep looking for an apprentice] knowing what the dietary of the workhouse was, well knew that he would be a nice small pattern, just the thing for register stoves.' It was appallingly hard work, and it is small wonder that Oliver Twist begged the parish beadle to 'starve him – beat – kill him' rather than abandon him to Mr Gamfield.

Initially the Poor Law Commissioners tried to ban apprenticeships altogether, but this proved impractical. Legislation in 1844 abolished compulsory apprenticeships and gave Whitehall the power to prescribe the duties of masters and the terms and conditions of indentures (the agreement between the master and the apprentice). No child under nine or who could not read and write his own name was to be bound; no one over fourteen was to be bound without their own consent. Further legislation in 1851 provided for the prosecution of cases of neglect or ill treatment. In addition, apprentices were to be visited twice a year.

Workhouse children tended to be apprenticed to local trades, where they existed. In places such as Norfolk and Northamptonshire, this was likely to be shoemaking; there were many small workshops and plenty of vacancies for apprentices. In Bromsgrove in Worcestershire, however, many children were apprenticed to the needle and fishhook makers of neighbouring Redditch. In smaller unions, such as Belford, where there were far fewer children, efforts were made to match individuals to a chosen career. Here, for example, in 1907 the 14-year-old William Cameron was offered the chance to join the training ship *Wellesley*, but he preferred to become a carpenter and was duly apprenticed to a local joiner.

The sea was indeed an option for some. The *Wellesley* was moored offshore in the Tyne at Newcastle and trained boys (workhouse children as well those from local orphanages) for the sea. As well as instruction in seamanship, climbing masts, weapons training, fencing and first aid, they received strict religious training. The boys slept in hammocks on the ship and were rarely allowed on shore, except for training purposes. Exceptional good behaviour was rewarded with a couple of days' leave so that the boys could visit their families. In London the Metropolitan Asylum Board maintained a former wooden battleship, the *Exmouth*, at Grays in Essex, which accommodated over 600 boys. Between 1876 and 1929, over 16,000 workhouse boys were trained on board; of these over 4,500 joined the Royal Navy, 6,400 joined the merchant marines and 1,600 became army musicians.

More problematic were the apprenticeships on board fishing trawlers at Brixham, Grimsby and Hull. Three-quarters of the apprentices at Brixham in 1882 came from local workhouses in south Devon, particularly Exeter, Totnes, Honiton and Brixham itself. At Hull they were recruited from the nearby industrial towns of Lancashire and Yorkshire, and from Holborn in London. By the mid-1870s over 300 apprentices a year were being taken on. The authorities thought that this was an ideal solution for 'disposing of the rougher classes of pauper boys', that is those aged 14 or 15 'who from having been brought up among vicious surroundings or from some defect of character are not fit for domestic service' and for whom 'an apprenticeship to the fishing trade is their last chance'.

A few took to the trade and prospered at it. There was always a shortage of skilled labour and once the indenture expired, normally at the age of 21, it was possible to make good money. One old boy from Hackney workhouse, James Plastow, told a parliamentary inquiry into labour conditions in 1882 that he now owned several smacks and had an extensive trade as a fish salesman: 'I believe every lad in the fishing trade has the same chance of a successful life as I have had, providing he saves his money instead of spending it.'

In 1897 the guardians at Bromsgrove apprenticed Frederick Broadley to the International Steam Trawling Company at Grimsby. He wrote to the board 'stating that he liked the sea and would rather be on the sea than on land', the first of several such letters that the board received from him. Most, however, found work at sea too hard and uncongenial and ran away. A third of the boys at Grimsby absconded between 1881 and 1893; and in Hull as many absconded as had been recruited. William Chance said that this was because the boys resented being paid only a pittance, while the other deckhands received a decent wage, without realizing the investment that was being made in them by their masters. A more likely reason was that the boys had little supervision when they were on shore – because of their bad behaviour, masters were generally unwilling to have them staying with their families. There was also no support available for the apprentices onshore, let alone training or any attempt to impose discipline – except through the courts.

New lives in the colonies

During the 19th century, many perceived emigration as a solution to the overcrowded cities and countryside, as well as making the colonies strong and thus able to buy British exports and contribute to imperial defence. In the words of the guardians at Petworth in Sussex, in the 1830s, it is 'only a removal from one part of the British Empire where there are more workmen than there is work to another fertile, healthful and in everyway delightful portion of the same empire, where the contrary is the case'. A trickle of pauper families had long been sent by parishes to the colonies, where it was hoped they would take the opportunity to start fresh lives without the taint of pauperism. Some guardians were keen on this idea, although Whitehall was much less enthusiastic, fearing a waste of public money and scandals in the making. Between 1835 and 1837, however, some 5,000 individuals were sent to Canada and Australia, with particularly high numbers coming from Norfolk and Suffolk. At the same time, Petworth Union sent several hundred labourers and their families to Canada, although the scheme depended on support from the Wyndham family, the major local landowners. Few parties of children were sent out. The Philanthropic Farm School at Redhill in Surrey (which took a number of boys from workhouses) sent just over a thousand boys abroad between 1850 and 1871, mainly to Canada and Australia.

In 1869 two spinster ladies of strong resolve, Maria Rye and Annie Macpherson, began taking parties of workhouse and orphan children to Canada. They received a small bounty for each child from the Canadian government, although most of the funds came from charities or fees paid by the Poor Law Unions. By 1874 just over 600 such children had arrived in Canada, mainly being settled with farming families in Ontario.

In the same year Poor Law Inspector Andrew Doyle was sent out to investigate. His report was highly critical, pointing out deficiencies in the training of children before they crossed the Atlantic and subsequently in the inspection of their new homes to prevent abuses. These were to be the worries expressed about the emigration of children throughout the existence of the scheme. Although battered by Doyle's report, Miss Rye continued to send out parties of girls to Ontario. In a newspaper interview in 1894 she said that:

> My children are not fitted for the refinement of the cities. They are better suited to the farm. We do not rescue them from the cities to return them to the same temptations. My aim is to find them good homes with farmers' wives, with whom they can grow up, working side by side, into honest smart capable girls, fit to be the wives of thrifty young farmers.

It was up to individual boards of guardians to approach Miss Rye, Miss Macpherson and the others who took parties of children to Canada. The boys and girls had to be under 16 and have signed a written agreement that they wanted to leave England. In 1873, for example, Hereford agreed to send with Maria Rye a small party of six girls aged between seven and twelve at a cost of £8 per child (including an outfit and 'free delivery at Liverpool'). According to the *Hereford Times*:

> The little girls now present [before the guardians] appeared highly pleased at the prospect before them. They were all smiling and cheerful and appeared healthy looking children, and did credit to their fare. The

Master said he had left a number of little girls in the workhouse crying because they had not been chosen to go.

The colonial authorities were always very concerned that pauper children were being dumped upon them. They wanted children of good character untainted by crime or connected with any criminal institution, who had received some training before emigration and who would be supervised until they had reached adulthood. But, as Will Crooks and others pointed out, these were the children who were equally likely to do well in England. It must have been quite a temptation for the guardians to get rid of their most difficult (and thus likely to be the most expensive) children overseas. In 1887 the immigration agent at Winnipeg, W.C.B. Grahame, complained to the authorities in Ottawa about a boy 'part negro ... who was smuggled on board by the Croydon Union authorities... There are two other boys of the same stamp here, quite incorrigible, who are rambling about the country like wild beasts.'

It would be too easy to condemn the sending of children to workhouses entirely. For every scandal that came to light, such as the appalling conditions of Drouet's School at Tooting, there were imaginative schemes to foster children and real attempts to provide a proper education and subsequently a secure job away from the poverty line. Above all, the workhouse authorities were determined to ensure that these children did not repeat the mistakes of their parents. They did this in several ways: through education and training for the outside world; through separation from the parents' 'baleful influences'; and later, in the 1880s and 1890s, through attempts to create a happy family life outside the workhouse. In the 1890s the Local Government Board laid down that no new workhouse should provide accommodation for children, and in 1913 it banned keeping children over three years of age in any institution containing adults. By the First World War almost every pauper child was looked after well away from the workhouse, and from the taint that it bestowed on those who entered its doors.

CHAPTER SIX

Sick Bodies and Old Bones

The look of the sick ward certainly takes away all the romantic notions of
ministration; everything most uncomely and meagre and some of
the old folk repulsive enough.

Lady Frederick Cavendish, St Martin in the Fields, 1850s

IN the workhouse considerable resources were spent on caring for the
sick, the infirm and the aged, as the elderly were then known. By the
end of the 19th century the inmates in most houses largely comprised the sick
and elderly.

The downside, as always with the Poor Law, was the institutional nature
of the care offered, particularly for long-term patients – one pauper is known
to have been kept in the same bed for 11 years. Also, the quality of care
was erratic, depending on how willing the guardians were to pay for the
service and the dedication of overworked and poorly paid staff. Conditions
improved from the 1880s, with the arrival of professionally trained medical
staff and the election of women and working-class guardians with imaginative ideas and the determination to improve the lives of the inmates.

There were charitably funded alternatives, such as voluntary hospitals
and almshouses for the elderly, but these institutions were not interested
in the undeserving poor and the destitute, and they made great efforts to
keep such people from their doors. In addition, the distribution of such hospitals and almshouses was patchy. In the early 1860s, Richmond in Surrey,
for example, had six almshouses and no hospital. The Poor Law did at least
offer a national network of institutions offering 'care'.

The burden of care

Increasingly, the greatest success of the workhouse lay in the care and treatment of the sick. Even today, most surviving workhouse buildings and sites are used by hospitals. Yet surprisingly this was not a duty laid down in the Poor Law Amendment Act of 1834, and the Royal Commission which preceded it hardly mentioned the provision of medical care for paupers.

Under the Old Poor Law, the care of the sick poor had been the responsibility of parishes. In most cases, the overseers of the poor employed elderly female paupers to nurse the sick in their homes, and occasionally provided food and paid for medicines or, in rare cases, trips to spas, in the hope that the patient would recover. If there was a local workhouse, the sick could be admitted and cared for by the matron and a team of pauper nurses.

Provision varied greatly. At the model workhouse at St George's Hanover Square in London's West End, built in 1725–6, the sick poor were attended daily by a doctor, apothecary and surgeon, and twice a week by a clergyman. More typical perhaps was the house at Louth, Lincolnshire, where the ill shared wards with the well. When Sir Frederick Eden visited in 1791, he found:

> There is one large lodging-room for the men and another for the women,
> each containing 14 beds which are partitioned from each other by
> deal-boards at each end, and on one side: the view of a sick neighbour
> is thereby, in a great measure, obstructed; but to a feeling mind, the sense
> of hearing must frequently convey disagreeable ideas; the smell,
> must also, be frequently offensive.

However, more workhouses provided isolation wards for victims of fever and other communicable diseases. As early as the 1720s St Giles in London had three separate wards for the itch (scabies), 'the foul disease' (venereal diseases) and smallpox and other malignant fevers.

It was expected that this arrangement of mostly out-relief would continue after 1834, particularly for the elderly. If the sick could not manage at home, it was suggested that they might be accommodated in separate buildings away from the punitive establishments for the able-bodied. Even so, the Poor Law Commissioners stressed to the guardians that it was important to 'prevent medical aid from generating or encouraging pauperism'. The

SICK BODIES AND OLD BONES

stigma of the workhouse must have been enough to discourage many poor people from seeking the medical treatment they needed.

Medical treatment was also provided by voluntary hospitals, supported by charitable donations. Most large towns had one or more such institutions, such as the London Hospital in the East End, the Radcliffe Infirmary in Oxford and, on a smaller scale, the York Dispensary, which provided outpatient services. Admission was generally by letter from a rich subscriber. Unfortunately, voluntary hospitals were choosy about the patients they took and were interested in neither the very poor nor the incurably ill. In Wakefield the Dispensary would not admit paupers. If patients on poor relief were discovered in the hospital, they were immediately dispatched to the workhouse. This happened ten times in 1854 and 1855 alone. Subscribers were warned in 1858 not 'to let their tickets of admission fall into the hands of improper objects'; it was recommended that such applicants be directed to the relieving officer. This meant that the tickets only went to 'the most deserving of the poor, and avoid[ed] the risk of being used merely as a relief of the general poor rate'.

There were also far fewer people in voluntary hospitals than in the workhouse. In 1861 voluntary hospitals looked after 11,000 patients, while Poor Law infirmaries cared for some 50,000. Increasingly, workhouse hospitals accommodated the bulk of sick children, the mentally ill, those with skin conditions, epilepsy, tuberculosis and venereal diseases and those who were just sick. In 1911 just over 120,000 patients were treated in Poor Law infirmaries. In part this increased number reflected changing medical practices. Traditionally, all but the most seriously ill were cared for at home. Even the vast majority of paupers were visited by medical officers in their homes. However, improvements in medical treatment increasingly made it better and easier for the sick to be treated in hospitals.

Housing the sick

Initially, the pauper sick were accommodated in the same buildings, occasionally even the same wards, as the able-bodied. In fact, conditions during the first few decades of the New Poor Law as a whole were far from good. Lady Frederick Cavendish, who was a regular visitor to St Martin in the Field's workhouse in London in the 1850s, noted that 'the look of the sick ward certainly takes away all the romantic notions of ministration; everything most uncomely and meagre and some of the old folk repulsive enough'.

A series of investigations in the mid-1860s revealed how bad the position was. In London, Poor Law Inspector Harry Farnall found that 13 of the 40 workhouses were unfit for use as hospitals:

> In each sick ward ... there is a great deficiency of cubical space for each patient... [M]ost of those workhouses are badly constructed and are closely hemmed in on every side by other buildings; the trades carried on in some of them taint the atmosphere; there is no facility for supervision on any other; there is no room to erect sufficient bathrooms and lavatories where required ... and there are no means of giving day rooms to the convalescent.

The government was stirred into action by a damning series of articles in *The Lancet* which exposed the truth about conditions in London's sick wards. The reports described the almost universal practice of 'mixing up sick wards in the body of the house'. Even paupers with 'contagious fevers of the most dangerous kind' were cared for in the ordinary wards.

In Huddersfield, which had five small workhouses in the Union, the *Leeds Mercury* in 1848 condemned the one in the town as being in every respect 'wholly unfitted for a residence for the many scores that are continually crowded into it, unless it be that desire to engender endemic and fatal disease. And this Huddersfield workhouse is by far the best in the whole union.' Little changed over the next decade. A special committee appointed by the guardians in 1857 reported that the lack of classification in the hospital wards of Huddersfield workhouse led to 'abandoned women' with diseases of a 'most loathsome character' being mixed up with idiots, young children and even lying-in cases. The hospital accommodation was crowded, damp, insanitary and 'utterly unfit' for lodging sick inmates. It took another 15 years before a satisfactory new building was built.

Cleanliness was another problem. *The Lancet* found only one workhouse in London where there was a sufficiency of bathrooms. Dr Edward Smith, the Poor Law Board's Chief Medical Officer, came across paupers at Kensington and Paddington who washed in their own chamber pots. He was told by one medical officer that his patients preferred to wash in this way, but he later established that they did so 'against their will and their former habits at home'. Few guardians provided lavatory paper on the grounds that the inmates were not in the habit of using it. Dr Smith found numerous instances of water closets being blocked with 'old towels, dusters and dishcloths' and pages torn from the Bible. 'One or more Bibles and sometimes a Prayer Book were found in each ward, but in a more or less dilapidated state – a circumstance connected with the subject just discussed.'

The reports by Smith and Farnall revealed how bad medical care for paupers could be. Farnall, in particular, made recommendations about how matters could be improved, arguing that, in London, Poor Law infirmaries should be built separately from the workhouse and paid for by a common rate across the metropolis. This proposal was taken up by Gathorne Hardy, the president of the Local Government Board, who, in introducing the Metropolitan Poor Bill into Parliament in 1867, explained:

> There is one thing … which we must peremptorily insist on, namely
> the treatment of the sick in workhouses being conducted on an entirely
> different system, because the evils complained of have mainly arisen from
> workhouse management, which must, to a great degree, be of a deterrent
> character having been applied to the sick, who are not proper objects for
> such a system. That is one thing I should insist on as an absolute condition.

The new Act set up the Metropolitan Asylums Board to run fever hospitals on behalf of the local boards of guardians in London and encouraged them to build new hospitals, such as the Poplar and Stepney Sick Asylum (now St Andrew's Hospital), which opened in 1871 for 592 patients from the East End. It cost £43,000 to build, boasted electric bells and telegraphic communications, lifts to each ward, hot-water heating pipes, and tubes to carry dirty linen to the steam-powered laundry in the basement. The Act was the first acknowledgement of the duty of the State to provide hospitals for the poor; this would eventually lead to the creation of the National Health Service. In the following year further legislation allowed provincial unions to establish separate hospitals if they so chose, although few unions in rural areas bothered.

In Manchester a new workhouse infirmary at Crumpsall opened in 1878 for 600 patients. It consisted of seven parallel three-storey ward blocks, four for women and children and three for men. The wards were lit by gas and not plastered but colour-washed, which meant they could be painted regularly. Mattresses were made of canvas and stuffed with straw; they were removed and burnt when a patient was discharged. There was also a dispensary (for outpatients), an operating theatre, offices for the medical staff and nurses' quarters. On its opening, the newspapers made much of its position on the edge of the city: 'Its elevated position site makes it peculiarly adapted for hygienic and sanitary purposes.' On fine days, patients' beds were pushed outside so they could enjoy the fresh air and sunshine. Over the entrance to the new buildings, the inscription 'Poor and Needy, the Lord Careth for Me' was carved in a prominent position.

Not all the new infirmaries met Crumpsall's standards. Between 1863 and 1865 a new union workhouse was erected at Marland, Rochdale. It was designed to accommodate 260 adults and 40 children. In 1870 it housed 194 paupers, none able-bodied, of whom 47 were imbeciles, mostly bedridden. Even by the low standards of most workhouses, Marland was badly run. Diets ordered by the medical officer were rarely provided. Infectious cases wandered at will through the wards. There were few means of washing clothes, utensils or bodies. Medicines were administered by paupers and kept in unlabelled bottles in a box, together with blacking and firewood. Although pauper nurses were supposed to be able to read, the guardians claimed that the medical officer never wrote prescriptions because the only medicine in the unlabelled bottles was cod-liver oil, as the illiterate nurses well knew. All inmates urinated into a tub in the corner of each ward – the urine was sold by the guardians for scouring cotton. The inmates had head sores and the itch and had all been dosed with sulphur, brimstone and cod-liver oil for eight months, but the scratching had not stopped. Diarrhoea was endemic.

Whatever their standards, the new hospitals were filled with patients who might previously have been treated at home. The authorities in White-hall saw this as a way of forcing the poor into the workhouse, thus reducing the amount paid as out-relief. And as medical officers were not paid extra for attending the poor in their homes, they naturally felt that the pauper sick would be better off in an infirmary. However, one group of medical officers argued against this, saying: 'Sickness, one of the most prolific and pitiable sources of pauperism, ought, we submit, to be placed upon a footing quite apart from that of ordinary causes of want and dependence on the rates. It is cheap and wise to cure the sick poor with the greatest promptitude.' This argument very largely fell on deaf ears. Over the last three decades of the 19th century, the numbers of sick paupers helped in their own homes fell and those admitted to Poor Law infirmaries rose. Even so, of the 60,000 sick paupers recorded by the Local Government Board on 1 July 1896 as being under the care of the guardians, 36,500 were still in workhouse sick wards rather than in separate infirmaries.

This was probably because it was more expensive to run a separate establishment. For a start, infirmaries tended to be more expensive to fit out and maintain. The greatest expense was, however, the staff. It was more difficult in infirmaries to use pauper labour to do the nursing, let alone cleaning or preparing meals, because there were few able-bodied or healthy elderly paupers available. Infirmaries also employed more medical staff, such as a medical superintendent at £400 with accommodation and an assistant superintendent at perhaps £160, plus an increasing number of trained nurses.

The medical men

At the heart of the new system was the medical officer, who was appointed from among local doctors. A union might employ a dozen or more such men. Unless directly employed at the workhouse, they were each assigned a district, supposedly containing about 15,000 people or, in rural areas, covering 15,000 acres in size; in fact their responsibilities were often much greater. Each officer visited sick paupers in their homes, prescribing the appropriate medicines and recommending admission to the union workhouse, if he thought fit. The cases dealt with generally concerned minor illnesses and broken limbs.

In rural areas the officer might also maintain a private practice or contract his services to other health care bodies such as friendly societies, or act as the local factory doctor or police surgeon. The 1909 Royal Commission on the Poor Laws, however, was told that 'the doctor takes these positions in order to further his private practice and I am afraid the poor very often have to suffer for that reason; he takes it too cheap'.

Medical officers were often young and inexperienced. They were underpaid for their responsibilities, often funding medicines from their own pockets. As late as 1909 it was reported that in most unions the district medical officers 'still have to find their own drugs and medicines and any dressings or bandages that are required, and they are paid fixed stipends which vary from as little as £10–£15 up to as much as £300 or £400, a very usual figure being £100, together with additional fees for midwifery cases and operations'.

The low wages were a constant source of friction. Seeking an increase in salary in 1857, Dr Palmer, the medical officer for Mortlake and Barnes, described his duties to the Poor Law Board:

> My case book informs that I have on average seldom less than fifty
> visits per week whom I see at my house and prescribe for as well as visit
> at their respective houses... This work requires the use of a horse as
> patients live some two, three or sometimes nearly four miles apart...
> My present rate of pay is not one pound per week to find knowledge,
> medicine, and the wear and tear incident upon these labours.

A pay rise was sanctioned, even though, compared with neighbouring unions, the medical officers in Barnes were well paid. Other medical officers were less successful, and grew bitter about the limitations they struggled with. One medical officer told a journalist in 1859:

> I can't do my duty to my patients for the simple reason that I can't
> afford it. The wards of my workhouse and its classification will not bear
> scrutiny. When I first put on harness here, I was young and enthusiastic,
> and tried hard to get the guardians to provide what I knew to be
> absolutely necessary. But I only gained ill-will for myself, and did no
> good for my patients, so I've just struggled on as well as I could... I could
> tell you of instances in which a really zealous man has been worried into
> resigning, and a selfish drone appointed in his stead, who has been
> popular because he let things alone... I haven't a doubt that deaths from
> medical neglect are far commoner than you'd suppose.

Low wages were a false economy because medical officers either resigned after a few months or persuaded the guardians or the authorities in London of the need for a rise. After a considerable row, the salary of Dr T.R. Tatham, who was the medical officer for the Huddersfield North District (which contained 25,000 residents as well as the workhouse), was doubled to £80 in 1847. Tatham remained in post for another ten years.

The low pay meant that the guardians often had to employ somebody who was incompetent or simply unqualified. In 1852 the Ripon (Yorkshire) guardians wrote to Whitehall about the appointment of one of their medical officers, William Armstrong: 'It is impossible to procure a person residing within the district ... duly qualified in any of the four modes of the order of the Poor Law Board ... because there is no person so qualified within the district.' A year later he was reprimanded for neglecting his patients.

It was also difficult to get rid of unsatisfactory men, because there was often no other person available. In 1848 Joseph Hesslegrave, the medical officer for Marsden in the Huddersfield Union, was dismissed by the Poor Law Board for failing to attend two paupers, one of whom subsequently died. Hesslegrave successfully reapplied for his post, supported by memorials from prominent ratepayers.

In Norfolk, when R.J. Tunaley was medical officer at both Henstead and Forehoe between 1839 and 1855, there was a constant stream of complaints about professional misconduct. In 1843, for example, he failed to visit a pauper woman who subsequently died. Three years later there were allegations that he neglected to call upon paupers despite being directed to do so by the relieving officer. As a result, three people died and one went blind. On both occasions, Whitehall tried to dismiss him, but he was defended by the guardians, in part because he was one of the few local medical men they could afford to employ.

For the conscientious officer, the work was onerous. In 1852 Frederick Chapman was appointed medical officer for the Richmond workhouse at a salary of £50 per annum. He was expected to inspect each new pauper admitted into the house and to care for the sick and infirm ones already there, as well as to monitor the sanitary provisions. Often the paupers were seriously ill. In 1857 he described his workload: 'The cases coming under my charge are not mere illnesses of short duration and trifling character, but such as cannot be properly treated at their own homes and require long, anxious and assiduous attention.'

Edward Smith reported that

the usual routine is for the medical officer to attend at or before midday for his principal visit, and then he visits the infirmary or sick wards and speaks to all the more important cases. He also walks into each infirm ward where there are some sick persons and asks if any wishes to see him.

Often the sick were not seen daily, but perhaps three or four times a week depending on the severity of the case and the numbers in the workhouse. Smith thought that on average medical officers spent between two and three hours a day in the workhouse. In rural workhouses it could be much less. A parliamentary inquiry of 1902 heard that in Wiltshire some medical officers spent just five minutes a day in the house, leaving the work largely to the paid nurses.

The medical officer had to report to the relieving officer and the guardians. The relieving officer directed him to the patients he saw outside the house and the guardians had to approve his orders for medicines and additional food. By the 1870s Whitehall had laid down that the medical officer's requests should be approved, but this still led to grumbling among the guardians.

The relationship with the master in particular was vital, for as in the case of George Catch at the Strand and Lambeth workhouses (p.84), the master could and did interfere in medical treatments. Catch certainly resented the medical officers' social superiority and, in a very class-conscious age, this could be a source of friction. *The Lancet* found it could lead to 'the most vexatious and mischievous interference by the master with the purely medical order of the surgeon'.

Relations with the board of guardians could also be difficult. The medical officer was responsible for suggesting improvements in the workhouse and requesting special diets for sick inmates. Unsympathetic as the guardians were to the needs of the paupers and aware of the need to keep the rates as low as possible, the medical officers' reports caused a great deal of grumbling amongst them. In particular, there was much discussion about the amount of spirituous liquors that were dispensed. It was widely believed that alcohol in moderation stimulated the system and was thus good for the sick. Patients might be prescribed a half pint of porter beer or wine. At Belford, Northumberland, in the early 1890s, the medical officer, Dr Balfour, prescribed four tablespoons of whisky to Isabella Watson, an elderly lady with a heart condition. He had tried stopping the whisky but restored it when she seemed to be dying. Another patient, James Elliott, was given three tablespoons to help him sleep. Temperance guardians on the board protested, one of whom said that 'the most eminent doctors of the day had pronounced it a useless thing'. In an experiment in 1876 Dr Edward Davies, the medical officer for Wrexham in north Wales, replaced alcohol with beef tea, eggs and milk. Not unsurprisingly, the result was a general increase in the health of the paupers. Medical science eventually confirmed that alcohol was not a stimulant and its use gradually declined.

Although historians have criticized the skills and qualities of these medical men – and it is true that some were poor doctors – most of them did an adequate job in often very difficult circumstances.

Drunkards and Nightingales

Initially, there were very few workhouse paid nurses. In 1866 the 40 London workhouses employed just 142 nurses to care for roughly 21,150 sick and infirm patients. There were just three paid night nurses across the whole of the metropolis. Outside the capital, very few guardians employed nurses. Chorlton in Manchester used a couple of Protestant sisters and in larger towns, such as Derby, nurses might be hired occasionally.

At Congleton in Cheshire a couple of nurses were taken on during the typhus epidemic of 1848, but they did not last long and were not replaced. In 1856 the Poor Law Inspector recommended that the guardians employ 'an educated and good woman as general nurse for the whole establishment, to be paid a good and sufficient salary and to be under the attention of the medical officer'. This recommendation was initially ignored, but, following pressure from Whitehall, the ominously named Mary Coffin was appointed in February 1858. She had previously been a pauper in the house and before that a dressmaker. Like subsequent appointments, she did not stay long. Only from 1864, when the guardians appointed Elizabeth Shaw, a nurse from Manchester, at a salary of £20, was there any real continuity; she stayed for 12 years. Her successor, Mary Bennett, had been the workhouse cook with, presumably, no nursing experience at all.

Well into the 1860s and, in many places, much later, nursing was generally undertaken by male and female paupers who had only the barest of training, under the supervision of the nursing staff (where it existed), the matron or the medical officer. They undoubtedly helped keep the costs low, which appealed to the guardians and ratepayers, but the care they offered was often worse than useless and in many cases actively endangered their patients' lives. As Poor Law Inspector Herbert Preston-Thomas pointed out, they 'had nothing to gain if they did the duty assigned to them well, nothing to lose if they did it badly; the fact that being able-bodied women, they were workhouse inmates proved *prima facie*, that they were not of high character'. As already noted, the nurses were usually semi-literate at best, so had difficulties reading medicine bottles, and had a fatal weakness for alcohol. Drunkenness was common, encouraged by 'the daily allowance of one pint, or a pint and a half of strong porter ... with one or two more glasses of gin for night duty or disagreeable work'.

Matilda Beeton (p.27) had four such nurses under her control at the Rotherhithe workhouse in 1864:

All of whom were old and inexperienced; two could read but neither could write. I had no night nurses or scrubbers; if patients were very ill I had to watch them at night myself or make the pauper nurse do so, who, perhaps, had been working or scrubbing hard all day. Under such circum- stances, what attention could I expect the sick paupers to get? Of the four nurses allowed me, three were all I could expect them to be, drunk only when they had the means or the chance of getting anything to drink; the fourth was a confirmed drunkard, so much so, that I was in constant fear of her doing bodily harm to the sick patients; she would beat them until they were black with bruises, more especially those who were unable to help themselves and friendless.

Just occasionally, the nursing care offered could be surprisingly good. *The Lancet* thought the nurses at Islington, London, 'zealous and well-managed, conscious that they are thoroughly looked after and anxious to deserve good opinion'. John Burnett, a guardian at London's Paddington workhouse, told a parliamentary inquiry in 1866 that he considered pauper nurses nine-tenths as efficient as paid nurses, although he felt that the standard of paid nursing was very low.

The younger nurses were often enthusiastic, possibly because it was the first time they had had a chance to learn a trade, but they frequently left

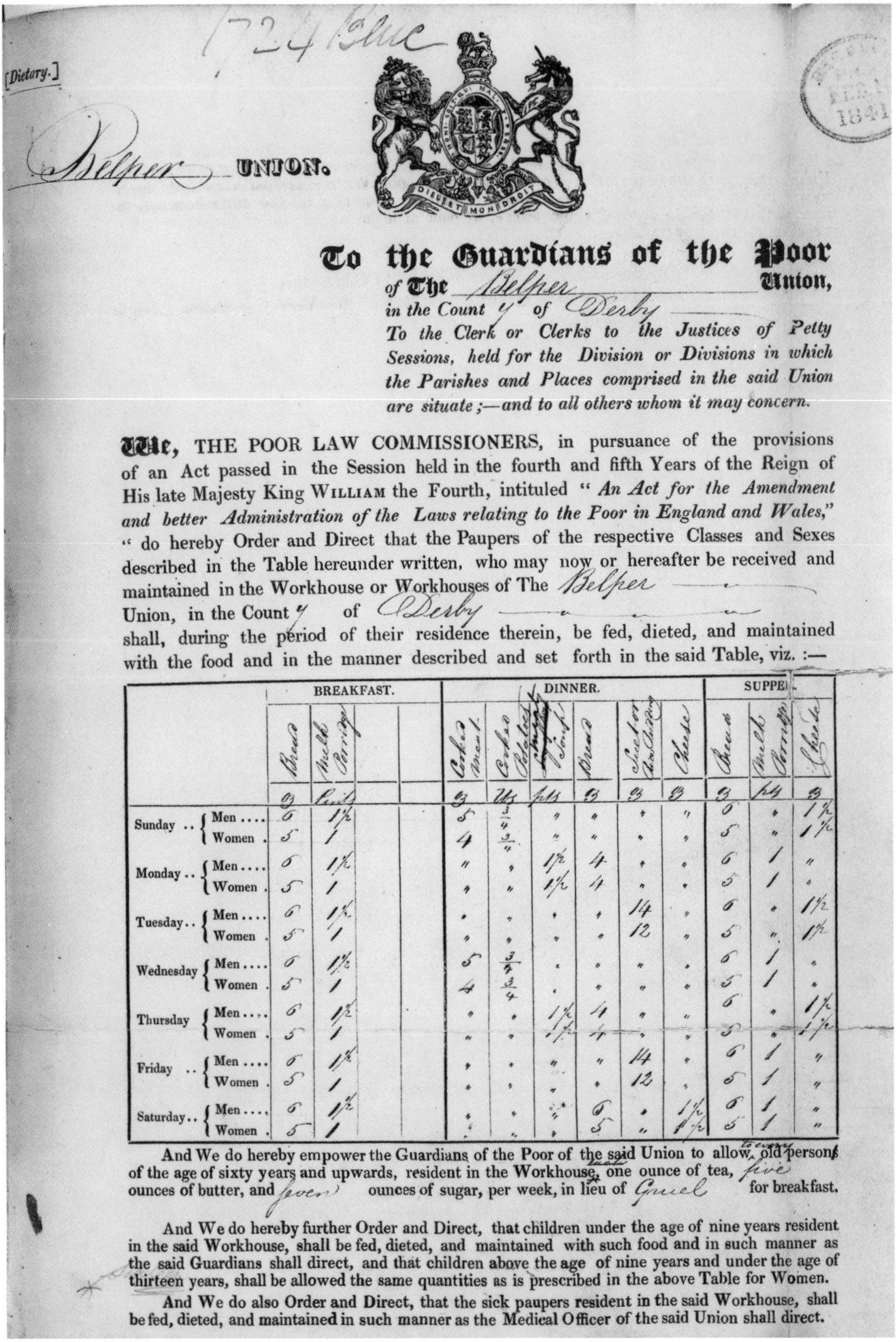

1724 Blue

Belper UNION.

To the Guardians of the Poor

of The *Belper* Union,

in the Count*y* of *Derby*

To the Clerk or Clerks to the Justices of Petty
Sessions, held for the Division or Divisions in which
the Parishes and Places comprised in the said Union
are situate ;—and to all others whom it may concern.

We, THE POOR LAW COMMISSIONERS, in pursuance of the provisions
of an Act passed in the Session held in the fourth and fifth Years of the Reign of
His late Majesty King WILLIAM the Fourth, intituled " *An Act for the Amendment
and better Administration of the Laws relating to the Poor in England and Wales,*"
" do hereby Order and Direct that the Paupers of the respective Classes and Sexes
described in the Table hereunder written, who may now or hereafter be received and
maintained in the Workhouse or Workhouses of The *Belper*
Union, in the Count*y* of *Derby*
shall, during the period of their residence therein, be fed, dieted, and maintained
with the food and in the manner described and set forth in the said Table, viz. :—

		BREAKFAST			DINNER						SUPPER		
		Bread	Milk Porridge		Cooked Meat	Baked Potatoes	Soup	Bread	Suet or Rice Pudding	Cheese	Bread	Milk Porridge	Cheese
		oz	pint		oz	lbs	pts	oz	oz	oz	oz	pint	oz
Sunday	Men	6	1½		5	¾	"	"	"	"	6	"	1½
	Women	5	1		4	¾	"	"	"	"	6	"	1½
Monday	Men	6	1½		"	"	1½	4	"	"	6	1	"
	Women	5	1		"	"	1½	4	"	"	5	1	"
Tuesday	Men	6	1½		"	"	"	"	14	"	6	"	1½
	Women	5	1		"	"	"	"	12	"	5	"	1½
Wednesday	Men	6	1½		5	¾	"	"	"	"	6	"	"
	Women	5	1		4	¾	"	"	"	"	5	1	"
Thursday	Men	6	1½		"	"	1½	4	"	"	6	"	1½
	Women	5	1		"	"	1½	4	"	"	5	"	1½
Friday	Men	6	1½		"	"	"	"	14	"	6	1	"
	Women	5	1		"	"	"	"	12	"	5	1	"
Saturday	Men	6	1½		"	"	"	6	"	1½	6	1	"
	Women	5	1		"	"	"	6	"	1½	5	1	"

And We do hereby empower the Guardians of the Poor of the said Union to allow old persons
of the age of sixty years and upwards, resident in the Workhouse, one ounce of tea, *five*
ounces of butter, and *seven* ounces of sugar, per week, in lieu of *Gruel* for breakfast.

And We do hereby further Order and Direct, that children under the age of nine years resident
in the said Workhouse, shall be fed, dieted, and maintained with such food and in such manner as
the said Guardians shall direct, and that children above the age of nine years and under the age of
thirteen years, shall be allowed the same quantities as is prescribed in the above Table for Women.

And We do also Order and Direct, that the sick paupers resident in the said Workhouse, shall
be fed, dieted, and maintained in such manner as the Medical Officer of the said Union shall direct.

17 The dietary in force at Belper workhouse, Derbyshire, in 1841. Each board of guardians had to
draw up a weekly rota of meals to be approved by the Poor Law Commissioners in London.
Although desperately dull, the food provided was reasonably nutritious, although portions were
always meagre (MH 12/1841).

18 RIGHT A member of the Blackett family talks to a pauper at a tea hosted by the family at Wickham House near Newbury, Berkshire, in the early years of the twentieth century.

19 BELOW LEFT Tea mugs used at Chepstow workhouse in south Wales. Visitors to workhouse dining rooms remarked on the battered, if scrupulously clean, pewter plates and utensils used by the paupers. Initially tea was only served to the aged paupers, without milk or sugar, which were regarded as unnecessary luxuries.

20 BELOW RIGHT Women inmates picking oakum, around 1900. This was the chore most closely associa with the workhouse. Old ropes were unpicked and sold to ship-builders to seal ship bottoms. Paupe sometimes used a large metal nail spike (hence the nickname for the workhouse) or as here just ba hands. Either way, it was hard on the fingers and very tedious (PRO 30/69/1663).

21 TOP LEFT A sack shirt worn by a pauper at Brecknock workhouse in mid Wales in about 1910. On their admission paupers would be issued with distinctive uniforms made of coarse cloth which would easily identify them if they tried to abscond.

22 TOP RIGHT Casuals picking oakum at an unidentified workhouse, around 1900. Each vagrant had to perform two or three hours' hard labour before they could leave in the morning. The tasks they were assigned were often pointless and the work was often not properly supervised (PRO 30/69/1663).

23 ABOVE The men's dining room at Marylebone in 1902. Men and women inmates were kept separate and in addition a rule of silence was usually enforced. Almost no other photograph of workhouses so effectively shows the soul-destroying nature of the Poor Law system, even though Marylebone was a model modern workhouse.

24 RIGHT The kitchen at Marylebone workhouse, about 1902. When the journalist T.W. Wilkinson visited, he was impressed by the machine which was used in 'artificially masticating the meat supplied to old and toothless paupers'.

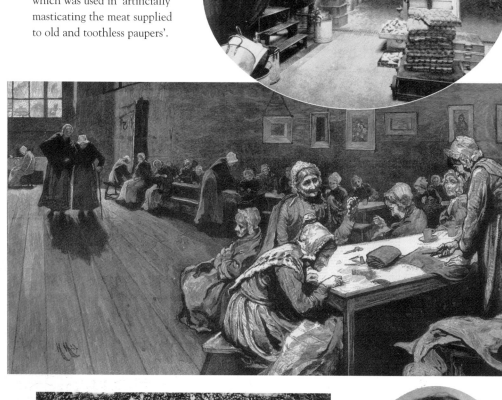

27 ABOVE A workhouse woman suffering from goitre in 1880.

28 LEFT In 1872 the first female Poor Law Inspector, Mrs Nassau Senior, roundly condemned the education of pauper girls as being extraordinarily limiting. Reforms in the 1880s and later gradually improved matters, although it is highly unlikely that workhouse schoolrooms, with their reputation for regimentation, were anything like the one here.

29 RIGHT Workhouse dolls made by an inmate of Walsingham workhouse, Norfolk, in about 1900 as presents for the master's daughter. Workhouse infirmaries pioneered an early occupational therapy, known as the Brabazon scheme, for the elderly, which was later extended to children.

30 BELOW RIGHT Dickens' *Oliver Twist* was thoroughly researched and his description of Oliver asking for 'more', graphically captured here in George Cruikshank's illustration, is based on fact. Charles Dickens had a lifelong interest in the Poor Law system and wrote about a number of his visits to workhouses.

OPPOSITE PAGE

25 MIDDLE 'Eventide: A Scene in the Westminster Union, 1878' by Hubert von Herkomer (1849–1914). Conditions for aged paupers were generally slightly better than those offered to the rest of the inmates. Even so most old people resented the loss of liberty and the humiliation of entering the workhouse and would only do so when there was no alternative.

26 FAR LEFT Elderly pauper ladies at a tea for workhouse inmates hosted by the Blackett family at Wickham House near Newbury in about 1905. As attitudes towards paupers softened from the 1850s, young children and the elderly in particular became the subject of charitable pity by local gentry and well-to-do ladies.

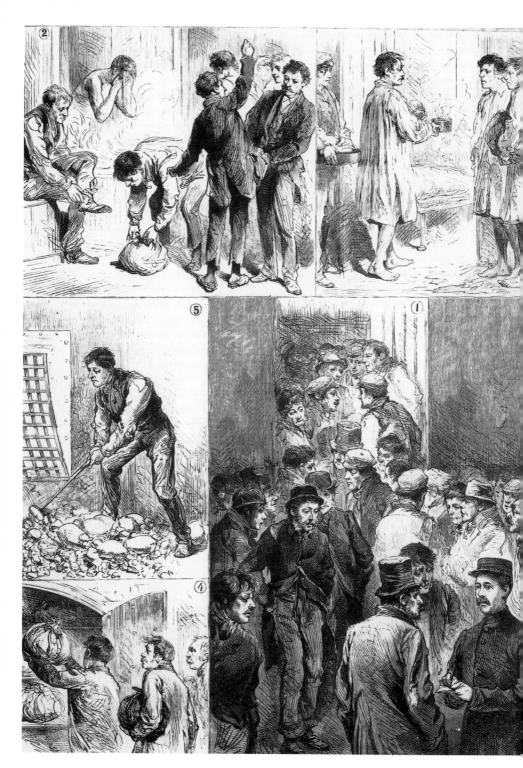

31 The Poor Law authorities were never able to satisfactorily tackle the problem of vagrancy, except to keep conditions as poor as possible as a deterrent. Here the *Illustrated London News* artist recorded a typical evening at a metropolitan casual ward showing what the applicants had to endure. By the 1880s there were few female vagrants (ZPER 34/91).

32 LEFT A completely destitute woman asleep on the stone steps of a workhouse, 1877. As conditions for admission were tightened in the 1870s, *The Times* and other newspapers carried stories about the deaths of destitute men and women who were turned away.

33 ABOVE A queue of casuals outside an East End workhouse, possibly Poplar. They may have queued for hours to guarantee a bed for the night. The porter, extreme right, was responsible for their admission. These men had considerable power over the applicants which was sometimes abused, for example in seeking sexual favours from young female vagrants (PRO 30/69/1663).

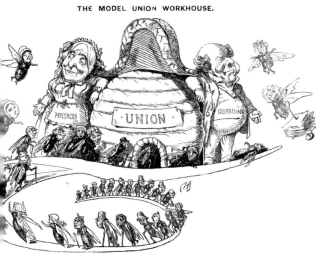

THE MODEL UNION WORKHOUSE.

34 LEFT For all its faults the Poor Law provided a minimal welfare state for the most destitute, who were either unable to help themselves or refused assistance by charities. This is acknowledged by this rather strange *Punch* cartoon, 1886.

35 ABOVE As well as the Poor Law there was a network of charitable bodies to assist the poor. At times of mass unemployment charities would be set up to help the destitute. Some of the largest were organised by the Lord Mayor at Mansion House. Despite the image here they were generally chaotically run and very inefficient (ZPER 34/50).

36 BELOW In order to prevent abuse by shirkers, unemployed applicants for out-relief sometimes, as here, had to demonstrate their skills before they were offered relief by the guardians. It was petty humiliations like this which made the Poor Law and the workhouse loathed by the working classes (PRO 30/69/1663).

before they could be properly trained. Older pauper nurses, however, could not cope with the long hours and physically hard work. Many were in their fifties or sixties and had already endured a lifetime of hardship.

The Poor Law Board and its successor, the Local Government Board, tried to clamp down on the practice of employing pauper nurses, but with mixed success. As late as the 1890s it was claimed that 'almost all provincial infirmaries are nursed by paupers under the control – or not under the control – of one paid nurse'. In London one matron of a Poor Law infirmary said that she 'did not expect nurses to do the nursing themselves, but only to superintend the paupers'.

Florence Nightingale was already showing the way forward in the nursing of sick paupers. In 1864, in response to an approach from William Rathbone, a Liverpool merchant and philanthropist, she sent one of her assistants, Agnes Jones, and eight nurses to run the Brownlow Hill Institution in Liverpool. Within a month Miss Jones had sacked 35 pauper nurses and quarrelled with both the master and the guardians, but over the next four years she introduced many improvements before dying of typhoid, almost certainly picked up at the infirmary.

In 1879 Louisa Twining founded the Workhouse Nursing Association to promote the training of nurses at workhouse infirmaries. By 1890 the Association had trained almost 100 probationers and appointed almost 300 staff. Even so, demand for its nurses outstripped supply. Each year it received requests for 200 or more nurses but could only supply 70 or 80.

In many infirmaries the working conditions for nurses were far from attractive. At the Central London Sick Asylum in the early 1890s, for example, 17 day and 7 night nurses were responsible for 264 beds. They commonly worked a 13-hour day. In the provinces one untrained nurse could be struggling with up to 28 beds. One nurse told Miss Twining that she had tried to keep up the traditions of her training, but had been defeated by her own fatigue. She was responsible for 120 beds with the help of a 61-year-old pauper assistant.

In the smallest unions the matron continued to nurse paupers when necessary. In 1868 Belford's medical officer, Mr Hunt, praised the matron, Jane Smith, for her care of children with cholera during an outbreak in the district: 'I believe all my treatment would have been futile but for the zealous and fearless way in which the matron washed and kept the Children clean, indeed she herself frequently suffered from nasty sores on her fingers clearly showing how communicable it is by contact.' Thirty years later the current and former matrons received a gratuity from a local company for their care of a drayman who had been seriously injured in an accident.

Because Belford Union was so small – there were no more than two or three patients in the sick wards – the guardians found it difficult to recruit a workhouse nurse for the workhouse. Mr Dawson, the Poor Law Inspector who visited the house in 1895, noted: 'The medical officer has reported that a nurse is greatly needed for the sick, but it would be useless to engage one permanently for this small primitive place.' The solution was to hire nurses when necessary from an agency in Newcastle.

The standard of care in rural workhouses was usually poor. In 1900 Miss Chapman, a guardian in Tisbury, Wiltshire, estimated that 9 of Dorset's 12 workhouses had fewer than 100 inmates in them; the only able-bodied women were the retarded, who had to be entrusted with the housework, nursing and the care of the newborn. Scalded babies were common. It is perhaps not surprising that one nurse wrote to Louisa Twining: 'Surely in no other branch of the nursing profession can the work be so unsatisfactory and discouraging as in a lone country union.'

The patients' experience
In the late 1850s Louisa Twining occasionally visited an old crossing sweeper, John Thomson, at London's St Giles's workhouse:

> He was in the basement ward, nearly dark, and with a stone floor; beds, sheets and shirts were all equally grey with dirt. To get in, I had to wait with a crowd at the office door to obtain a ticket, visitors being allowed only for one hour a week. The sick in the so-called infirmary, a miserable building, long since destroyed, were indeed a sad sight, with their wretched pauper nurses in black caps and workhouse dresses.

At about the same time, an investigation by *The Lancet* condemned the arrangements and particularly commented on the provision for nurses:

> Disorder and neglect appeared to be in authority as a direct consequence of the so-called system of nursing which obtains here, directed by an

aged female, 63 years old, with a salary of £20 per annum. Under her supervision there are fourteen pauper assistants or helpers, with two night-nurses, selected from those who perform the day-nursing, none of whom receive remuneration for their labours.

In 1866 the workhouse nurse at Rotherhithe, Matilda Beeton, told a committee of inquiry about her experiences. She had charge of 50 sick and infirm patients 'which is as much as one paid nurse can do with satisfaction to herself or those who employ her'. (Miss Nightingale recommended a maximum of 12 patients per nurse.) She found that there was an 'insufficiency of everything throughout the infirmary'. In particular, 'there was a bad supply of towels, the same used for wiping the patients on had to serve for a teacloth and every clean and dirty purpose'. She remembered that she had once had an old man sent to her from one of the wards:

> On my going to the bedside one of the patients called out 'don't go too near that bed, nurse as he' meaning the patient, 'is swarming with vermin'; and on my removing his clothes I found his body covered with them; his hair and whiskers were matted and he looked the picture of distress and misery. I at once reported the case to the master, when he said 'Dirty old Irishman; he is not fit to be down here; I shall have him brought back'.

Miss Beeton washed the man and cut his hair and whiskers – he 'did not forget to thank me a hundred times over for what I had done'.

Although conditions in the new infirmaries were considerably better than in the sick wards, they were still soulless places and little attempt was made to entertain the patients. A journalist who visited the Crumpsall Infirmary in 1898 found: 'In the ward itself the patients can do little more than sit in company with their own reflections. The view of the painted wall opposite is not cheerful... As regards reading, taste appears to incline principally towards newspapers and plain tales.' He suggested that readers might like to donate pictures and books to enliven the stay of the inmates.

It is difficult to know how effective the care of the sick in the workhouse was. It was probably no worse than that available in the charitably funded voluntary hospitals. It is important to remember that medical knowledge was still very primitive – it was only in the 1850s, for example, that anaesthetics were widely introduced – and most medicines were only one step away from folk remedies.

For most patients, the enforced rest and perhaps a better diet were more effective cures than any amount of medical care. The journalist James Grant reported in the late 1830s that:

> the best regulated workhouses are conducive to health rather than otherwise… A guardian in one of the workhouses in the centre of the metropolis, lately mentioned to me some singular cases of paupers having entered these establishments in a very bad state of health, brought on by irregularity of living, and of their complete restoration to health after being a short time there.

Conditions in the infirmaries improved from the 1870s to such an extent that they began to attract non-pauper patients. They were asked to pay something towards their treatment, the maximum being 10s 6d a week, rather less than might be charged in a private hospital. One witness told the Royal Commission on the Poor Laws of 1909 that 'a great many people go into sick asylums now who would not have gone into them in the old days'. Indeed at Camberwell in south London it was alleged that 'the ordinary "infirm" cases have largely been driven out of it [the infirmary] … in order to make room for the better off patients'. The Camberwell infirmary may, however, have been so popular because it was the only hospital in a densely populated area.

Poor Law infirmaries also had to admit accident cases. Mr Manton of the Birmingham Union described to the Commission how his hospital was in the centre of an industrial area, 'for in the midst of great works and street risks, casualties cannot be refused admittance, though the interests of ratepayers are safeguarded as much as possible'.

One commissioner visiting a rural union was told that the matron

> recently had the pleasure of nursing a Member of Parliament who happened to have an accident of a serious nature while motoring in the district. He was exceedingly well pleased with the attention he received. He sent a cheque to the clerk for his maintenance and £10 to the master to be spent on the inmates at the master's discretion.

Lunatics and simpletons

Almost every workhouse had a number of mentally ill and mentally disabled paupers among the inmates, who were, for the most part, harmless both to themselves and to their fellows. Nathaniel Hawthorne describes a visit to a Merseyside workhouse in the mid 1850s:

> A character came under our notice which I have met with in all almshouses, whether of the city or village, or in England or America. It was the familiar simpleton, who shuffled across the court-yard, clattering his wooden-soled shoes, to greet us with a howl or a laugh, I hardly know which, holding out his hand for a penny, and chuckling grossly when it was given him.

They were treated much the same as the other adult paupers and expected to work, as far as they could. Dr Nairne, a Commissioner in Lunacy, visited the workhouse at Walsall in June 1863 and found that lunatics

> associated with the other inmates … all were quiet and orderly, and several of them were occupied; they were well clad; five of them have extra diet, and all have tea and bread and butter for supper. All of whom who are able attend Divine service and all walk out regularly twice a week beyond the premises.

A good number spent many years in the house, often because there was nobody able to care for them outside. In 1890 the master of Ripon reported the death of Ellen Spencely: 'The poor idiot woman who had been an inmate of this House for 34 years died this morning aged 55 years.' Further north at Belford, Mary McDougal spent over 50 years in the workhouse. In 1875 her situation was described by the local Commissioner in Lunacy thus: 'She has been here for more than 30 years, and is quite harmless, fairly intelligent and makes herself very useful.'

Inevitably, these unfortunates were mocked and teased by the other inmates. 'The Indoor Pauper' found that 'it is a common amusement of the jokers to excite the idiotic temper as often as possible'. He cited the examples of 'Jack Queedom', with 'his extreme credulity on the one side and his capacity in the extreme for recounting every single incident in his life exactly as it occurred', and 'General Booth', who, when teased, 'bursts out into a roar, reciting a series of hymns and passages of Scripture mixed up with canting ejaculations. He utters these pious scraps in exactly the same order on every occasion.'

A much more serious problem concerned those paupers who were violent. It is safe to say that a large proportion of the trouble that occurred in workhouses was caused by people in a mentally unstable state. Some were casuals whom it was possible to get rid of after a day or two, but others eventually ended up being transferred to the county asylum. The guardians were often reluctant to do this because of the additional charge to the rates.

One such at Belford was Sarah Taylor, who, on her brother's death in June 1888, was found in his house dirty and unable to walk. Miss Taylor was admitted to the workhouse, where she began to complain to the Local Government Board that she was being held against her will. The guardians, however, advised her that 'she was much better there [in the workhouse] than she could be outside'. However, she chose to leave and soon began to bombard relatives with demands for money. Eventually she entered the county lunatic asylum at Morpeth.

A rather more serious case was that of Harriet Kettle, who was in and out of Gressenhall for many years and spent some time in the Norfolk county asylum. She was a difficult inmate and was sent to prison several times. Aged just 14, she was sentenced in January 1853 to 42 days' imprisonment along with several other girls for 'destroying the food and property of the Guardians and by wilfully disobeying the orders of the Master and by making a great noise and disturbance and by using obscene and violent language'. In 1856 she spent a year at the Thorpe asylum near Norwich, afterwards returning to the workhouse. In 1858 she was accused of setting fire to the house and was sent back to Thorpe, having told the magistrates that she had not meant to burn the building down but to kill herself. However, the authorities could not agree on whether she was insane or not – the master at Thorpe thought she was not insane but subject to violent fits of passion when thwarted, but the prison authorities argued that she should be in the asylum. Eventually she was sent to the government asylum for the criminally insane at St George's in the Fields in London. Harriet Kettle only spent a couple of months there, before returning to Norfolk. She again entered the workhouse in January 1863 and soon fell out with the assistant matron,

Mrs Butcher. Indeed the antagonism was so great that Mrs Butcher's husband, Thomas, felt he had to accompany his wife to protect her when she did her rounds at night. A year later Harriet married a William Head, an agricultural labourer in Dereham. Marriage seems to have agreed with her, and she disappears from the records, presumably much to the relief of the guardians.

Ending their days

There was a far greater mismatch than for any other class of pauper between the harsh reality of the experience of the elderly and the vision propagated by the authorities. The poor were very well aware of this, which is why their response to the suggestion that they should spend their declining years in the house was overwhelmingly hostile.

In the course of his survey of the aged poor in 1894, Charles Booth talked to many poor people about their experiences of the Poor Law. In the Cambridgeshire village of Oxham he found 'intense abhorrence of the workhouse. The old people do not feel that they have done anything to deserve being "locked up".' One person told him: 'I would rather be hung than go in again.'

The author Robert Roberts remembered his parents telling him about a man with a large family struggling to look after his sick father.

At last the old man insisted that he be taken to the workhouse…
En route, they stopped to rest a while on a stone seat. 'It was here,' said
the old man, 'I too rested carrying my father to the workhouse.' The
son rose, took the burden on his back again and turned with his wife
for home. 'We'll manage somehow,' he said.

In his evidence to the Royal Commission on the Aged Poor in 1893, Major Frank Ballantine, the master of Crumpsall, north Manchester, said that he had spoken to many people as they were admitted to the house: 'I have sometimes heard them very much regret that they have been allowed or compelled by circumstance to come to the workhouse; they have repeatedly told me.'

If they could, aged paupers preferred to die at home. Mrs Fordham, a guardian in Royston, Hertfordshire, described one old man of 80 who had been persuaded to enter the workhouse: 'He was well looked after there, but the dreariness and the routine of the place together with immense home-sickness drove him almost crazy.' In despair, he discharged himself and, although frail and almost lame, walked the six miles home, 'wishing for nothing better for his old life to flicker away there in sight of the trees and surroundings which were so much part of his life, that it was impossible for him to live away from them'.

It did not help that the late Victorians had a romanticized view of the elderly poor, of rosy-cheeked old ladies and proud old men bent after decades of selfless and deferential labour, resting comfortably in the twilight of their years in the comfortable surroundings of the workhouse. A not untypical account of a visit to Marylebone in about 1903 is by T.W. Wilkinson for *London Lives*, in which he describes the 200 octogenarians, the majority of whom were women: 'Veritable dear old creatures many of them are! The feeling they produce must needs be one of sadness and yet there is something pleasing in the spectacle they present when hob-nobbing over their tea in the afternoon.' Yet on the opposite page of the book is a photograph of the dining room at the workhouse, showing row upon row of elderly men staring blankly at the camera.

In 1834 the Poor Law Report recommended that under the New Poor Law the regime for the elderly and infirm should be less rigorous than that for the able-bodied; the workhouse should be a place where 'the old might be indulged without torment from the boisterous'. Claims were soon made that conditions inside the house were better than those experienced by the elderly outside. The Commissioners noted in 1838 that 'the warmth and cleanliness of the workhouse, as well as the regularity of the diet, could scarcely fail to be manifested in the general health of the aged and infirm'.

Nearly 60 years later Herbert Preston-Thomas reported to the Commission on the Aged:

When one sees knots of old men gossiping by the fire or basking in the sun; when one finds the bed-ridden old women carefully nursed and appropriately fed; it is difficult to help contrasting their condition with some of the out-door poor who, failing under the weight of years and infirmity, pass almost solitary lives in miserable dwellings and are half starved on the pittance which they obtain from their scanty earnings or from private charity… It is common to hear an old inmate say that he could not bear the notion of entering the house, but that had he known it was so comfortable he would have come there long ago.

In the 1890s theorists liked to separate the elderly into two categories, replicating the wider division between the deserving and the undeserving. In evidence to the Commission, George Bartley – a guardian at Ealing during the 1860s and 1870s – divided the destitute into those whose earnings enabled them to provide sufficient for their old age, but who had not done so, and those whose earnings rendered it impossible, or nearly impossible, for them to do so. In the case of those who had failed to save, he urged that they be left to the mercy of a deterrent Poor Law, while those who had been unable to save should receive a small state pension.

Again the reality was rather different. Henry Broadhurst, a member of the Royal Commission on the Aged Poor, concluded: 'There are without doubt a certain number of deserving aged persons who are in workhouses for reasons other than sickness or infirmity; but the general effect of the evidence we have received distinctly tends to the conclusion that they are few in number.'

Mrs Fuller, a London guardian in the 1890s, argued that few respectable paupers would seek admission because of the monotony of workhouse life, the abrasiveness of its discipline, the uncaring staff, and the unwelcome association with the rough and retarded. But she stressed that the worst aspect was the loss of individuality; respectable elderly women who had managed their own homes for decades found it especially demeaning to enter a workhouse where one was a 'nobody'.

Working-class men and women continued to work for as long as they could, because they had no savings and, until 1908, there was no such thing as a state pension. It was easier to find employment in rural areas, where men could continue to do a little gardening or work on the roads, and women did charring or washing. In Ely, Cambridgeshire, Charles Booth was told that the average labourer 'works until he can work no longer, i.e. to 70 or 75. Some take light work, or do odd jobs, earning small pittance. If quite broken down or worn out, they go to the workhouse.' In towns, however, work was increasingly skilled and mechanized and unskilled labour was more successfully performed by the young. In York, Booth found that 'masters grow less willing to employ any but young men'.

In the 1850s Henry Mayhew found that

> the aged ... often pretend to sell small articles in the street – such as boot-laces, tracts, cabbage-nets, lucifer-matches, kettle-holders, and the like; and that such matters are carried by them partly to keep clear of the law, and partly to evince a disposition to the public that they are willing to do something for their livelihood.

Charles Booth found many widows residing in cramped rooms in the worst slums. In one London district, described as being 'almost solid poverty', Booth describes the various, but poorly paid, occupations they pursued, such as those of hawker, paper kite-maker, watercress-seller, coster and washerwoman. At their most abject, widows could be found 'begging or picking up odds and ends in the street'.

Most of the elderly poor who received out-relief from the guardians remained outside the workhouse; only about a third entered the house. For those who could continue to work, out-relief was often used to supplement earnings or support from their families. In late-Victorian rural areas claimants seem to have received about 2s 6d per week, with more sometimes being offered in urban areas.

The introduction of old age pensions in 1908, for men and women over 70, transformed the lives of the very old. Provided they earned less than thirty guineas a year, they were entitled to receive five shillings a week of right. It was collected from post offices and administered by Customs and Excise in order to remove the stigma of the Poor Law. Initially, however, applicants were to be turned down if they had ever received support from the guardians. In practice, this was widely ignored by the local committees which administered the new system. Between 1908 and 1912 the number of elderly people receiving out-relief fell by a quarter, because the old age pension was more generous than out-relief, although numbers in the workhouse remained constant because the pension on its own was not enough to enable the infirm to support themselves. The lowering of the pension age to 65 in 1926 further reduced the need for out-relief for the elderly.

Despite their reluctance, for the very old and the very poor there was an inevitability about entering the house. As a verse from Yorkshire put it:

Hush-a-bye baby, on the tree top,
When you grow old, your wages will stop,
When you have spent the little you made,
First to the Poorhouse and then to the grave.

In 1900 about 30 per cent of the population over the age of 70 were in the workhouse. Indeed the older the individual was, the more likely it was that he or she would be cared for by the Poor Law authorities. In 1906 about 6 per cent of the population aged between 60 and 65 received some sort of assistance, and this rose to 35 per cent for men and women who were over 85.

Elderly men and women entered the workhouse mainly because they could no longer look after themselves, were not respectable enough to secure election to a charity-run almshouse or had nobody either willing or able to care for them. Charles Booth gives a number of examples taken from London's St Pancras admission register for 1889:

Old Woman. Age 90. Had outdoor relief for many years; friends and relatives very kind to her, but in consequence of severe illness she had to go in. A very respectable old lady. Married man. Age 70. Formerly a horse-keeper. His wife has 2s 6d out-relief. Admitted through paralysis. Respectable old man.

If the guardians discovered that an aged pauper had children, they tried to make them pay for the care of their elderly parents. For example, the guardians' minute books for Whitechapel, London, contain details of many orders made for the care of elderly people. On 4 February 1888 alone the sons of Elizabeth Young were ordered to pay 2s 5d each and the two sons of Sarah Langleben were ordered to pay 3s 5d each for the maintenance of their respective mothers in the infirmary, and John Newman and his son were ordered to pay 1s each for the care of John's wife, Elizabeth.

George Bartley grumbled that he had 'seen well-to-do women, keeping large shops and public houses, allowing their old parents to get the parish half-crown and refusing all aid. "For why," they say, "should we save the rates?"' He also complained that his fellow guardians and the magistrates, before whom enforcement cases came, were sentimental about the elderly and failed to enforce the rules, allowing out-relief when the individuals could earn enough or be supported by their family. Bartley believed that 'married daughters, grandchildren and even nephews and nieces, should, if they are in good circumstances and their own natural feelings do not prompt them to do what is right, be compelled by law to help to support their flesh and blood'; and that if they did not wish to help their elderly relations, the solution was 'to firmly offer the [aged pauper the] house and decline outdoor relief' in the hope of shaming them into making a contribution. In practice, the families of the old men and women who entered the house were usually too poor or too indifferent to make any such contribution.

Robert Roberts notes the lengths to which the guardians might go to make aged paupers and their families pay towards their upkeep. He quotes from a report in a local newspaper in Salford about the case of an elderly lady inmate who had received letters from a daughter containing small amounts of money:

> 'She refuses,' the clerk told the board, 'to let the workhouse master see the letters.' Mr Brownrigg, of the board, said that 'if the master believed an inmate had money he should have a search made.' Mr Simmons stated that 'if the master found an inmate with money he should turn out that inmate'. The old woman, who is paralysed on one side said that she had been in the workhouse for two years.
>
> Chairman: 'Can't you see that it is your duty to give up the money to the workhouse people for your maintenance here?'
>
> Old woman: 'No, I can't see that.'
>
> The guardians ordered a search to be made and said she could ask the workhouse master for a shilling or two from time to time.

A few old people voluntarily went into the workhouse and paid towards their stay. One such man was James Hammett, the only one of the famous Tolpuddle martyrs who returned to the Dorset village. As his sight deteriorated, he chose to go into Dorchester workhouse so as not to be a burden on his family. He died there in 1891 and was buried in the churchyard at Tolpuddle. One elderly miner entered the house at Ashby because he 'could not stand the noise made by his grandchildren and wanted peace and quiet'.

Small privileges

In 1850 Charles Dickens, writing an article for his journal *Household Words*, visited the aged wards of London's Whitechapel workhouse:

> In all of these Long Walks of aged and infirm, some old people were
> bedridden, and had been for a long time; some were sitting on their beds
> half-naked; some dying in their beds; some out of bed, and sitting at a
> table near the fire. A sullen or lethargic indifference to what was asked, a
> blunted sensibility to everything but warmth and food, a moody absence
> of complaint as being of no use, a dogged silence and resentful desire to
> be left alone again, I thought were generally apparent. On our walking
> into the midst of one of these dreary perspectives of old men, nearly
> the following little dialogue took place … 'All well here?'
>
> No answer. An old man in a Scotch cap sitting among others on a
> form at the table, eating out of a tin porringer, pushes back his cap a
> little to look at us, claps it down on his forehead again with the palm of
> his hand, and goes on eating…
>
> 'How are YOU to-day?' To the last old man. That old man says
> nothing; but another old man, a tall old man of very good address,
> speaking with perfect correctness, comes forward from somewhere,
> and volunteers an answer.
>
> 'We are very old, sir,' in a mild, distinct voice. 'We can't expect to be
> well, most of us.' 'Are you comfortable?' 'I have no complaint to make,
> sir.' With a half shake of his head, a half shrug of his shoulders, and a
> kind of apologetic smile.

His visit was not untypical. When a newly elected guardian, Mrs Fuller, visited the aged wards in the early 1890s, she found them 'more like a prison for criminals than a lasting home for aged men and women'. The inmates sat in ill-fitting workhouse dress on hard benches around the walls.

Most observers agreed that the worst aspect of life was the boredom and the air of hopelessness. Fred Copeman, who grew up in the workhouse at Wangford, Suffolk, during the First World War, remembered:

> Most of the two or three hundred inmates were very old, and many were
> treated as hospital patients. Looking back through memory's years, I see
> an atmosphere of hopelessness which gave me, surrounded as I was by

the old, the infirm and even the insane, the feeling that all had come here to die. Life was a continuous repetition of work, sleep and funerals.

Conditions varied greatly between workhouses. In most places the old men and women had separate wards, with perhaps a sitting room, but in the smaller unions, or at times of overcrowding, they might have to share wards with the able-bodied. The elderly were granted small privileges in terms of diet. The Poor Law Commissioners, for example, allowed local guardians to provide each week 'one ounce of tea, five ounces of butter and seven ounces of sugar per week in lieu of gruel for breakfast ... if deemed expedient to make this change'. Few unions did. Indeed, sugar or milk were rarely provided. Even then, as one pauper John Law found at Whitechapel, tea might not be served until supper and the bread scraped with the merest suspicion of butter.

Although the majority of aged paupers were in declining or poor health, there were many for whom the dietary was not sufficient. 'The Indoor Pauper' said: 'I have known "old men" beg and pray to be restored to the "young men's" dietary, and to congratulate themselves when the request was granted, and for no better reason than because they had a better chance of filling their stomachs.'

Where possible, the elderly were expected to undertake tasks in the same way as the younger men and women did. Allowances, however, were made for their frailness. At Crumpsall in Manchester, the Master, Major Frank Ballantine, told the Royal Commission on the Aged Poor that half of the inmates

> were fit for work of a very light description, such as picking beaten oakum, something which requires very little moving about, and which can be done while they are sitting in their seats. Then the remainder of them do work, such as chopping and sawing firewood, some of them carrying coals, cleaning up their wards, running as messengers from one part of the house to another for the men; and the women sewing and doing domestic work of any kind which may be required.

By 1900 some 180 workhouses adopted Lady Brabazon's scheme of occupational therapy, whereby lady visitors helped the aged and infirm make wickerwork baskets, rugs and quilts and even wrought ironwork. The scheme was designed to encourage the inmates to be creative and to stop their constant grumbling. It proved so successful that it was soon extended to children as well.

Many unions tried to moderate the effect of the Poor Law on the elderly inhabitants, at least informally. As early as 1836 the guardians at Aylsham in Norfolk, for example, agreed to provide long waistcoats for the old men, because the existing ones were not long enough to protect them from the cold. Others provided beer and tobacco or privileged access to the work-house garden. A blind eye was sometimes turned to the more stringent of the regulations. In his report for 1892, George Douglas, the master of Maryle-bone workhouse, revealed: 'At least twenty years ago I quietly permitted the old women to have a private teapot and make their own tea, condi-tionally that it was done at the same time, four o'clock, and that the pot and the tea was supplied by friends.' He added: 'A cup of tea is a wonder-ful comfort to an old woman who, in the ordinary way, would have to wait until the evening meal at six for it.'

In a sentimental exception to the strict rule which separated the sexes, aged couples who had been married for many years could ask to share a room. At St Marylebone, T.W. Wilkinson found ten rooms, one per couple, with 'brightly-painted walls, the pictures, the official furniture … the pho-tographs and the knick-nacks belonging to the inmates who are allowed to bring in such property as they choose… If an old couple must spend their last days in the workhouse one could wish them no brighter or more healthy quarters.' However, very few couples seem to have requested this privilege. One such case was reported by the Poor Law Inspector at Ripon in 1859:

> There was a couple in the workhouse sleeping separate by consent, at least, so far as the husband was concerned. The wife was becoming quite an imbecile. The master sanctions a considerable extent of smoking even among the women, and this old woman had set fire to her clothes in smoking a few days before my visit.

Where there were no rooms in which couples could live, the strict rule of separation was occasionally broken if either the husband or the wife was dying. At Andover, of all places, 76-year-old pauper William Norris told the parliamentary inquiry into the scandal that he and his wife had entered the house together:

My wife was ill and died here. I was allowed by the master to go and sit by my wife ... whenever I liked. I went to see her at dinnertime twice, whilst she was in the day hall. I cannot tell you when she was removed into the sick. I went to see her there... When I left the house ... I said to him: 'Good Bye God bless you; I shall always be thankful to you for my wife.' He behaved very well to me.

As mentioned above, the increase in the number of women and working-class guardians in the 1880s and 1890s led to an improvement in conditions. Previously bleak rooms were decorated, more comfortable furniture provided, the diet improved and the Brabazon scheme introduced, with figures such as Emmeline Pankhurst – a new Poor Law guardian at Chorlton (Manchester) – making a considerable impact in 1894 (p.31).

But not everything was sweetness and light. A number of elderly paupers were troublesome individuals who had to be handled with care and could cause trouble for the staff. 'The Indoor Pauper' attested to the aggressive nature of many of the old men, who 'are some of the most irritable and cross-grained beings in existence. They are perpetually on the watch for the slightest invasion, of what they consider any infringement of "their rights" and as perpetually vindicating the rights by growl and snarl and venomous remark.' Nonetheless, they were much better behaved than the old men and women whom John Sutton, master of Barham workhouse in Suffolk and former master of Covent Garden, had to deal with. He told the Poor Law Commissioners in 1832 that his experience:

would lead me to say that the character of the aged paupers maintained in the old workhouses was generally vicious; and the aged inmates of Barham workhouse when I arrived were in no respect better. When I first arrived at Covent Garden workhouse, the aged paupers were permitted to go out on Sunday, and it was no common thing, at the hour when they ought to have returned, for me to be summoned to have some aged male or female paupers removed from the street, having fallen down in a state of great intoxication... It was common for me to call in the assistance of three or four policemen to quell the riotous state of the house, in consequence of the intoxication of those who had been out on Sunday.

By the 1890s behaviour of this kind seems to have largely died out. At Crumpsall, Frank Ballantine said that fewer than a dozen paupers returned in a drunken state each year, out of the hundreds allowed leave each week. They were punished by not being allowed out for two months. As leave, or indeed any contact with the outside world, was highly prized, this must have been a particularly effective punishment

There seem to have been relatively few cases of deliberate mistreatment. Even at Andover, although the elderly were underfed, they suffered no more than the other inmates. A number of cases were investigated by the Poor Law Commissioners. In June 1846, at the height of the Andover scandal, an inspector was sent to look into the death of James Jarvis, a 75-year-old pauper at Barrow-upon-Soar, Leicestershire. He had been put on 'a short diet' of bread and water for refusing to pump water and subsequently died. Jarvis was described by witnesses as being of an 'irritable disposition' and difficult to manage. The master and matron, Joshua and Eliza Derry, were sacked for the infringement of the rules which said that paupers who had previously been ill could not be put on a reduced diet, although a number of witnesses, and the board of guardians, testified to the couple's long service and 'their humanity and attention to the duties of their office'.

Yet the Commissioners did not care to investigate a case reported in *The Times* in October of the same year, concerning the pauper lunatic John Webb (aged 74), at Risbridge, Suffolk. His daughter told Haverhill coroner's court that when she visited him in the workhouse, she found him '"lying on the bed on his back. He appeared senseless and blood was trickling down his face." She asked Slater [a male pauper nurse] what he had been doing to her father? Slater said, nothing. She then asked how it was that blood was trickling down his (her father's) face? Slater said "You are a d-d sight worse fool than your brother." She went and told the mistress. Her father was quite helpless. He had received several injuries on different parts of his body and was very filthy.' Witnesses attested to Slater's mistreatment of Webb. The coroner's jury recorded a verdict of natural death but they noted 'their horror and detestation of the cruel and inhuman treatment' provided by Slater, and criticized the 'highly reprehensible' actions of the guardians 'for employing a pauper nurse for the sake of paltry economy ... instead of an efficient and responsible female nurse'.

177

'Rattle his bones'

For the Victorian poor, the worst fate of all was to receive a pauper funeral 'on the parish', with the minimum expense. Indeed, under the Anatomy Act of 1832 an unclaimed pauper's body could be denied a decent Christian burial and handed over to the medical school for dissection by medical students. Always hard-hearted, the Brixworth (Northamptonshire) guardians once suggested that if they sold the cadavers of recently deceased paupers to local anatomy schools, such as the one at Downing College, Cambridge, then the poor who claimed welfare could be made to pay their financial debts to society in death. The idea was rejected out of hand by Whitehall.

Even the poorest person expected a decent send off. All but the very poorest contributed a penny or two to a funeral club, which would ensure that they and their families would receive a proper burial and have enough to pay for the wake. And for those who did not have such insurance, there might be a whip-round. Robert Roberts remembered how his mother would often give a sheet to make a shroud, and women went from door to door collecting for a wreath.

The social investigator Maud Pember Reeves found that the poor in Lambeth were determined to do well by the dead, particularly dead children. They would scrimp and save from an already meagre budget to pay for a funeral, the expense of which roughly equated to a week's pay for the father, rather than turn to the Poor Law. She noted:

> The pauper funeral carries with it the pauperisation of the father of the child – a humiliation which adds disgrace to the natural grief of the parents. More than that, they declare that the pauper funeral is wanting in dignity and in respect to their dead. One woman expressed the feeling of many more when she would as soon have the dust-cart call for the body of her child than that 'there Black Mariar'.

The poem 'The Pauper's Funeral' by Thomas Hood, written in the early 1840s, is a graphic condemnation:

> There's a grim [one-]horse hearse in a jolly round trot,
> To the church yard a pauper is going, I wot,
> The road it is rough, and the hearse has no springs,

And, hark! to the dirge the sad driver sings.
> Rattle his bones, his bones, his bones,
> Over the stones, the stones, the stones,
> He's only a pauper, who nobody owns,
> Nobody owns, nobody owns...

Oh! Where are the mourners? Alas, there are none,
He has left not a gap in the world, now he's gone;
Not a tear in the eye of child, woman or man,
To the grave with his carcase as fast as you can.
> Rattle his bones, his bones, his bones,
> Over the stones, the stones, the stones,
> He's only a pauper, who nobody owns,
> Nobody owns, nobody owns.

Hood's poem was soon set to music and became a popular favourite with audiences. The *Manchester Guardian* reviewed one recital in November 1845, where 'The words, "Rattle his bones, over the stones," are sung by three of the vocalists, and there is a sort of sepulchral response on the words "his bones" and "'the stones," by the bass voice, which is quite new and thrilling in its effect.'

Few unions spent much on pauper funerals. After all, anybody who spent their last days in the house was regarded as a failure. Yet workhouses were obliged by convention and the fear of popular reaction to provide a modicum of respect. The guardians at Brixworth were roundly criticized in 1888 for failing to bury a respectable pauper, Elizabeth Simons. They rejected pleas from her unemployed 74-year-old husband and their family. While they wrangled, the body festered at Simons' home and became a public nuisance. Eventually, two guardians paid for a pauper funeral from their own pockets.

When, in the eyes of the public, the minimum respect was not shown to the deceased, there could be protests in the papers and occasionally on the streets. In February 1864, the workhouse matron at Tadcaster, Catherine Leivers, decided to humiliate for one last time a pauper woman, Elizabeth Daniel, by ignoring most of the funeral conventions (p.85). The *Tadcaster Post* reported:

The matron of this institution, not content with making her feel in a ten-fold degree that she was a pauper determined to inter her in a manner she thought fitting of a pauper's grave.

The poor woman (a native of Tadcaster) had been in the workhouse twelve months or thereabouts and on the day appointed for her intern-ment a number of poor women offered to carry her to her grave. But no! This was too good for a pauper! Her body was placed in a rough unplaned, deal coffin blackened over without either tie or handles and was pushed head foremost into a sweep's donkey cart, tied in with a rope and driven by one of the lads belonging to the workhouse, who was nearly as black as the cart in which the remains were conveyed.

At the church-yard gates, the corpse was met by the undertaker's apprentices in their working clothes, with their white aprons on, who, ashamed of the proceedings, had come by some other route and was carried by them into the church followed by the father of the deceased (a very old man who inhabits one of the Bede Houses) and a large congregation of people who denounced the proceedings in unmeasured terms.

Mrs Leivers had overstepped the mark and she was eventually forced to resign.

Coffins were cheaply made by a local joiner under contract. In 1888, at Mile End, there were complaints about the funeral of 'an old man named Young' who had been 'buried in a roughly marked "box", the bottom of which was not even painted black'.

The union might maintain a hearse to take the body to his or her home parish when there was no graveyard attached to the workhouse or when the pauper's family paid for the body to be brought home. In *Far from the Madding Crowd*, Thomas Hardy tells of how Fanny Robin and her illegiti-mate child were taken from Casterbridge workhouse:

Whilst the chimes were yet stammering out a shattered form of "Malbrook", Joseph Poorgrass rang the bell, and received directions to back his waggon against the high door under the gable. The door then opened, and a plain elm coffin was slowly thrust forth, and laid by two men in fustian along the middle of the vehicle.

One of the men then stepped up beside it, took from his pocket a lump of chalk, and wrote upon the cover the name and a few other words in a large scrawling hand. (We believe that they do these things more tenderly now, and provide a plate.) He covered the whole with a black cloth, threadbare, but decent, the tailboard of the waggon was returned to its place, one of the men handed a certificate of registry to Poorgrass, and both entered the door, closing it behind them. Their connection with her, short as it had been, was over for ever.

The clothes worn by the driver and any bearers were likely to be second-hand, if not threadbare. There was rarely a tombstone: the family could not afford one and the guardians would not commemorate an individual brought to the workhouse.

Things could be rather different at the larger unions. As if to try to combat the negative publicity of pauper funerals, Frank Ballantine boasted that at Crumpsall there were

> four inmates who wear distinctive black dress, which is furnished to
> them, to act as bearers or carriers. The coffin is provided with a pall, and
> there is a coffin painted with the name and age and date of death of
> every person interred and the name is also sewn on the shroud inside…
> All our internments are conducted with the very greatest decorum.

If there was a New Poor Law success story it concerned the care of the sick and to a lesser extent the elderly. The 1843 Act made almost no mention of provision for these people, the Poor Law Commissioners assuming that the new boards of guardians would take over the duties of the parish overseers. However, it took thirty years for matters to improve. A number of well publicised investigations into conditions in the mid-1860s forced White-hall to act. By 1900, in London and the larger cities at least, workhouse infimaries were almost as good as voluntary hospitals supported by chari-table donations and certainly cared for more patients.

CHAPTER SEVEN

Casual Encounters at the 'Spike'

The majority of these men, nay, all of them, I found, do not like the spike,
and only come to it when driven in… Of course, this continuous
hardship quickly breaks their constitutions.

Jack London, *The People of the Abyss*, 1903

THE worst-treated people in the workhouse were undoubtedly the vagrants or 'casuals', as they were often called. The way in which they were housed and cared for shows that they were generally despised. Casual wards, or 'spikes' as they were nicknamed by the inhabitants, were colder and dirtier and the food even drearier than that offered in other wards. And while conditions improved in the rest of the workhouse, in the casual wards they remained largely unchanged during the 90 years of the New Poor Law. But then vagrancy was a problem that the Poor Law authorities did not effectively tackle.

Society in general, and the authorities in particular, were convinced that the vast majority of vagrants were worthless men and women whose sole purpose in life was to cause trouble and do as little work as possible. Most shared the views of the early 19th-century writer Thomas Walker, who wrote that they 'will not have households of their own, who have but one object in all their wicked and perverse lives – to exist without work at the expense of their industrious neighbours' and went on to complain that 'we are taxed to provide board and lodging'. The term 'vagrant' was a catch-all definition used to cover anybody from the tramp who spent his life on the road and only entered the workhouse in the worst of weathers to the semi-employed and semi-criminal 'mouchers' who lived off their wits, for whom the workhouse was an all-too-familiar refuge, to the genuine job-seeker forlornly tramping between towns looking for work.

There was a divide, although not always a clear one, between those men and women who were actively seeking work and those who were not. In 1864 the editor of *Hiscoke's Richmond Notes* divided vagrants between those

> really in search of work, but by far the greater are a set of useless vagabonds who detest work and pick up a living by attending fairs, races etc, to whom of course anything that comes in their way is fair prize, in obtaining which they have as few morals as the Emperor of Austria or the King of Prussia.

The 1906 committee on vagrancy identified four distinct types of vagrants: people tramping the country for work, those unable to hold down a job except in times of exceptional prosperity who survived on a mixture of temporary work and begging, and the workshy and the criminal who have no intention of working but for whom the casual ward provided a convenient base. The most desperate were the

> old and infirm persons who wander about to their own hurt; they are 'unemployable' and crawl from vagrant ward to vagrant ward; only entering the workhouse infirmaries when they are compelled to do so; many of them are crazy, all of them live by begging and they give much trouble to police and magistrates.

Because of their obsession with the 'undeserving' vagrant, the Poor Law authorities constantly underestimated the number of men in casual wards looking for work. The master of Potterspury workhouse in Buckinghamshire, S.H. Hardwick, thought that very few genuine jobseekers stayed in his casual wards despite it being on the main road between Birmingham and London, and the 1906 committee on vagrancy estimated that less than 3 per cent of the residents of the casual wards were seriously looking for work. This was an absurdly low figure.

Perhaps a more accurate view, although based on anecdotal evidence, was that of the American Josiah Flynt, who tramped through Britain for a month in the mid-1890s. In this time he estimated that he had met more than 200 vagrants, over half of whom were looking for work. His figure tallies with a survey conducted by the Ministry of Health in the late 1920s. It found that wards were almost equally split between those seeking work and the habitual vagrants who had no intention or were incapable of working, although the survey acknowledged there was an overlap between the two (many vagrants began as jobseekers, but it was all too easy for them to end up as habituals).

At Potterspury the admission book for the early 1890s revealed that the great majority of the applicants were labourers if they were men, and charwomen if they were women. But among their number were a schoolmistress and 2 (female) mantlemakers, 18 cabinetmakers, 5 gunsmiths, 3 electricians, 2 penmakers and 2 sailmakers. The wards at Belford, which lay on the Great North Road between Newcastle and Edinburgh, were regularly visited by miners. In September 1893 the master noted that a great many Staffordshire miners had stayed at the house. Thirty years later, in 1926, it was reported that a number of miners had passed through on their way back to the mines after the conclusion of the General Strike.

The periods after the two world wars saw an increase in the number of vagrants using the casual wards; many were veterans who could not settle down after their experiences in the trenches. In 1946 the Rev. Frank Jennings, who ministered to tramps on the road in the 1920s to 1950s, talked to one man at the St Albans 'spike' who had won a DSO at El Alamein. On his return to 'Blighty', he found that he was unable to settle down, so he divorced his wife, sold his house and, feeling bitter and disillusioned, took to the road. This disillusionment is recorded in a piece of doggerel found on the wall of a casual ward at Yeovil:

The master has the meat
Inmates the bones
The men who fought for Empire
Hundredweights of stones

The casual wards swelled at harvest time, when the guardians – often local farmers – were happy to accommodate the poor from the towns seeking work in the fields. Working in the hop-fields was particularly popular. In 1904 the average number of casuals relieved in Kentish workhouses on

Friday nights at harvest time was 1,087, compared with an average for the year of 559. One tramper told Henry Mayhew: 'In the autumn, [vagrants] are mostly in Sussex or Kent; for they like the hop-picking. It is not hard work, and there are a great many loose girls to be found there. I believe many a boy and man goes hop-picking who never does anything else during the year but beg.'

But for jobseekers, staying at the workhouse was often the last resort. Paradoxically, although the casual wards were originally meant for workers on the tramp, conditions were such that a stay of more than a few nights could destroy the ability to get work. Mary Higgs, who had several stays in casual wards in the early 1900s and went on to campaign for improved conditions, found that, after being discharged, 'one thing we could not do – we could not work for an honest living. It is physically impossible... Strength to work has gone.' Henry Mayhew's informant noted:

> I have known many an honest, industrious, working man, however, made a regular beggar and vagrant by continued use of the casual wards. They are driven there first by necessity, and then they learn that they can live in such places throughout the year without working for their livelihood. Many a hard-working man, I am convinced, is made idle and dishonest by such means: yes, that is the case... They were originally labouring men, or mechanics, and had given over all thoughts of working, finding that there was no necessity to do so in order to live.

In many places there was often no alternative place to lay one's head, particularly if the individual had little or no money. As Jack London astutely observed:

> The majority of these men, nay, all of them, I found, do not like the spike, and only come to it when driven in. After the 'rest up' they are good for two or three days and nights on the streets, when they are driven in again for another rest. Of course, this continuous hardship quickly breaks their constitutions.

S.H. Hardwick was harsher. He described the circumstances of four jewellers who had stayed at his house: 'Is it probable that any merchant would employ them? They, like the others, are on the road through some fault of their own, which will forever remain a secret, but to a few.'

A familiar sight in the countryside 150 years ago would have been the moucher (a cross between a petty thief and a beggar) travelling alone, perhaps as a couple or, worst of all, as part of a gang. Mouching seems to have been largely seasonal. The onset of spring saw crowds leave the cities for the countryside, intent on making a living until the onset of bad weather drove them back to the slums or the urban workhouses. Mouchers generally supported themselves by scrounging, begging and wheedling, doing best at fairs, markets and race courses. They were often known as cadgers, particularly by the authorities, who grumbled bitterly about the money they made from the generosity or gullibility of ordinary people.

Josiah Flynt said that mouchers had innumerable 'lurks' (con tricks). 'One day he is a "shallow cove" or "shivering Jimmy"; another is a "crocus" (sham beggar); but not very often is he a successful mendicant pure and simple. He begs all the time to be sure, but continually relies on some trick or other for success.' The writer W.H. Davies spent time with one cadger whose lurk was to sing hymns badly out of tune until he was paid by annoyed householders to shut up. But they never seemed to earn very much; Flynt thought that they might make two shillings a day.

Captain Amyatt Amyatt, the Chief Constable of Dorset in the 1860s, interviewed a number of mouchers, including the Devonian Thomas Washott:

> This man ran away from his master at 19 years of age, commenced by offering bootlaces and matches for sale as a pretext for begging, and found the business so profitable that he said: 'I could make enough in three days to keep comfortably for the rest of the week. My plan was to go to a common lodging house, pick up information from my pals, as to the houses in the neighbourhood, and what they were good for, and then make the round. At races I could do a good deal better. When I had worked the neighbourhood I went on to the next place. I was never in a tramp ward but once in my life.

It was not just men who took to this life. Henry Mayhew met one woman of about 22 'who had lost all traces of feminine beauty'. She told him: 'I went down into the country, down into Essex, sir. I travelled all parts, and slept at the unions on the road. I met a young girl down in Town Malling, in Kent

... we used to go begging together, and tramp it from one union to another.' Families, too, were to be found on the road. Josiah Flynt was surprised by the number of couples and families he found: 'I should far sooner have looked for a New York hobo in clergyman's robes. But tramping with children and babies is a fad in English vagabondage.'

By the first decade of the 20th century, mouching was dying out and had largely disappeared by the Second World War. Even so, Susan Lawrence, Parliamentary Secretary at the Ministry of Health, found a moucher staying at Newmarket workhouse during a tour of inspection of East Anglian work-houses in 1931: 'He was going down from London for races at Newmarket ... lives in London – and went about the country to race meetings. Looked a professional tough.'

Tramps as such were a relatively rare sight in casual wards, particularly in urban areas, as they usually preferred to sleep rough. The 1930 Com-mittee on the Casual Poor was told:

The men you meet in the casual ward in a town and men you meet
in the country are two different classes altogether. There is a class of man
whom I have met roaming around the country that will not go inside
a town to live, they keep on going circulating round the country
casual wards year in, year out.

Many seem to have had psychiatric problems or experienced a traumatic event in their lives that forced them to tramp the roads. Josiah Flynt thought in general they were a 'trifle insane' and wrote about walking with one for an hour who said nothing but constantly wetted his cheek with a finger. An investigation by a psychologist in the late 1920s of inmates of casual wards identified over a quarter with some sort of mental instability; others were chronic alcoholics.

Some seem to have come from well-to-do families: men who had fallen on hard times as a result of drink or foolish investments. Frank Jennings met a well-educated man, who had been a successful accountant, at the spike in Bishop's Stortford. Bad speculation and loose living had been the cause of his downfall. '"I went through £5,000," he said bitterly. "Life has no evil left to inflict on me."'

The tramp could easily be identified by his clothing: usually layers of dirty and partly decayed garments which, according to S.H. Hardwick, were 'generally in shreds and tied with pieces of string or lace'. Another thing which commentators remarked upon was the smell, particularly in the summer when they often spent nights sleeping in barns or in open fields. The only time they had a bath was when they were admitted to the casual ward. During the 1950s Frank Jennings came across one vagrant:

> garbed in a wondrous assortment of clothes that, seemingly, had not left his body for many a long day, who grumbled about being made to take a bath: 'That's all they blurry-well fink of! 'Ave a bath, 'ave a bath! Gets on your bleedin' nerves! An' when yer catches a blurry cold, wodder they care? It's a bleedin' cruelty, that's wot it is!'

Basic accommodation

The casual wards provided extremely basic shelter for vagrants of all kinds. They were generally about 20 miles apart, which was a fairly easy day's tramp. Those on the main routes between the industrial north and London (for example, near the Great North Road from London to Edinburgh) attracted more vagrants than those which were not.

Despite some pressure from Whitehall, guardians and masters had little incentive to improve conditions for the casuals. Workhouses where facilities were better than average were likely to get more than their fair share of visitors. When news broke that oakum had run out at North Witchford Union in rural Cambridgeshire, within three weeks there was a surge in applicants from 20 a week to 75. Conversely, when conditions suddenly worsened, numbers could fall dramatically. At St Saviour's, Southwark, London, in 1842 the introduction of compulsory stone breaking reduced numbers considerably. In the previous three weeks, some 11,111 persons were relieved; in the three weeks after, the figure was 776.

In the 1840s it was not unknown for the better wards to be besieged by applicants. At the height of the flight from the Irish Famine, Mayhew was told of Irish men and women at Holborn workhouse in London who 'besieged the doors incessantly; and when above a hundred were admitted, as many were remaining outside, and when locked out they lay in the streets stretched along by the almshouse close to the workhouse in Gray's-inn-lane'. In Richmond, Surrey, the relieving officer complained to the guardians in May 1848 'of the great annoyance he and his neighbours were subjected to by the great and increasing number of mendicants and the riotous and violent conduct in applying for tickets'. Eighty years later George Orwell came across tramps who knew the merits and faults of spikes up and down the country. The one in Chelsea was particularly praised for its blankets.

Tramps would find out about the better casual wards by word of mouth or even from graffiti on casual-ward walls. In 1866 the Poor Law Inspector Andrew Doyle noted down some of the graffiti he found in workhouses he visited. In one ward he found the following doggerel about the Seisdon Union workhouse at Trysull in Staffordshire:

Dry bread in the morning, ditto at night
Keep up your pecker make it all right.
Certainly the meals are paltry and mean
But the beds are nice and clean.
Men don't tear these beds, sheets or rugs
For there are neither lice, fleas or bugs
At this clean little union at Trysull.

New instructions were occasionally issued by Whitehall to toughen the regime offered, particularly at times of high unemployment, to act as a disincentive to potential vagrants. This meant that the genuine workseeker was penalized, while the 'loafers' and 'shirkers' were hardly affected.

Wherever possible, the casual wards were kept physically separate in order to prevent contamination from potentially disease-carrying applicants, as well as to keep potential troublemakers well away from the supposedly more placid pauper. Separate wards were provided for men and women. Often the wards were situated to one side of the main gate and close to the porter's office, the porter being responsible for admitting tramps to the house.

There were surprisingly few women vagrants. In 1845 women made up roughly 15 per cent of people staying in casual wards. Of the 9,768 vagrants in the casual wards on the night of 1 January 1906, only 886 were women. The numbers were so small that the 1906 Departmental Committee on Vagrancy recommended that vagrant women, and their children where appropriate, be accommodated in the female wards in the main workhouse.

Why the number of women was so low is difficult to understand. It may be that women had more domestic responsibilities which tied them down. Women's work was also more readily available. And as Mary Higgs suggested, women could always fall back upon prostitution if desperate.

In 1840 the typical casual accommodation was described as comprising single-storey buildings attached to the back yard. One observer found:

> In general they have brick floors and guard-room beds, with loose straw and rugs for the males and iron bedsteads with straw ties for the females. They are generally badly ventilated and unprovided with any means of producing warmth. All holes for ventilation in reach of the occupants are sure to be stuffed with rags and straws; so that the [e]ffluvia of these places is at best most disgustingly offensive.

Initially, the casual ward was one large room with rudimentary beds and bedding, perhaps with a bucket in the middle. In the mid-1840s in Richmond the authorities provided straw and rags for bedding, although beds and bedding were made available for the sick. Such conditions facilitated the spread of disease, which all too often the vagrants brought with them. The most common disease was the itch (scabies), but occasionally the diseases were more serious. In 1842, 14 children died when tramps introduced measles into the workhouse at Thirsk in Yorkshire. By the end of the century hygiene had generally improved; vagrants were made to bathe on arrival and some provision was made to treat those who were obviously ill.

In 1865 the Poor Law Board laid down regulations for the design and layout of tramp wards, although they were slow to be adopted. Separate wards for men and women had to be provided, together with a yard 'containing a bathroom and a water closet attached to each apartment and a shed provided for the vagrants to work in'. Each ward 'should be fitted up with a sleeping platform or barrack bed of adequate depth along each side of it with a convenient gangway down the middle. The platform should be divided by means of boards and the space allocated to each person should be at least two feet three inches wide.'

These regulations were not often followed. Arriving just before 9 pm at Lambeth workhouse in January 1866, the journalist James Greenwood was shown to a shed:

a space of about 30ft. by 30ft. enclosed on three sides by a dingy whitewashed wall, and roofed with naked tiles which were furred with the damp and filth that reeked within. As for the fourth side of the shed, it was boarded in for (say) a third of its breadth; the remaining space being hung with flimsy canvas, in which was a gap 2ft. wide at top, widening to at least 4ft. at bottom. This far too airy shed was paved with stone, the flags so thickly encrusted with filth that I mistook it first for a floor of natural earth.

A decade later Whitehall recommended the introduction of the cell system, whereby the inmates would sleep, and ideally work, in one or two-person cells. In introducing the new regulations in 1874, the Local Government Board argued that the traditional casual ward had 'afforded the opportunity for the interchange of information and for the communication of plans for evading the operation of the law'.

The new arrangements were obviously too luxurious for 'A Lambeth Guardian' who wrote, in a pamphlet published in 1875, that he had recently visited the new casual wards at Plumstead, where everyone

> who wishes for a night's lodging is provided with a warm bath, and with a clean shirt and a clean bed, in a room heated by hot water and with a gaslight all to himself, disturbed by no neighbour. Should he want anything in the night, there is a bell in a room, by which he may ring a valet appointed to attend upon him.

Fifty years later, in 1929, George Orwell had a very different experience in an East London workhouse:

> The cell measured eight feet by five by eight high, was made of stone, and had a tiny barred window high in the wall and a spy-hole in the door, just like a cell in a prison. In it was six blankets, a chamber pot, a hot-water pipe, and nothing else whatever. I looked round the cell with a vague feeling that something was missing. Then, with a shock of surprise, I realised what it was and exclaimed: 'But I say, damn it, where are the beds?' 'Beds?' said the other man, surprised. 'There aren't no beds! What yer expect? This is one of them spikes where you sleep on the floor. Christ! Ain't got you used to that yet?'

Casuals had a reputation for being troublesome, and small rural houses, in particular, lived in fear of gangs of vagrants arriving, because the master and his staff had no effective way of controlling them. Even in the large metropolitan wards, tramps were a constant source of trouble. It did not help that conditions in prisons were often better than at the workhouse; food was certainly more generous and the beds better. A report prepared for Lincolnshire Quarter Sessions in 1903 found:

> tramps in the casual ward when threatened with prosecution before the Magistrates ... have openly avowed their preference for prison life, and cases are also noted where, after sentence, the prisoners have made a similar statement as to their having no dislike for prison... Prison conditions indeed, to persons with so low a standard of physical comfort as the average vagrant, must be extremely comfortable and even attractive.

The daily grind

Although the experiences of the casuals varied greatly depending on the workhouse and when they were admitted, the procedure for their admission and treatment seems to have been much the same. Admission was by ticket, which could be obtained from a workhouse official (usually the relieving officer or his assistant) or, in some places during the 1850s and 1860s, from the local police station. However, most applicants preferred to turn up at the workhouse itself, if for no other reason than that they were less likely to undergo searching questions. Even so, the porter, who was responsible for admissions, was obliged to complete a register of entrants and ask where an individual had come from, where he was going to, and his occupation.

Casuals were admitted between 4pm (5pm in summer) and 8 or 9pm. It was not unknown, however, for the wards to close earlier because they were full or to stay open later on the whim of the workhouse porter on the door. Generally men and women were admitted for one night, although in 1881 regulations were imposed which said that they had to stay for two nights (three nights if admitted on a Friday or Saturday night). Under pressure from Whitehall, more and more unions adopted this regulation, although in practice it was often unworkable, since most workhouse masters were keen to get rid of troublesome inmates.

192

Many men welcomed the new arrangements, because it gave them a few nights' shelter. Jack London tried to persuade a fellow inmate at Poplar to run off without undertaking his task, but was told 'Aw, I came 'ere for a rest... An' another night's kip won't hurt me none.' Mary Higgs, admittedly from a middle-class background and unused to the vagrant's life, was less sure. After her short stay she 'felt a mere wreck. Only two days ago I was in full health and vigour. It was not absolute cruelty, only the cruel system, the meagre and uneatable diet, the lack of sufficient moisture to make up for loss by perspiration, two almost sleepless nights, "hard labour" under any circumstances.'

At busy times there might be a queue for admission. In 1903, outside the Whitechapel workhouse, Jack London found 'a most woeful picture, men and women waiting in the cold grey end of the day for a pauper's shelter for the night'. At Poplar, Jack London's companions were nervous about ringing the workhouse door for fear of upsetting the porter:

> The Carpenter stealthily advanced a timid forefinger to the button, and gave it the faintest, shortest push. I have looked at waiting men where life or death was in the issue; but anxious suspense showed less plainly on their faces than it showed on the faces of these two men as they waited on the coming of the porter. He came. He barely looked at us. "Full up", he said and shut the door.

Women vagrants were most at risk. Mary Higgs, when spending a week with a friend in lodging houses and workhouses, was shocked by the reception she received from a porter at a northern house:

> He kept me inside his lodge, and began to take the details. He talked to me in what he supposed was a very agreeable manner, telling me he wished I had come along earlier, and he would have given me a cup of tea. I thanked him, wondering if this was usual, and finding I was a married woman (I must use his exact words), he said, 'Just the right age for a bit of funning; come down to me later in the evening.' I was too horror struck to reply; besides I was in his power with no one within to call but my friend and all the conditions unknown and strange.

At another workhouse she and her fellow applicants had to undergo a barrage of insults before they were admitted:

If the unfortunate applicant stated the facts in a meek and ordinary voice, this official asked 'have you been here before?' If the reply was 'no' 'See that you don't come here again' 'Sponging upon the rates!' and various other expressions not to be repeated were used in a hectoring tone of voice. If the reply was 'yes' he became threatening and violent in language.

Each person admitted was thoroughly searched and any possessions taken away. Tramps made a great deal of being able to hide a wad of tobacco or a penny from the prying eyes of the workhouse staff, either in their boots (which traditionally were never searched) or in nooks and crannies outside the house. If they were caught, they could be turned out of the workhouse or even imprisoned. In August 1868 the *Berwick Advertiser* reported the case of George Williams, who was caught with 1s 3d when seeking admission to Belford workhouse and was sentenced to a week in Alnwick prison.

Vagrants were made to undress and bathe, usually in dirty tepid water which had previously been used by other residents. George Orwell described the scene at his fictional 'Romton' spike (in East London):

> Fifty stark-naked men elbowing each other in a room twenty feet square, with only two bath-tubs and two slimy roller towels between them all. I shall never forget the reek of dirty feet. Less than half the tramps actually bathed... When my time came for the bath, I asked if I might swill out the tub, which was streaked with dirt, before using it. [The porter] answered simply 'shut yer f- mouth and get on with yer bath!' That set the social tone of the place and I did not speak again.

A few years earlier, at Cannock, Staffordshire, an inspector found 'one bath only in use, men who may have skin diseases dry themselves on the one and only towel provided'.

Their clothes would be taken from them and fumigated by being heated in an oven, or 'stoved' as the phrase was, or possibly disinfected with chlorine, and were then stored to be collected the following morning. Mrs Higgs pointed out that, particularly for women, having crumpled and unironed clothes made it even harder to find work, as it marked out applicants as having just come from the workhouse.

Men and women were supposed to be issued with blue nightshirts made of a coarse material. Often they were very threadbare as a result of many months' wear and tear. At smaller rural workhouses, vagrants might well sleep in their own clothes.

Eventually, the casual would be given eight ounces of dried bread (Jack London thought it was a brick) and perhaps a bowl of skilly (gruel), before being shown to the ward itself. An Irish tramp told George Orwell that skilly was nothing more than 'a can o' hot water wid some bloody oatmeal at de bottom'. Food was important for half-starved casuals, even skilly. James Greenwood recorded this conversation: '"You was too late for skilly, K. There's skilly now, nights as well as mornins" "Don't you tell no bleeding lies," K. answered, incredulously. "Blind me, it's true! Ain't it, Punch?" "Right you are!" said Punch, "and spoons to eat it with, that's more!"' Few unions provided spoons and it was quite an art to drink skilly from a large bowl without wasting any. Naturally there could be lively debates about which spike did the best skilly. According to a couple Jack London met: '"You do get good skilly at 'ackney," said the Carter. "Oh, wonderful skilly, that," praised the Carpenter, and each looked eloquently at each other.'

Visitors often remarked on the noise made by the sleeping casuals, the loud snores and the talking in the sleep which kept them awake. Occasionally there might be a group which disturbed the others by talking, singing and rough-housing.

Breakfast was more bread and skilly. James Greenwood wrote:

> I was glad to get mine, because the basin that contained it was warm and my hands were numb with cold. I tasted a spoonful, as in duty bound, and wondered more than ever at the esteem in which it was held by my *confrères*... But it was hot, and on that account, perhaps, was so highly relished, that I had no difficulty in persuading one of the decent men to accept my share.

Mary Higgs was pleased to be offered a mug of coffee at a workhouse where she was staying. A few workhouses provided tea or coffee instead of gruel, although it was contrary to regulations. She was told that 'the tramps never eat the gruel and frequently throw it about, and even at each other, making a great mess! Also, being made in summer overnight, it turns sour and "is not fit for pigs".' In general she commented about the lack of water, let alone coffee or tea, to wash down the food.

Every day vagrants undertook three or four hours of work, known as 'the task', before they could leave the workhouse. Most unions wanted inmates to contribute to their upkeep, and it was supposed to be a deterrent for the indolent. It was made compulsory in 1873, although most casual wards already required inmates to undertake such work. For men the task was often breaking stones, for women cleaning and tidying. Either sex could be required to pick oakum. The worst task was stone-pounding, using four-foot bars with square ends. The journalist Everard Wyrall said that 'only men in good health can use them properly'. No protection was given for the eyes, and after half-an-hour he was exhausted with sore and bleeding hands.

In Lambeth James Greenwood was required to turn a crank. He described it as:

> like turning a windlass. The task is not a severe one. Four measures of corn … have to be ground every morning by the night's batch of casuals. Close up by the ceiling hangs a bell connected with the machinery, and as each measure is ground the bell rings, so that the grinders may know how they are going on.

There were complaints about the pointlessness of many of these tasks. In the 1840s Henry Mayhew pointed out:

> for what was easy work to an agricultural labourer, a railway excavator, a quarryman, or to any one used to wield a hammer, was painful and blistering to a starving tailor. Nor was the test enforced by the overseers or regarded by the paupers as a proof of willingness to work, but simply as a punishment for poverty, and as a means of deterring the needy from applying for relief. To make labour a punishment, however, is *not* to destroy, but really to confirm, idle habits; it is to give a deeper root to the vagrant's settled aversion to work. 'Well, I always thought it was unpleasant,' the vagabond will say to himself '*that* working for one's bread, and now I'm *convinced* of it!'

Nearly 100 years later a witness told the Committee on the Casual Poor in 1930:

The work I saw in the casual wards was a farce. I was only in one ward where the work was well organised. We chopped firewood like the Church Army – that seemed to be entirely good – but as a rule it was loitering about waiting to get out. It was simply being bored stiff, waiting and waiting and waiting.

At least by 1925 the picking of oakum had ended and few places were insisting on stone-breaking, largely because there was a falling demand for stone chippings for roads.

At about 11 am the casuals were released to look for work or to make their way to the next workhouse, where the whole experience would be repeated. Often it was too late for serious jobseekers to find employment, and in any case the tasks they had to perform had exhausted them. Workhouse masters had the discretion to release serious jobseekers early, but few did.

The casual ward and the experience of the vagrants there was an example of the Poor Law authorities' misjudgement. Convinced that the majority of casuals were shiftless and feckless, they constructed a system which made them so. Mary Higgs called the casual wards 'National Tramp Manufactories' and said that 'all this rough hard work naturally made our clothes dirty and would soon wear them out. We were, after only two nights in the workhouse tramp wards far more dirty and disreputable in our clothing than when we left home... We felt completely tired out.'

As so often with the Poor Law, prejudice had overcome objectivity.

Alternatives

By no means all vagrants spent time in casual wards; indeed, conditions were generally so bad that entering the house was usually the last resort. Even a night or two in a prison cell could be preferable; it was generally more comfortable and the food was usually better. It was easy enough for a tramp to break a window or cause an affray and be sentenced by a magistrate to a few days inside. It was only the fear of their loss of freedom which kept many a vagrant out of prison.

In the countryside a vagrant could sleep in barns or woods and beg food from sympathetic locals or work a few hours for a night's accommodation. Details of householders who could be relied upon to help tramps were spread by word of mouth, occasionally marked on maps passed from beggar to beggar, or scrawled on the walls of casual wards.

Another alternative was the lodging house or 'dosshouse', where for a penny or two you could lay down your head and perhaps share a meal in a communal kitchen. The Medical Officer of Health for London claimed in 1905, without much evidence, that only failed thieves were found in the casual wards, for the successful ones used lodging houses. Originally known as 'netherskens', low lodging houses were at their peak in the half century or so before the 1860s, when the authorities began to close down the most foul and to license the rest. In their defence, they provided very cheap accommodation, but the police regarded them as sinks of depravity and criminality. They were extremely widespread. The small Lancashire market town of Ormskirk had 60 such premises in 1849. In Old Buildings Yard, off Burscough Street, there were six such houses, which were described as being 'wretched beyond description' with a sickening smell, both inside and out.

Although lodging house conditions improved during the last years of the 19th century, as late as 1910 the Rev. Zachary Edwards gave a description of the cheapest house in Preston, Lancashire: for a penny, 30 to 60 men slept each night in a room measuring 25 by 18 feet, and there were no washing, heating or cooking facilities. Each man was assigned a space on the floor with a wooden block as a head rest. Twenty years later George Orwell spent a night in a dosshouse off the Waterloo Road in London which cost him a shilling: 'It had a sweetish reek of paregoric and foul linen: the windows seemed to be shut tight and the air was almost suffocating at first... [T]he sheets stank so horribly of sweat that I could not bear them near my nose.'

Charities, notably the Salvation and the Church Armies from the 1880s, increasingly provided another option, but they were not popular because the tramps found them dreary and oppressively religious. One vagrant, W.A. Gape, recalled enduring a sermon lasting an hour and ten minutes on the evils of gambling, drink and idleness. The walls of the 'Sally Ann' homes were adorned with gloomy, religious homilies, which were lost on the weary derelicts. Both George Orwell and W.H. Davies severely criticized the Salvation Army hostels. Around 1900 Davies spent many months at the Salvation Army hostel in Southwark Street, known as 'The Ark': 'I have nothing to say in its favour... Certainly the food was cheap, but such food was not fit for a human being.'

However, these charitable hostels seem to have had a greater appeal to the more respectable people on the tramp who had a few pence spare for a bed, but who did not want to spend a night in a nethersken. Mary Higgs was impressed by her stay in a women's hostel run by the Salvation Army. On her way to it she met several women who had stayed there:

> One said 'it was right enough', another said, 'I should think it was better than going into the common lodging house among a lot of "riff-raff"; you can put up with it for a night anyhow'. A third, with a child in her arms, said that she had lived there some time and 'was very comfortable'.

Others, without even the penny or two for a bed, slept rough. In London the Embankment was a popular destination. In 1910 at least 1,500 vagrants gathered each night in the search for a hot meal, and this attracted dozens of different charities offering soup or a bed for the night in return for an hour's work. It was claimed that scroungers slept during the day and arrived at night for a hand-out, that meal tickets were being sold by those who had already fed, and that left-wing agitators were causing trouble among the disaffected. John Burns, president of the Local Government Board, visited one night and found himself being offered a meal by an undiscriminating charity worker.

If conditions inproved for other pauper inmates, they hardly changed at all for the casuals who spent a night or two in the wards. The authorities thought that vagrancy was impossible to solve, and that vagrants and tramps were almost an irredeemable underclass, who should be shown no sympathy. Yet, as often with the New Poor Law, they ignored the evidence before their eyes. Many, perhaps most, casuals tramped the roads for work, but instead of helping them find it, the authorities actively made it as difficult as possible, almost inevitably forcing the honest work-seeker on a downward spiral to destitution.

CHAPTER EIGHT

Closing the Doors At Last

The small [out-relief] allowance which we make to them is not
sufficient to sustain nature, and the horses, nay the dogs, of our aristocracy,
are better stabled, kennelled and fed than our deserving poor
are housed, clothed and fed.

Joseph Turnell, relieving officer for Sheffield, 1872

THE workhouse only accommodated a small fraction of the people the Poor Law authorities helped. Two-thirds of the men and women assisted by the guardians probably never saw the inside of the workhouse. Most were given a small weekly pension, sometimes called a dole, and perhaps a loaf of bread and a ticket to be handed over to a named local grocer in exchange for a few essential goods.

In rural areas this support might be delivered by the relieving officer or his staff. In towns, however, recipients were often expected to attend the workhouse to receive the dole and bread. As a child before the First World War, Ted Harrison used to go to Shoreditch workhouse in London to collect his grandmother's ration:

Everyone was lined up, coughing, and one of the old inmates used to come along and shout out your name. He was a bit pompous. He was like Dickens's Mr Bumble, but he was only a workhouse inmate himself. He'd say, 'Follow me!' so I went after him and he'd say, 'Hold your arms out!' and he gave me four loaves, which was Granny's ration for the week. She got no butter, or anything else, just four loaves of bread.

Both the guardians and the authorities in London were wary about too great a provision of out-relief because they were concerned about the burden on the ratepayers. But as important, at least until the end of the 19th century, was the moral argument. Many commentators, such as George Bartley, thought that unnecessary provision would lead to permanent dependency on the parish. He wrote in 1876 that:

> Englishmen as a rule are proverbial for their independence, courage and reliance on themselves, and if anything tends more than another to condemn the present administration of the Poor Law, it is the fact that so many thousands ... are kept chronically in this state of abject dependence upon the dole of relief.

Modern critics of the welfare state still talk about 'welfare dependency', although in less patriotic terms.

Inevitably, there was an element of social control. For instance, some unions only made awards to individuals or their families who kept themselves neat and tidy. Others insisted that widows with two or more children deposit them in the house while they sought work, and unmarried mothers always found it difficult to get any relief. Nonetheless, the guardians and relieving officers were generally less censorious than the relief charities, who made grants to those whom they regarded as deserving, such as people temporarily down on their luck or the elderly. This may have been because in towns and cities only the most desperate and destitute applied to the Poor Law for assistance, so there was little point in the authorities wagging a finger at them.

The amount to be granted to individual claimants was not fixed by Whitehall (they had no powers to do so), which meant that the sums offered varied greatly from union to union and claimant to claimant. Members of the Royal Commission on the Poor Law of 1905 who attended a meeting of rural guardians found: 'The relieving officers and the chairman stated the cases so confusedly and incompletely that it was almost impossible to form any opinion as to the methods on which out-relief is distributed.'

Even the amount provided to two applicants in the same difficulties varied greatly. By 1905 most unions offered either 2s or 2s 6d per adult per week and about 1s 6d per child. To an extent this could be controlled by proper record-keeping and the advice of the relieving officer, but the board, and especially the chairman, could be swayed one way or another by a particularly piteous case or, conversely, take against an applicant. One investigator for the 1905 Royal Commission sat in on board meetings and found that: 'Cases are seldom discussed with reference to their needs. "She will be content with that" or "That is what the other old women are getting" or "She is over 80 give her another sixpence" were the sort of considerations brought forward.'

In many places the amount offered, even to the elderly, was clearly inadequate. In rural areas, clergymen told the Royal Commission that, after rent had been paid, claimants often had no more than 6d a week to live on and relied on charity. Critics argued that offering these small amounts was just a salve to the guardians' conscience rather than any effective way to manage the poor. Mr Cleaver, the clerk to the guardians at West Derby on the outskirts of Liverpool, told the Commission that, by giving out-relief of this kind, the guardians felt that

> they have dealt with the case… I consider that there are numberless cases in the West Derby Union, who ought to be receiving considerably more than they are receiving; but it is very difficult to get guardians to understand that it is better to have 500 on outdoor relief at 7s 6d than 1500 at 2s 6d.

By the 1920s local discretion was increasingly out of place in an emerging welfare state in which benefits were set nationally and were equal wherever the claimant lived. It was clear that, for all its faults, the new system was fairer and easier to administer.

The job of the relieving officer

Every union had one or more relieving officers, who would be assigned a district, either several parishes in the countryside or a ward in a town. It was his job to assess applicants and recommend to the guardians what relief, if any, should be granted. This might include 'the house' as well as out-relief. George Bartley thought that relieving officers needed tact and management, 'which is not always found', together with 'great firmness coupled with a great kindness of manner'.

Officers were expected to visit applicants in their homes and to make repeated visits, ideally unannounced and at different times, to make sure that the relief was needed and was being used. If they thought that the applicant needed immediate assistance, they could provide a note recommending that the individual or family should be admitted directly to the workhouse or offer small amounts of money or goods to tide them over to the next meeting of the guardians. In cases of sickness or serious injury, they could summon the union medical officer. In rural villages, the officers would ride out once or twice a week to investigate new claims, check on existing cases and pay out pensions. In between times, parish officers would deal with emergencies, such as the sudden loss of work.

The relieving officers were usually overworked. Poor Law Inspector Andrew Doyle reported to the Local Government Board in 1873 that 'it is impossible to avoid the conclusion that the duties imposed upon the officers is in the majority of cases so onerous that no man, however active and intelligent, can satisfactorily discharge them'. He found that it was difficult for relieving officers to be personally acquainted with each case and to administer the relief which had been ordered by the guardians, and he recommended that the maximum number of cases they dealt with should be about 500. Very few unions, however, adopted this figure.

Inevitably, the numbers of relieving officers grew. In West Ham, the second largest union in the country (after West Derby on Merseyside), there were, in the late 1920s, a superintendent relieving officer; 2 assistant superintendent relieving officers; 6 clerks; 24 relieving officers, including a female officer assigned to deal with sensitive cases concerning women, and 58 assistant relieving officers in six districts or stations. In addition, there was a department of 30 investigators under a relieving officer. In 1925–1926 they dealt with approximately 58,000 cases involving 120,000 individuals at a cost to the ratepayer of nearly £1.5 million or £28,189 per week.

Relieving officers came from a variety of backgrounds. Many had been former servicemen or policemen, others had had posts elsewhere in the Poor Law service (a few had even been workhouse masters), and some had no obvious qualifications at all. It was not unknown for local farmers, publicans or small traders to be appointed to posts by friends among the guardians. In the 1920s guardians in Bedwellty in South Wales were appointing their friends and relations. By the 1880s and 1890s a degree of professionalism was being introduced and there was an opportunity to make a career of social work. One of the first women relieving officers, Miss Mabel Bhose, who was appointed at Poplar, London, in 1910, had previously been a health visitor in Acton.

At times, life as a relieving officer could be hazardous. Because they were the visible representatives of the hated Poor Law, they were occasionally attacked by disgruntled agricultural labourers. And no doubt they were abused and threatened by the men and women whom they declined to help. They often carried the money to be paid out to the elderly or the sick and so became targets for robbers. In 1835 William Holt, the relieving officer for Swaffham, Norfolk, was assaulted by a horse-dealer called Henry Riches, who attempted to stab him in the throat. And in May 1922 *The Times* reported that Henry Fearne, a relieving officer in Lambeth, London, was assaulted and robbed of £200 by a 23-year-old chauffeur, Herbert Reeves. Fearne was lucky. Back in 1836 a Norfolk relieving officer by the name of Cunningham was robbed of £12 by William Buck, who attempted to cut his throat and was later described by Cunningham as being '33 years of age, five feet six inches high, of dark hair and complexion, lame and turns his feet out when walking'.

It was also tempting for relieving officers to embezzle money from their employers, either by fiddling the books or by not paying the paupers the correct amount. In March 1837 Edmund Bailey, relieving officer at Salisbury, was tried at Bury St Edmunds sessions for embezzling £23 by falsely entering the amounts into his books. Although he did not contest the charges, Bailey was found innocent by the jury, which, according to the *Suffolk Chronicle*, not unnaturally 'excited the greatest surprise in the court'. He seems to have been the beneficiary of the popular feeling against the Poor Law which ran deep in East Anglia.

Thomas James Lewis, a relieving officer at Canning Town, London, was tried in April 1908. A man named Winchester should have received 5s cash, 2s in kind and 6d per week for coal, but Lewis only gave him tickets for groceries. In other cases, the coal money was not given out. His defence counsel said that he had recently been burgled and lost £80 and 'after that he gave way to drink and became neglectful and careless'. Lewis was sentenced to three months' hard labour.

There seems to have been an upsurge in court cases after the First World War, perhaps a sign that the Poor Law could no longer cope with the changed social conditions. James Handford, an assistant relieving officer in Southwark, London, who stole £42 7s, was fortunate. *The Times* reported that, at his trial in May 1927, the guardians felt compelled to prosecute, but they appealed for leniency because of his 'splendid war record'. Even so, Handford was sentenced to three months.

Medical officers could order medicine and food for their pauper patients outside the workhouse. Realizing that the root cause of many of the ailments that their patients endured was starvation or semi-starvation, doctors attempted to remedy this situation by issuing orders for additional food, such as meat and milk. Francis Bonney, the former medical officer for Brentford, Middlesex, told a parliamentary inquiry into medical poor relief in 1844 that he thought that many of the cases he dealt with were caused by poor diet or housing conditions and so ordered food for the sick as he thought fit. He was eventually sacked by the local guardians for being overgenerous in issuing these orders. Echoing the view of many boards across the country, Henry Pownall, chairman of Brentford guardians, told MPs that his experience was that 'not one in ten who come for medical orders require them… They want the cook not the doctor.'

Medical orders could be a convenient way of subverting the stricter regulations regarding the payment of doles to able-bodied paupers and their families. Many guardians in rural areas used medical orders to pay what were, in effect, unemployment benefits to agricultural labourers over the winter period. This kept a pool of labour available for work in the spring. A loophole in the 1834 Act allowed guardians to pay allowances to the family of an able-bodied pauper, provided a member of the family was ill. This loophole was widely exploited in East Anglia. Edwin Chadwick, secretary to the Poor Law Commissioners, gave an example of a scene at a board of guardians:

> A man presented himself for relief, and said that he must have an
> addition to his wages; that he could not go on with these wages.
> The ordinary reply was, 'but the prohibitory order [of 1834] forbids
> your having relief in aid of wages'. But they went on to say. 'Have

you got none of your family sick?' 'No' 'Think again?' 'Yes, there is
my boy has got a sore eye.' 'Well you shall have an order for medical
relief for him, and an allowance on account of the sickness of a part of
your family.

Before the guardians

All applicants for out-relief, unless they were too ill or infirm, were expected
to appear before the guardians, who would make a decision on the amount
they would be given or offer them the house instead. The relieving officer
would be present to explain the background to each case and recommend the
amount of relief to be offered. George Bartley noted:

> The table in the Board-room in the larger Unions is usually in the
> shape of a printed U, the members sitting round the outside of it and
> the space up the middle being reserved for the poor unfortunate
> creatures who present themselves for relief. By this arrangement every
> member may have a good look at the applicant who is as it were
> obliged to run the gauntlet before the whole assembly.

Writers such as Bartley urged that the guardians investigate as many applicants as they could and suggested that newly elected members spend a day
or two with the relieving officer. In most places this did not happen. Where
it did, such as Brixworth, the amount paid to individuals was generally cut.
But many guardians were not really interested – few had much sympathy
with applicants and it was a chore investigating cases. Most unions spent
little time in dealing with the cases of individual applicants and that often
incompetently. George Bartley calculated that the average time spent on
a case, often involving relief to half-a-dozen people or more, was less than
45 seconds. And one of the first women guardians, Miss Alexander, found
when she was elected to the Kensington guardians that 'the chair merely
confirms every admission by a stroke of a pen, while the committee dis-
cusses politics or the latest war news'.

Even those men and women, the aged for the most part, who received
a regular pension of a few shillings a week were expected to attend at least
once a year to have their cases reviewed. Albert Pell, one of the guardians at
St George-in-the-East, London, told a parliamentary committee that the

elderly came 'well-dressed and with very good manners, and no appearance of living in a squalid or uncomfortable manner'. To do otherwise would probably have resulted in the loss of their precious pension.

Charitable overlap

In urban areas, relieving officers and the guardians often worked closely with charities, such as the Charity Organization Society (COS). This was encouraged by the Poor Law Board in the Goschen minute of 1869 (named after the president of the Board at the time), which argued that, in order to prevent duplication of effort, charities should attempt to care for men and women who were not absolutely destitute, because local guardians were forbidden to help them under the doctrine of 'less eligibility'. The guardians, for example, could not redeem tools or clothes in pawn, assist in purchasing tools or clothes, or pay rent or fares.

There was meant to be no overlap, but inevitably there was; the more enlightened guardians sometimes referred cases to the local visiting charity, while charity workers told relieving officers about people they thought suitable for the workhouse. In 1902 the Rev. L.R. Phelps explained how things operated in Oxford, where he was a guardian and where most cases were sent to a charity for consideration: 'The poor themselves, I believe, prefer help to be given in this way and in this spirit to being a charge on their neighbours [i.e. as payers of the poor rates], some of whom have often a hard struggle to keep themselves.'

From the early 1870s, the Charity Organization Society was the dominant charity in London. It prided itself on thoroughly investigating each case through a system of volunteers, known as visitors, who would call on households that required assistance. By 1904 there were some 10,000 such persons in the capital alone, by no means all associated with the Charity Organization Society. As the charity historian, Frank Prochaska, has put it: 'Armed with the paraphernalia of their calling – Bibles, tracts, blankets, food and coal tickets, and love – these foot soldiers of the charitable army went from door to door to combat the evils of poverty, disease and ill-religion.'

The Charity Organization Society had a justified reputation for hard-heartedness and inflexibility, although it would prefer to have been described as rigorous and thorough. The visitors were regarded as interfering middle-class busybodies, not just by the poor families they visited but also by many boards of guardians. For all their faults, the relieving officers were rarely judgemental.

In addition, these visiting societies were not widespread and many only lasted a few years. The Guilds of Help, for example, were set up in a number of provincial centres during the first decade of the 20th century as a more humane version of the Charity Organization Society, and volunteers were asked to 'endeavour to become the personal friends of those whom they visit[ed]'. At their peak in 1911, they had branches in about 50 towns but were only really effective in Bolton and Bradford.

The problem of the unemployed

The biggest problem facing the Poor Law authorities throughout the period of the New Poor Law was how to deal with the unemployed, or the able-bodied poor as they were known. This became a major factor in the downfall of the workhouse system in the 1920s. The authorities were lucky that for approximately 80 years, between about 1840 and 1920, there was no economic slump to cause a huge rise in people seeking work.

One of the major elements of the 1834 reforms was the ban on out-relief for the able-bodied. The Poor Law Commission of 1832 argued that out-relief had become a major problem: it both dissuaded able-bodied paupers from working and increased the burden on ratepayers. Under the so-called 'Speenhamland system', poor rates were used to subsidize the wages of agricultural labourers. This had disadvantages: it depressed the wages paid by farmers and removed an incentive for labourers to seek work.

The reforms meant that all cases were to be 'offered the house' and nothing else. Less than a quarter of the able-bodied applicants in Norfolk who were given this opportunity entered the workhouse in 1835 and 1836. As a result, the amount spent on the Poor Law in the county fell from £307,000 in 1834 to £181,000 in 1839, and spending per head fell from 15s 4d in 1834 to 9s 10d in 1839. The reduction was not dissimilar across the rest of England and Wales.

Out-relief was only to be offered in cases of 'sudden and urgent necessity; sickness, accident or infirmity; burials; widows in the first six months of widowhood; widows with legitimate children and with no illegitimate children since widowhood; imprisonment [that is, to dependants of prisoners]; family of soldiers, sailors or marines; and resident family of non-resident head'. Over 85 per cent of applicants for outdoor relief were described as being able-bodied in the 1850s, although this fell to just over two-thirds by the 1890s. The rest were the elderly, the chronically infirm, widows with one or two small children (those with larger families had to place their children in the workhouse until such time as they were earning enough to support them) or people who required tiding over short-term crises, such as funerals.

The new policy caused great hardship, forcing many labourers and their families to emigrate or move elsewhere in search of work. In November 1838 *The Times* reported that respectable residents of Haverhill had petitioned the local board of guardians to ask them to pay out-relief to local labourers who earned only a 'pittance of two shillings a week to support themselves, their wives and generally a family of three or four children'. The petitioners were told by the guardians that their hands were tied by the authorities in London, 'having by their general orders forbidden upon principle, all outdoor relief to the able-bodied labourer, no matter however poignant his and his family's sufferings may be'.

The intentions of the authors of the 1834 Act were, however, soon modified; indeed the Act was almost unworkable, because it was so inflexible. It was clear to most guardians that there were deserving cases who needed support. The surviving files of correspondence at the National Archives are full of letters from guardians seeking exemptions and guidance about individual cases. Even after 150 years, the inflexibility of the officials in London and their ability to waste ratepayers' money in order to make a point remain staggering.

One such case, found in the volumes relating to Southwell Union, concerned Mary Cook of Ossington. It was raised by Evelyn Denison, the MP for North Nottinghamshire. Mrs Cook's husband had been sentenced to transportation for sheep stealing, leaving her to fend for herself and four dependent children. She went to live with her parents in nearby Arnold, where two of her children could find employment as framework knitters, but was refused out-relief unless she returned to the Union. Even though the cost to the Union would be 11s a week if she went to the workhouse, but only 5s if she stayed in Arnold, the Southwell board stated that they could not relieve her in Arnold because of a recent order from Whitehall. If she came back to Ossington, or another parish in the Union, out-relief could be offered: if she became destitute, she could go into the workhouse. A copy of this letter was also sent to Denison, who replied that Ossington was supporting Mrs Cook at 5s a week, that she had no house to return to and that in her circumstances it would be difficult to find housing within the Union.

The Poor Law Commissioners replied to Denison that he had 'urged on them the expediency of the allowance of relief proposed for Mary Cook under a misapprehension of the source from which it can be legally derived' and that, as long as she resided at Arnold, that parish solely was primarily responsible for her relief, if she was found to be destitute; the Southwell Union had no powers to relieve non-resident paupers. Furthermore, no official application had been made, but if it had been, the Commissioners would have refused it. In the end, Mary Cook seems to have left the area, perhaps to find work in nearby Nottingham, leaving the younger of her children with her grandparents.

The obvious inhumanity and inefficiency of the system meant that there was widespread evasion and every loophole was exploited by the guardians. In 1856 Poor Law Inspector Sir John Walsham remarked: 'With scarcely an exception, the tendency everywhere is to substitute outdoor relief for indoor relief whenever the guardians may legally do so.'

In 1852 the Outdoor Relief Order stated that with certain exceptions able-bodied male paupers out of employment were to be set to work in return for poor relief, at least half of which was to be given in kind. The unemployed were to be offered work by the guardians in return for a small amount of out-relief, often referred to as 'a dole'. At times of unemployment, work-yards were established where the unemployed were set to breaking stones or picking oakum for a few shillings a week. During the Lancashire Cotton Famine in the early 1860s, when cotton supplies from the southern states of America were disrupted by the Civil War, hundreds of mills across the county closed, and the local guardians provided work and relief for many of the men and women who had worked in them. In Clitheroe, cotton operatives were employed in draining a neighbouring moor and gathering stone.

This was hard work for men used to operating sensitive machinery and led to some ineffectual grumbling. One man, John O'Neill, noted in his diary that 'if any one complains to the master of bad work, he says, If you don't like [it] you can leave ... and that is all the satisfaction we can get.'

During the 1860s and 1870s spending on out-relief began to rise again, as a result of trade slumps and industrial crises in Lancashire and London. Instead of accepting the economic reasons for this rise, the Local Government Board blamed recalcitrant boards of guardians who supposedly insisted on paying out doles to undeserving cases. They issued a series of circulars which promoted the efficacy of the 'workhouse test' and stated that guardians should cancel all outdoor relief payments. Outdoor relief was again made illegal and Poor Law Unions were encouraged to recover welfare costs where possible. Between 1871 and 1876 the total number of paupers relieved nationally on out-relief orders fell by around a third, with expenditure decreasing by some £276,000. Thereafter, numbers stabilized to an average of 542,000 claimants nationally between 1877 and 1892, despite the general rise in the population.

The elderly, in particular, lost out: the number receiving some form of public assistance in 1890 was less than half of what it had been in 1870. Some probably entered the workhouse, while others were forced to fend for themselves when they were no longer capable. In a pamphlet, Joseph Turnell, the relieving officer for Sheffield, pointed out the human cost of this policy:

> Hundreds of our aged infirm poor are in a most miserable condition: that the small [out-relief] allowance which we make to them is not sufficient to sustain nature, and the horses, nay the dogs, of our aristocracy, are better stabled, kennelled and fed than our deserving poor are housed, clothed and fed.

In January 1875 a coroner held an inquest on the death of 77-year-old Thomas Nolan, who had died in Soho. According to *The Times*, he and his wife had been reduced to begging in the streets, 'dangerous to the neighbourhood from a sanitary point of view', because their out-relief of three shillings had been cut off, as the relieving officer felt that it was being used by their son ('a lazy, drunken vagabond') and the couple refused to enter the workhouse: 'Mr Warren, the relieving officer, ... said that he had seen the deceased and his wife occasionally since the discontinuation of the out-relief, but had not spoken to them. He did not consider it necessary to look after them, because they had a son.' Warren was castigated by the coroner, who told him: 'Unquestionably, it was the duty of the relieving officer to see that they did not die through want or live in such a way as to endanger the health of others.' But guidance from Whitehall had given Warren little choice.

Most guardians modified the instructions from the centre and boards varied widely in the relief they offered to paupers. In his 1876 manual for new guardians, George Bartley pointed out: 'Nothing will strike a new guardian ... more than the slight circumstances which often decide boards as to the form in which relief shall be given, without regard being had to any fundamental principle or systematic rule of action.' He urged that the 'wishes of the individual applicant should not be considered nor the imme-diate cost to the union', but the guardians should decide whether they were 'likely to be encouraged or discouraged by one form of relief or another, both in the persons themselves and among the inhabitants of the union generally'.

Under the influence of Albert Pell MP, Earl Spencer and several other local guardians during the early 1870s, the small Northamptonshire Union of Brixworth stopped paying out-relief. It was one of only a handful of unions, including Farringdon and Bradfield in Berkshire and London's St George-in-the-East (where Pell was also a guardian), where this policy was adopted. Pell was convinced that out-relief created a culture of welfare dependency:

> The administration of the Poor Laws is a matter of policy, not
> sentiment, and should be applied unswervingly in obedience to fixed
> principles, and not become the haphazard display of sentiment and
> counterfeit charity... [Otherwise] the incentives of industry are
> weakened; the fear of the consequences, such as cold, hunger and
> distress, is diminished or vanishes; and a distinct and pernicious induce-
> ment offered to the practice of deceit and fraud, and the total abandon-
> ment of conscientious, honest effort for self-maintenance unfolds.

In implementing the new policy, the guardians began by visiting all the people receiving some form of out-relief and immediately struck off a quarter.

They published a list of cases to whom out-relief would no longer be paid, concerned more with social control than any economic motivation: 'wives and families of convicted prisoners, single women with illegitimate children … able-bodied women with one child only' and 'persons living in cottages or premises reported by the sanitary officer as unfavourable to health'.

Perhaps the cruellest of Brixworth's new restrictions was that able-bodied widows with two or more children should be separated from them. The children would be placed in the workhouse, where 'they will be better fed, better disciplined, and better and (to the ratepayer) more cheaply taught'. In turn she would be 'set free for work' and could save enough to make a comfortable home for her children when they left the workhouse.

Out-relief was reduced to a maximum of four weeks, except for the very old or chronic cases, to whom it was now to be provided for no more than six months. Children were expected to pay for the upkeep of their aged parents. It also became much more difficult to get medical relief. Relieving officers were expected to visit the sick often and at irregular intervals in order to spot malingerers. No relief was to be given except with the authority of a medical officer, and no medical extras (that is more nourishing food and drink than applicants normally enjoyed) were allowed except with the approval of the guardians.

In 1871 the Brixworth Union helped 1,067 outdoor paupers; by 1895 this figure had fallen to just 97, out of a total population of 12,200. The amount spent fell from around £6,000 in the late 1860s to just £140 in 1895. These reforms, the guardians hoped, would 'encourage providence, truth-fulness, industry, independence; [provide] … a legitimate reason for demand-ing fair and full wages, with the corresponding ability on the part of the employer to meet that demand; … re-establish the acknowledgment of parents to maintain their children, children their parents and well-to-do persons to assist their poorer relatives'. Unfortunately, they achieved none of these aims. The result was social tension and bitterness, because the measures were deeply unpopular among the poor, who had had no say in their implementation. Local problems were exported elsewhere because labourers were forced to move to Northampton and other neighbouring towns to look for work. As a result, the population of the district fell by over an eighth between 1871 and 1901.

Revenge, however, was sweet when it came. In 1893 shortly after the property qualification required to become a guardian was reduced, the Brixworth District Outdoor Relief Association was formed. Within two years, over 7,500 local people had joined, or two-thirds of the adult population. In the elections of 1896 they formed the majority on the board. Their first act was to reintroduce out-relief.

Transfer of powers

The out-relief problems identified above came to haunt the Poor Law authorities in the years after the First World War and ultimately led to the abolition of local Poor Law Unions on 1 April 1930. Their powers were transferred either to county councils (in regard to workhouses and related bodies such as infirmaries and children's homes) or to central government in the shape of the new Unemployment Assistance Committees, which took over the responsibility for out-relief. Time was moving on, leaving the workhouse behind as little more than a grim historical throwback.

By 1930, the Poor Law had already lost many of its powers and the guardians their clientele, as a result of the welfare reforms introduced by the Liberal government in the decade before the First World War.

This was partly due to changing attitudes. Old certainties were disappearing. In the world of 1834 paupers were seen as a morally weak underclass who had forfeited the sympathy of society because of their inability to stand on their own two feet, but nearly 100 years later society had become more democratic, and all citizens were able to have a say in the running of the country (even if they were not always very equal). The election of working-class guardians from the mid-1890s was an early sign of this change.

There was also an acceptance that the State had a responsibility for its citizens and how they lived. Attitudes changed even towards the least considered of the workhouse's clients: vagrants. The tone and conclusions of the Departmental Committee on the Casual Poor of 1930 were very different from those of its predecessor of 1906. The 1906 committee thought that 'the army of vagrants ... is mainly composed of those who deliberately avoid any work and depend for their existence on almsgiving and the casual wards; and for their benefit the industrious portion of the community is heavily taxed'. Two decades later the Departmental Committee concluded that

> a general raising of the standard of accommodation and treatment would not tend to attract men to a life of vagrancy, but would have the result of improving the self-respect of the casual population and making it easier for them to regain their proper places in the life and work of the community.

One of the first signs of the new world was the provision in 1906 of free school meals to the children of poor parents. They were administered by local authorities, thus preventing any association with the Poor Law. Then in 1908 came the introduction of old age pensions for men and women over the age of 70, as discussed above in Chapter 6.

Children had been all but removed from the workhouse by 1909 to children's homes and other establishments, where it was hoped that they would grow up as normally as possible. Illegitimacy rates had also fallen, and in the large cities charitable agencies, such as the Girls Friendly Society, sought to help girls in trouble, with the result that fewer single mothers were entering the workhouses to have their babies.

Another change was that in 1911 the government had set up a National Insurance scheme. Initially, it was for the better-off manual workers in a few trades, but by 1920 it had been extended to almost everybody in employment over the age of 16, other than agricultural labourers and domestic servants.

This meant that, in theory at least, the temporarily unemployed no longer had to seek out-relief for himself and his family. Unfortunately, the scheme could not cope with the scale of the problem: there was massive unemployment after the First World War which was even greater than that experienced in the 1830s. In a mirror image of the position a century before – when relief was needed most in the rural south – the problem after the war was concentrated in the industrial cities of the north and the Midlands and in London's East End. One in eight of the working population was out of work by 1926.

The result was that unemployment benefit was cut and restrictions introduced to make it harder to claim. The unemployed inevitably turned to out-door relief (doles) to make ends meet. Boards of guardians in the depressed areas complained bitterly about the excessive number of applications, because their finances could not cope with the demands being placed upon them.

In South Wales a report to the Ministry of Health noted in February 1929:

> A minority are dependent on outdoor relief. In most of the Poor Law Unions the outdoor relief given to unemployed married men, unless there is sickness in the household, is granted at a weekly rate of a shilling or two below the amount which would be received in unemployment benefit if it were available… [T]here is [also] a smaller class of single men who have ceased to be entitled to unemployment benefit.

Here men were offered the house, or in some unions relief was offered if the applicant was over 30. The Poor Law had been hijacked to become a replacement for the failed system of unemployment benefit. But just as the Old Poor Law was found wanting in the 1830s, so the New Poor Law was found wanting in the 1920s. The report admitted that in most unions 'the primary duty of the guardians in relieving able-bodied men, namely, to set them to work, has almost entirely been lost sight of since 1921'.

As unemployment rose, so did the poor rate. By 1926 it had reached £1.5 million. While it was often an increasing burden on the ratepayer in the poorest areas, an increasing proportion of the poor relief now came from the centre. By the time of the abolition of the Poor Law in 1930, about half of all out-relief was paid by Whitehall. The new Public Assistance Committees run by the local authorities had much less control over how this money was spent than had previously been the case.

As a way of cutting public expenditure, a means test was introduced in September 1931 and, with good reason, was hated as much as the old workhouse test. Another measure in 1934 established the centrally directed Unemployed Assistance Boards, which took away responsibility for the unemployed from the Public Assistance Committees.

Out-relief was not just expensive, it was inconsistent. The amounts paid varied from union to union, seemingly with no good reason. *The Times* found in September 1925 that the relief offered to a family of a man, wife and

four children varied from 39s a week in Bethnal Green and 45s in St Marylebone to a very generous 65s in West Ham. Outside London it was generally much less; for instance, Birkenhead in Merseyside paid out 30s, while in
one of the most generous, Walsall in the West Midlands, the rate was 41s.

In some unions, particularly West Ham, Bedwellty in south Wales and
Chester-le-Street in Durham, the generous rates were as much a political
statement as a reflection of the poverty of local people. At Bedwellty,
Assistant General Inspector Arthur Broadley found that out-relief was
'administered in an extravagant manner, no regard at all being paid to the
resultant cost' and that people had been attracted to the district 'by the
prospect of receiving out-relief without difficulty'.

In many less progressive unions, the guardians banned out-relief to
strikers and their families. They could get away with this when strikes were
organized and fought locally. But by the 1920s most strikes covered whole
industries across many counties and had nationwide popular support. The
Ministry of Health had to step in to prevent a potential political disaster,
when in 1921 the guardians at Lichfield, Staffordshire, declared their intention to withdraw all relief, indoor as well as out, from striking miners' families
– on the grounds that there was work for the miners to do and it was the
duty of the guardians to see that they did it. The Ministry told Lichfield
that it was their duty to relieve destitution, whatever the cause.

During the General Strike of May 1926 the Ministry issued instructions to guardians warning them about taking into account political
considerations in relieving destitution: 'They cannot, therefore, properly
give any weight to their views of such merits in dealing with the applications made to them.' But the Poor Law guardians in industrial areas were
now largely working class, the small businessmen and shopkeepers who had
traditionally run these unions as parsimoniously as possible having been
replaced. They could see nothing wrong in using the resources to help their
fellow workers. As George Lansbury, both a senior Labour politician and a
long-serving guardian, wrote in 1927:

> Nobody thinks poor relief is the true remedy, but every baby's life saved,
> every mother rescued from the thralls of suffering and death, every aged,
> infirm, sick person brought out from the vortex of destitution, and

> every widow saved from the terrible consequences of starvation and
> semi-starvation, all are a tribute to the humanity and rightness of
> policies pursued by labour guardians.

Officials at the Ministry of Health must have occasionally felt that the
lunatics had taken over the asylum. In a report on the worst offenders, a
bemused ministry official wrote: 'In none of the unions has there yet been
time to counteract the tradition which has grown up ... that resort to the
guardians is the obvious and first step for an able-bodied man, whatever
the cause of his unemployment might be.'

It would, however, be wrong to assume that there had been a total sea
change in the attitudes of the guardians, or of those in Whitehall. Many
boards still regarded the paupers much as they had always done. In 1927,
for example, the Ministry of Health circulated the details of an experiment
at Dudley, which had reduced the numbers of long-term unemployed. In
the spirit of 1834 the guardians there had resolved that outdoor relief should
cease for all men under 50 who had been unemployed for five years or more.
After a fortnight's warning, several of the men obtained work, but 87 were
offered the house and relief was to be provided to wives and families only
if their menfolk were inmates in the house. Only 11 admission orders were
issued, and in all cases the men discharged themselves after a day or two.

It was a long-standing complaint that social problems and the ways of
paying for them were not spread equally. Traditionally there was more
destitution in the inner cities which naturally cost more to relieve, but the
unions with the most problems often had the fewest and poorest ratepayers.
This was especially the case in London, where many small unions were
located in areas containing great poverty. This problem had been partly
solved in the mid-1860s by the establishment of the Metropolitan Poor
Fund, which redistributed poor rates from richer unions like Westminster
to poorer ones like Poplar, and the Metropolitan Asylums Board, which
provided hospitals, asylums and training for pauper children accros London.

Matters came to a head in 1921, when councillors and guardians in
Poplar spent six weeks in prison for failing to set a legal rate. Poplar was
one of the poorest areas in London and the Labour council elected in 1919
was determined to improve conditions for local people. They campaigned for

the equalization of rates across London, which would have considerably benefited the poorer councils. The dispute embarrassed the government, which was unsure what to do but eventually caved in. Lansbury, who coordinated the successful campaign, later wrote:

> Our crime ... is that we have refused to believe in the necessity of starvation. We have taught our people that it is no more wrong for a workman's widow and family to receive from the community the means of life than for a king's widow and family to receive sums varying from £10,000 to £70,000 a year.

The government, however, had its revenge. In 1926 Neville Chamberlain, the Minister of Health, assumed powers to take over boards of guardians if they failed to live within their means. He did so in the case of three unions: Bedwellty, Chester-le-Street and West Ham, where the guardians were ignoring the rules and paying out-relief to men and women who did not warrant its grant. (They were not the only unions to do so; the auditors were sent in to investigate Poplar, Manchester, Tynemouth, Rhondda and other places as well.) In all three unions the majority Labour group among the guardians had used its position to increase the amounts paid as out-relief and the numbers to whom it was paid, as was perfectly within its rights. At Bedwellty, Assistant General Inspector Arthur Broadley found 'out-relief administered in an extravagant manner, [with] no regard at all being paid to the resultant cost', and that the guardians 'have taken every opportunity of giving the greatest amount of relief which could be made to appear consistent with the rules'. The same could be said of West Ham and Chester-le-Street. In addition, the guardians overruled the staff, particularly the relieving officers, who were in an invidious position; while they were aware of the law, they were also at the mercy of their employers. At West Ham, the relieving officers were 'over-ridden in every direction by individual guardians and relief was demanded of them by applicants who, if refused, were then brought to a relief station by a guardian and given relief over the head of the ... officer'.

At Chester-le-Street, Henry Knight, a relieving officer, told an inquiry that, at the beginning of the miners' strike in early 1926, the relieving officers were instructed 'not to ask for any documentary evidence as to means and not to demand the production of share books in the co-operative societies nor savings bank notes. I felt bound to obey this order of the board, although I had considerable doubt as to the legality of it.' One Chester-le-Street guardian, Alexander Henry, was eventually sent to prison for three months for intimidating Cuthbert Laws, an assistant relieving officer. Laws had pointed out that it was illegal to relieve single men without a medical certificate. Henry exploded: 'To hell with the Minister. They are going to get it. No — is going to leave this room until they get what they want.' Laws and his staff were then locked in their office for nearly an hour.

Simple capitalist economics brought the guardians at these 'problem' workhouses to their knees. They could not afford to pay the additional amounts required from the rates and so were forced to borrow from banks and the government. Eventually, the creditors began to refuse extra credit and no amount of special pleading and moral blackmail softened their hearts. The government refused to help, unless economies were made. In June 1926 new guardians were appointed at West Ham, and then at Chester-le-Street in September and Bedwellty in February the following year. The newly appointed administrators drastically pruned back spending on out-relief in order to pay off the loans. In part this was done by reducing the amount payable to individuals, but in most cases claimants, particularly single men, found that they were no longer eligible under the new stricter guidelines now in force. At West Ham the number of people receiving support fell by 90 per cent from 66,700 in April 1926 to just over 6,700 in June 1929. In the same period, cases at Bedwellty fell from 4,582 to 1,640. However, in each union there was no notable decline in the number of inmates in the work-house, although staff numbers employed there and elsewhere on the boards were generally reduced.

The abolition of the Poor Law system in 1930 came almost without protest. Firebrands among members of the Association of Poor Law Guardians tried to stir up resistance but with little success. Their president P.S.G. Probert argued at their annual conference in November 1929 that the issue had brought down the Conservative Party at the previous May's election and that – with perhaps more justification – the proposals 'indicated the defeat of democracy and the triumph of bureaucracy'. However, the members cheered the Minister of Health, Arthur Greenwood, when he addressed the Association. He flattered them when he said that many guardians would be co-opted onto the new authorities and that he would endeavour to ensure that they were not under the thumb of 'hordes of bureaucrats'. After he had sat down, the Association unanimously agreed to wind itself up.

The fate of the workhouse buildings

As a result of the changes introduced by the Liberal government of 1906 and later administrations, the workhouses increasingly housed only those for whom no other provision could be made, either public or voluntary: old people who could no longer look after themselves, the chronically infirm, including the mentally ill, and vagrants.

In most places conditions hardly changed. George Orwell's experiences as a casual in 1929 were much the same as those of Jack London 25 years earlier, or even of James Greenwood in the late 1860s. Some institutions had knocked down the tall brick walls which had surrounded the work-house, but, as George Orwell remarked, they were still prisons. And people still dreaded entering them. One boy, Steve Tremeere, remembered many years later seeing this scene outside his local workhouse:

> an old bloke come up with an old girl, his wife. He had a little handker-chief tied around his little things what they had got left, the old girl on his arm was crying her bloody eyes out. We watch them till they got up to the Union. She was hanging back as they got up near the big doors – didn't want to go in there, but at last they had to go in... Wicked that was, parting them at that old age, when they had been together all their lives.

The abolition of the Poor Law, the transfer of powers to local authorities and the renaming of workhouses as public assistance institutions seem to have made little difference to the care and treatment offered, even if the workhouse was now an 'institution' and the paupers 'patients'. Many of the same people remained in place; most former guardians became members of the new committees nominated by county councils to supervise the new public assistance institutions, and many workhouse staff members remained in post.

The junior minister Susan Lawrence toured the workhouses of eastern England in April 1931. At Huntingdon she found the institution:

> horrid beyond description. An air of dirty sordid neglect over the
> whole place. Children's quarter in the workhouse horrid. A little handful
> of miserable dejected children playing in a dirty grass patch littered with
> dirty newspapers ... paint peeling off the walls. Stone floors. Casual
> ward – no beds – not even hammocks – an empty room – as many as
> 35 lie on the floor. Beck, chairman of House Committee, loud in
> his objection to spending money.

In some institutions much the same routines were in place until the 1950s and later. Over time, however, the atmosphere changed as the rules were relaxed and amenities slowly improved. Libraries and social clubs were organized, wards were redecorated, and comfortable beds and chairs, as well as wirelesses and televisions, were provided.

Conditions for vagrants also improved. At the Guildford spike, Nan Hammond, who was responsible for the female vagrants after the Second World War, remembered that when one arrived: 'I'd go across with a clean nightie, a comb, a bar of soap and a towel.' Her husband Joe, a maintenance man at the workhouse, disagreed with George Orwell's description of the conditions in a spike as disgusting, degrading and tyrannical. He told a local historian, Russell Chamberlin, that 'It wasn't a bit like that. The last Master was an old soldier. He was a disciplinarian – but you got your rights.'

Along with many other workhouses, Gressenhall became a county home for the elderly in 1948. For a time it also provided people with temporary accommodation. They found it demeaning that they were living in the house, for the Poor Law cast a long shadow. In London the St Marylebone workhouse came under the London County Council and was designated as a home for the elderly. Over time the maternity ward moved to Hammersmith hospital, and the nursery and the wards for the mentally ill closed. After the Second World War it also housed two parties of 250 displaced persons who had come to Britain in search of work. The vagrant wards closed in 1953, when a special hostel opened in Southwark. The rather gloomy Victorian building opposite Madame Tussaud's finally closed in 1965 and was demolished to make way for the campus of the

Polytechnic of Central London (now the University of Westminster).

By the 1970s the use of workhouse buildings to house the elderly was increasingly regarded as unacceptable, and they were gradually closed down and the residents transferred to new homes. At Gressenhall the last 45 residents were moved to a new residential home at Holt in 1974. It was noted that they tended to leave their doors open in order to re-create the dormitory atmosphere they were used to. One old gentleman sat on the staircase and flatly refused to move to 'foreign parts'; eventually he was found a place at a home in Fakenham.

Workhouse infirmaries were also transferred, first to the local authorities and then, in July 1948, they were merged with voluntary hospitals in the new National Health Service. In some places the new owners made much-needed improvements. At Crumpsall in north Manchester, the *Evening News* reported in 1953 that during the 1930s '[t]he Corporation carried on a steady programme of improvements until the war, converting old wards into out-patient, blood transfusion, physiotherapy and dental departments; and making life a lot quieter – and safer – for patients and staff by laying miles of rubber flooring on ward floors and staircases'.

During the Second World War much of the site at Bishop's Stortford, Hertfordshire, was turned into a temporary hospital for American servicemen from the nearby USAAF base at Stansted. The original buildings housed the mentally ill and did so until at least the mid-1970s when your author worked at the hospital.

Southwell remained in use until the early 1990s, providing temporary accommodation in 'bed-sits' for mothers and children awaiting more permanent housing. Both Gressenhall and Southwell ended up as museums – Gressenhall being the site of the Norfolk Museum of Rural Life from the late 1970s. Southwell was recognized by the Royal Commission on Historic Monuments as 'the best preserved workhouse standing in England'. It was imaginatively rescued by the National Trust with the aid of a £2.25 million grant from the Heritage Lottery Fund. The casual wards at Charlotteville in Guildford are being turned into a community centre, again with the help of lottery money.

Many workhouses remain in use as hospitals – the ones at Tonbridge in Kent and Guisborough in Yorkshire house the local hospitals – or as premises for NHS activities, such as the one at Ripon, Yorkshire, which has been converted into offices or the one at Falmouth in Cornwall, which accommodates the Budock home for people with learning disabilities. Other buildings, such as those at Richmond in Surrey and Bishop's Stortford, have been turned into private housing, as indeed have many of the smaller rural workhouses. But even if the buildings no longer survive, the reputation and the archival record remain to remind new generations of a period of neglect (and sometimes cruelty) to older generations of men, women and children who were rarely able to look after themselves.

Learning from the Poor Law

In the Introduction I wrote that this book was an attempt to answer three questions. Why was the Poor Law regarded with horror? Was every work-house as bad as the one at Andover? And, lastly, were the pauper inmates really as badly treated as we suppose?

Perhaps the greatest problem that faced the Poor Law was its structure. There were 650 or so Poor Law Unions, and each board of guardians could do more or less as it liked. As a result, conditions varied greatly. Although the Poor Law Commissioners and their successors in Whitehall could make a lot of noise, they had surprisingly few direct powers over the guardians. Most guardians were happy to follow the Commissioners' lead, as there were many benefits in doing so – but even then they often did not do things properly or misinterpreted the regulations.

The Poor Law and the workhouse were emotive subjects: people of all classes felt strongly about them. The policymakers whose views appear in the Parliamentary Papers largely defended the Poor Law during the 19th century, but in the 20th century there was a subtle shift as new, more humane ways were developed to help the very poor.

As far as the newspapers were concerned, a nice workhouse scandal was good for circulation, but the editorial comment was almost always in favour of the status quo. Their middle-class readers might grumble about the pet-tiness of Poor Law officials ('bumbledom' was the word much used to describe their actions), but they were reluctant to pay more to look after the paupers. Readers were united in the view that the paupers should have done more to look after themselves and that they brought their fate upon themselves. The Poor Law guardians were very aware of these opinions and it was a rare board indeed that was profligate with ratepayers' money. Before the 1920s

225

there were few grants from central government; money for paupers came directly from the ratepayers, and it was an unwise guardian who forgot this.

The poor themselves had different views. There was immense pity and concern for the innocent old people and children who were forced into 'the house' because they had nobody to look after them, or for the unemployed man who received a loaf of rock-hard bread or two from the relieving officer. But there was a clear sense of what was right and proper and what was wrong. The miserly allocation of out-relief to genuine applicants or the humiliation of the elderly or infirm in the workhouse were clearly not fair play. But George Lansbury, Will Crooks and the other working-class guardians also spoke for their electorates when they attacked the sponger and the loafer.

Some workhouses were awful, particularly during the 1830s and 1840s, and even in the 1890s conditions in a few – those exposed in the papers – were dreadful. The problems in most, however, were often relatively minor; one of the commonest criticisms that could be made against the workhouse was that life for the inmates was extremely dull and unnecessarily regimented. As we have seen, there was little enough stimulation generally and on Sundays almost none at all.

Yet some workhouses made reasonable efforts, and a few were very good. The guardians and staff in Richmond in Surrey or Belford in Northumberland were on the whole caring men and women, with just about adequate resources behind them. This was the luck of the draw, however; it was decidedly unpleasant to be elderly or without work in Brixworth, Northamptonshire, or in the desolate workhouses of London's East End.

It soon became clear that workhouses were not the right place to care for the elderly, the infirm and children, who swiftly became the majority of their inmates. Within a decade of the introduction of the New Poor Law, few able-bodied poor entered the workhouse. What is worse, the Poor Law was designed to deter applicants and cause misery to the very people – the sick, the elderly and the deserted – whom it should have been helping. Central government and the guardians were slow to understand this, and it was not until the 1870s that things began to change.

Reports, such as Dr Edward Smith's of 1866 on infirmaries in the metropolis and Mrs Nassau Senior's report of 1873 on the education of girls in barrack schools, exposed the conditions in two major areas of Poor Law implementation. Thereafter, new infirmaries conforming to modern principles began to be erected and children were increasingly looked after away from the workhouse. It was a process that took decades.

Conditions for the elderly also changed slowly, not as a result of a damning report but because of a change in society's perception of the old as a whole. The introduction of the old age pension in 1909 meant that many more very old men and women could live without recourse to the guardians. The sick, too, benefited from better techniques in nursing and surgery, as well as new technology which forced the guardians to employ more and better professionally qualified staff. By the time the Poor Law was abolished in 1929, workhouse infirmaries were hospitals in all but name and were mostly absorbed into the National Health Service in 1948.

In 1930 the Poor Law faded into history. No one has seriously suggested reviving it, and rightly so, because it was cruel and, even in the 1830s, largely inappropriate to people's needs. The politicians were lucky that the Poor Law was generally accepted (if loathed) by the people it most affected. There were surprisingly few serious protests against it and no effective political movement campaigned for its replacement.

Nowadays, we are horrified by the treatment people received in the workhouse, but we should remember that occasionally its modern successors can be just as cruel. For example, in July 2006 inspectors at Budock – the old Falmouth workhouse – uncovered alleged 'widespread institutional abuse' that might have been familiar to workhouse inmates. But today such cases are, fortunately, infrequent. The universal provision offered by Britain's welfare state is, for all its faults, a far better and far more humane solution. It is still a prize to be defended and nurtured. The alternative has been tried and found wanting.

Workhouse Museums

There are three workhouse museums in England at Southwell, Gressenhall and Ripon, each showing a different aspect of the workhouse. They are all well worth a visit, although sadly very little workhouse furniture survives, so visitors have to use their imaginations to visualise the life behind doors: a challenge when we have almost no connection with the routine and conditions in the workhouse. It is a world which, fortunately, has gone forever. The museums at Southwell and Gressenhall partially overcome a lack of artefacts through the use of re-enactors.

Both Southwell and Gressenhall were built before 1834, the year of the introduction of the New Poor Law: Gressenhall in 1776 and Southwell in 1824. Gressenhall was originally a House of Industry, a prototype workhouse which took in all the local unemployed men, women and their families. Today it houses the Norfolk Rural Life Museum.

Southwell was restored and reopened by the National Trust in 2002. It is important because it was the brainchild of a local vicar and social reformer, John Becher, who was one of the architects of the New Poor Law. The building clearly reflects his ideas on how paupers should be treated.

The Ripon workhouse opened in 1854, a date proudly emblazoned on the entrance building. Here only the casual wards are open and look more or less as they were a century ago. The rest of the workhouse complex now accommodates offices for the local Social Services.

Southwell and Gressenhall both have small research study areas, staffed by knowledgeable and helpful volunteers. Although the vast majority of records relating to these unions are at either the local record office or the National Archives (TNA), these museums have built up some interesting collections. Both are in the process of listing all the inmates and workhouse staff, and welcome enquiries from people whose ancestors had a connection with the house. In addition, Southwell is working with TNA to provide a detailed calendar of the records at Kew and elsewhere. The centres are open to the public, although you need to make an appointment.

The Workhouse,
Upton Road, Southwell, NG25 0PT
Tel: 01636 812250
www.nationaltrust.org.uk/workhouse

Gressenhall Farm and Workhouse,
Gressenhall, East Dereham, NR20 3DR
Tel: 01362 860563
www.museums.norfolk.gov.uk

The Workhouse Museum,
Allhallowgate, Ripon, HG4 1LE
Tel: 01765 690799
www.riponmuseums.co.uk

There are also plans to restore the workhouse at Llanfyllin in the heart of Wales and to open at least part of it as a museum. For details see www.llanfyllinworkhouse.com.

Workhouse records

Records of the New Poor Law are split between the National Archives (TNA) and local record offices. Material relating to the day-to-day operations of individual Poor Law unions are generally to be found locally, while TNA has documents on relations with the Poor Law Commissioners and their successors.

THE NATIONAL ARCHIVES

The major source is the correspondence between the Poor Law Commissioners and individual unions in series MH 12. The records begin in 1834 and finish in about 1900. Most later records were destroyed in the Blitz; what little survives is in MH 68.

They contain considerable correspondence about the workhouse, particularly at times when building work was planned in order to expand or improve the house. This material can give a vivid idea of what it must have been like to have been a resident of the workhouse. Incidentally, series MH 14 contains plans of lands and buildings, listed alphabetically by union between 1861 and 1918.

Among this correspondence you will probably also find returns to circulars sent out by the Commissioners. They include lists of people who had been vaccinated against smallpox in the union, paupers granted money to emigrate, and details of pauper lunatics and where they were looked after.

If the union ran a workhouse school, there will often be reports from Poor Law inspectors about the quality of tuition and the abilities of the schoolmaster or mistress. A few unions ran joint school districts, particularly in London. Records of districts are in series MH 27. They relate to the administration and control of the schools, including the appointment of managers and teaching and nursing staff, inspection of schools, construction and financing of buildings and related medical services. MH 17 contains similar papers of the Sick Asylum Districts in London, and the Metropolitan Asylum Board.

Whitehall had to approve the appointment of staff employed by local unions. Correspondence can be found in MH 12, while registers of people employed by unions are in MH 9. They cover the period between 1837 and 1921, although the vast majority of entries are for the last half of the 19th century. The registers are arranged by union. They contain dates of appointments and the salaries awarded. Reasons for leaving employment are noted, if they were known.

Scattered through MH 12 are application forms from people seeking employment as workhouse master, teacher or medical officer. Initially, these forms were introduced in 1842 for medical officers and then extended in the mid-1840s to other staff. There may also be letters from employees complaining about conditions or seeking pay rises.

Reports from Poor Law inspectors on conditions in workhouses and the problems faced by local boards of guardians are mostly in MH 32, with some in MH 12. The reports in MH 32 are generally arranged by name of inspector, which can be frustrating if you are looking for an individual union. From the 1870s specialist inspectors were increasingly recruited for buildings, infirmaries and schools (including a few women).

LOCAL RECORD OFFICES

Collections of Poor Law union records at local record offices are patchy. So it is not possible to give any clear idea of what might survive for a particular union or workhouse. On the other hand, many of the forms and registers completed by officials duplicate each other, so if one set of records has been lost, another similar type may be equally suitable.

A comprehensive list of the records that survive for each union can be found in the three volumes of Jeremy Gibson, *Poor Law Union Records* (2nd edition, FFHS, 2000). Brief details are also to be found on the appropriate individual workhouse page at www.workhouses.org.uk.

The most important series of records are:
- Minutes of the board of guardians and its various subcommittees. They may contain minutes about troublesome inmates or the apprenticing of individual children. You may occasionally find lists of paupers or, with the appropriate committee papers, lists of pauper children.
- Registers of indoor relief granted. These records come in various forms, for example registers of admission and discharge from the workhouse, or printed indoor relief lists published every six months. Not dissimilar are the creed registers which, from 1876, contain religious and other personal details about paupers.
- Registers of children, including admissions to the workhouse school. There may also be registers of the employment of children or where they were boarded out.
- Registers of lunatics in asylums.
- Registers or books of paupers receiving out-relief. There may also be printed outdoor relief lists showing where every recipient lived and giving the reason why they received support. Also of considerable interest are application and report, or case, books in which details of applications for relief are given.

Records less than 75 years old (sometimes 100 years) may be closed to public access.

PARLIAMENTARY PAPERS

Parliamentary papers are another useful and underused source. A general introduction can be found in the online research guide *Printed Parliamentary Papers* at www.nationalarchives.gov.uk/catalogue.

The National Archives has a set of these papers. They are now available online in the reading rooms at Kew, in a fully searchable form.

Parliamentary Papers are well indexed. The best index is online at **www.bopcris.ac.uk**, although it is not 100 per cent complete.

There are several types of record that may be of use:

Reports and papers of Royal Commissions, parliamentary select committees and other inquiries There were numerous Royal Commissions and other inquiries into the condition of the poor, the most important of which were the Royal Commissions of 1832–4 and 1905–8. As well as detailed reports, both Commissions ordered that accompanying evidence be published.

As part of the evidence presented to the Commission of 1832, overseers or Poor Law officials were asked to complete a questionnaire about the provision made for poor relief in their parish, but only a fifth of parishes bothered to reply. Disappointed by the poor return, the Commissioners decided to send a number of Assistant Commissioners around the country in 1832 and 1833 to report on the position locally. Another fifth of parishes were visited in total. Although sketchy, this evidence offers a unique view of the lives of poor people at the time 1830s.

There were also a number of select committees which looked at aspects of the Poor Law or indeed the condition of the poor in general. The evidence presented can offer a vivid insight into the life of the pauper. The best known of these inquiries examined conditions in Andover workhouse in 1847.

Annual reports of the Poor Law Commissioners and their successors The Poor Law Commissioners, and their successors, presented an annual report to Parliament summarizing their work during the previous year. Particularly in the early years, these reports provide another illuminating insight into how the Poor Law operated.

Individual returns and circulars Individuals made returns to Parliament, normally at the request of an MP. Often they are just for a single year or a few years. Among this material is a return of officials employed at Lady Day, 1848, listing people by union, with details of salary, age and period of service with their present employers, and lists for a number of years during the 1860s of paupers who had been in the workhouse for more than five years.

NEWSPAPERS

Newspapers are another important – and underused – resource. You may find almost verbatim accounts of the meetings of the boards of guardians. Local newspapers are also likely to feature in great detail debates about the treatment of the paupers, especially such minor issues as whether inmates should be allowed beer with their Christmas dinner. National newspapers, particularly *The Times*, also took a keen interest in the Poor Law, especially in the 1830s and 1840s.

Local record offices and study libraries are likely to have newspapers for their areas. The biggest collection of newspapers, however, is held by the British Newspaper Library, Colindale, London NW9 5HE (www.bl.uk). Many libraries (including the National Archives) have access to The Times Digital Archive with digitized images of each article and a comprehensive index.

GENERAL WORKS

Australian Dictionary of Biography, entries for Grace Elizabeth Jennings Carmichael, James Joseph Crouch, Worthy Worthington, George Nicholls (www.adb.online.anu.edu.au)

Dictionary of Canadian Biography Online, entries for John George Donkin, Maria Susan Rye (www.biography.ca/EN)

Imperial Calendar, 1844, 1864

Oxford Dictionary of National Biography, entries for George Bartley, Will Crooks, Andrew Doyle, Joseph Gutteridge, James Hammett, George Lansbury, Martha Merrington, George Sclater-Booth

Brian Abel-Smith, *The Hospitals 1800–1948: A Study in Social Administration in England and Wales* (London: Heinemann, 1964)

Amyatt Amyatt, *On the Repression of Vagrancy and Indiscriminate Almsgiving* (4th edn, Weymouth: H. Wheeler, 1878)

Anon. *Indoor Paupers by One of Them* (London: Chatto and Windus, 1885)

Ian Anstruther, *The Scandal of Andover Workhouse* (London: Geoffrey Bles, 1973)

Thomas Archer, *The Pauper, the Thief and the Convict* (London: Groombridge, 1865); online at www.perseus.tufts.edu

Max Arthur, *Lost Voices of the Edwardians* (London: Harper Press, 2006)

George Bartley, *A Handy Book for Guardians of the Poor* (London: Chapman and Hall, 1876)

John Belchem, *Merseypride: Essays in Liverpool Exceptionalism* (Liverpool: University Press, 2000)

Christine Bellamy, *Administering Central–Local Relations 1871–1919: The Local Government Board in Its Fiscal and Cultural Context* (Manchester: University Press, 1988)

Virginia Berridge, 'Health and Medicine' in F.M.L. Thompson (ed.), *The Cambridge Social History of Britain 1750–1950: vol. 3 Social Agencies and Institutions* (Cambridge: University Press, 1990)

Charles Booth, *The Aged Poor in England and Wales* (London: Macmillan, 1894)

Charles Booth, *Life and Labour of the Poor* (3 vols, London: Williams and Norgate, 1889–1891)

Charles Booth, *Old Age Pensions and the Aged Poor: A Proposal* (London: Macmillan, 1899)

Charles Booth, *Pauperism: A Picture and the Endowment of Old Age* (London: Macmillan, 1892)

J.M. Bowen, 'A Poor Little House…' *The Story of Belford Union Workhouse and Its People from 1836 to 1930* (Belford: Bell View, 2005)

Anthony Chadwick, *From Workhouse to Welfare State* (Ripon: Museum Trust, 2003; Life in the Workhouse Booklet 7)

Anthony Chadwick, *Yorkshire Workhouses* (Ripon: Museum Trust, 2003; Life in the Workhouse Booklet 1)

W. Chance, *Children under the Poor Law* (London: Swan Sonnenschein, 1897)

Valerie E. Chancellor (ed.), *Master and Artisan in Victorian England: The Diary of William Andrews and the Autobiography of Joseph Gutteridge* (London: Evelyn, Adams and Mackay, 1969)

Charles Chaplin, *My Autobiography* (London: Bodley Head, 1964)

S.G. and E.O.A Checkland (eds), *The Poor Law Report of 1834* (London: Penguin, 1974)

Kellow Chesney, *The Victorian Underworld* (London: Pelican Books, 1972)

John Cole (ed.), *Down Poorhouse Lane: The Diary of a Rochdale Workhouse* (Littleborough: George Kelsall, 1994)

Jacqueline Cooper, *The Well-Ordered Town: A Story of Saffron Walden, Essex 1792–1862* (Clavering: Cooper Publications, 2000)

Fred Copeman, *Reason in Revolt* (London: Blandford Press, 1948)

John Coveney, *Food, Morals and Meaning: The Pleasure and Anxiety of Eating* (London: Routledge, 2000)

Jeffrey Cox, *The English Churches in a Secular Society: Lambeth 1870–1930* (New York: Oxford University Press, 1982)

Bernard Crick, *George Orwell: A Life* (London: Secker and Warburg, 1980)

Frank Crompton, *Workhouse Children* (Stroud: Sutton, 1997)

M.A. Crowther, *The Workhouse System 1834–1929* (London: Batsford, 1981)

F.G. D'Aeth, *Report to the Chairman of the Liverpool Council of Voluntary Aid on the Charitable Effort in Liverpool* (Liverpool: Council of Voluntary Aid, 1910)

W.H. Davies, *Autobiography of a Super-Tramp* (Oxford: University Press, 1980), first published Jonathan Cape, 1908

Charles Dickens, 'The Wapping Workhouse' in *An Uncommercial Traveller* (London: Chapman & Hall, 1861)

Anne Digby, *Pauper Palaces* (London: Routledge and Kegan Paul, 1978)

Anne Digby, *The Poor Law in Nineteenth Century England and Wales* (London: Historical Association, 1982)

Felix Driver, *Power and Pauperism: The Workhouse System 1834–1884* (Cambridge: University Press, 1993)

Frederick Eden, *The State of the Poor* (London: Routledge, 1928)

Friedrich Engels, *The Condition of the Working Class in England* (Moscow: Progress Publishers, 1973, first published 1845); available online at www.marxists.org/archive/marx/works/1845/condition-working-class

William J. Fishman, *East End 1888* (Nottingham: Five Leaves, 2005)

Judith Flanders, *Consuming Passions: Leisure and Pleasure in Victorian Britain* (London: Harper Press, 2006)

Judith Flanders, *The Victorian House* (London: Harper Perennial, 2004)

Josiah Flynt, *Tramping with Tramps: Studies and Sketches of Vagabond Life* (London: Fisher Unwin, 1900)

Simon Fowler, *Philanthropy and the Poor Law in Richmond 1836–1871* (Richmond: Local History Society, 1991)

W.R. Garside, *British Unemployment 1919–1939* (Cambridge: University Press, 1990)

Frank Grace, *Rags and Bones: A Social History of a Working Class Community in Nineteenth-century Ipswich* (London: Unicorn Press, 2005)

Frank Gray, *The Tramp: His Being and Meaning* (London: Dent, 1931)

David R. Green, *From Artisans to Paupers: Economic Change and Poverty in London, 1790–1870* (Aldershot: Scolar Press, 1995)

William Grisewood, *The Poor of Liverpool and What Is Being Done for Them* (Liverpool: Egerton Smith, 1899)

Susan Hall, *Workhouses and Hospitals of North Manchester* (Manchester: Neil Richardson, 2004)

Hugh Hanley, *Apprenticing in a Market Town: The Story of William Harding's Charity, Aylesbury 1719–2000* (Chichester: Phillimore, 2005)

S.H. Hardwick, *Our Tramps* (Wolverton: McCorquodale, 1895)

Thomas Hardy, *Far from the Madding Crowd* (London: Smith Elder, 1874)

George Haw, *From Workhouse to Westminster: The Life Story of Will Crooks MP* (London: Cassell, 1907)

Nathaniel Hawthorn, *Our Old Home: A Series of English Sketches* (Boston: Houghton, Mifflin, 1883); available online at www.eldritchpress.org/nh/ooh.html

[Mary Higgs], *Five Days and Five Nights as a Tramp among Tramps… Social Investigation by a Lady* (Manchester: John Haywood, [1904])

Mary Higgs, *Glimpses into the Abyss* (London: PS King, 1906)

Tim Hitchcock, *Down and Out in Eighteenth Century London* (London: Hambledon, 2004)

Philip Hoare, *Spike Island: The Memory of a Military Hospital* (London: Fourth Estate, 2001)

Patricia Hollis, *Ladies Elect: Women in English Local Government 1865–1914* (Oxford: Clarendon, 1987)

Robert Humphries, *No Fixed Abode: A History of Responses to the Roofless and Rootless in Britain* (London: Macmillan, 1999)

David James, *Bradford* (Halifax: Ryburn, 1990)

F.J. Johnson (ed.), *Edwardian and Great War Cheadle 1905–1918* (Cheadle: Cheadle and Tean Times, 1997)

Valerie Johnston, *Diet in Workhouses and Prisons* (New York: Garland, 1985)

Jennifer Jones, *Macclesfield Workhouse* (Macclesfield: Graveyard Press, 1999)

Steven King, *Poverty and Welfare in England 1700–1850: A Regional Perspective* (Manchester: University Press, 2000)

Steven King and Alannah Tomkins (eds), *The Poor in England 1700–1850: An Economy of Makeshifts* (Manchester: University Press, 2003)

Marjorie Kohli, *The Golden Bridge: Young Immigrants to Canada 1833–1939* (Toronto: Natural Heritage, 2003)

'A Lambeth Guardian', *The New Pauper Infirmaries and Casual Wards* (London: Frederic Norgate, 1875)

Neville Land, *Victorian Workhouse: A Study of the Bromsgrove Union Workhouse 1836–1901* (Studley: Brewin Books, 1990)

Marlene and Graham Langley, *At the Crossroads: A History of Arclid Workhouse and Hospital* (Nantwich: Langley, 1993)

George Lansbury, *My Life* (London: Constable, 1931)

Robert Lea, *Unquiet Country: Voices of the Rural Poor 1820–1880* (Macclesfield: Windgather Press, 2005)

Lincolnshire (Parts of Lindsey), *Report of the Vagrancy Committee Adopted by Quarter Sessions on Friday 23 October 1903* (Lincoln: Morton, [1903])

Jack London, *The People of the Abyss* (Miami: Synergy International, 2000; first published 1903)

Norman Longmate, *The Workhouse* (London: Pimlico, 2003)

Sophia Lonsdale, *The English Poor Laws: Their History, Principles and Administration* (London: P. S. King & Son, 1902)

Sean McConville, *English Local Prisons 1860–1900: Next Only to Death* (London: Routledge, 1995)

John Macnicol, *The Politics of Retirement in Britain 1878–1948* (Cambridge: University Press, 1998)

Hilary Marland, *Medicine and Society in Wakefield and Huddersfield 1780–1870* (Cambridge: University Press, 1987)

Henry Mayhew, *London Labour and London Poor, volumes 3 and 4* (London: 1862); available online at www.perseus.tufts.edu/cache/perscoll_bolles.html

Kathryn Morrison, *The Workhouse: A Study of Poor Law Buildings in England* (Swindon: English Heritage, 1999)

National Trust, *The Workhouse Southwell* (London: National Trust, 2002)

Alan R. Neate, *St Marylebone Workhouse* (London: St Marylebone Society, 2003)

Julie O'Neill, *The Life and Times of J.T. Becher of Southwell* (Nottingham: the author, 2002)

George Orwell, *Down and Out in London and Paris* (London: Penguin, 2003; first published by Victor Gollancz in 1933)

Ruth Paley and Simon Fowler, *Family Skeletons* (The National Archives, 2005)

Robert Pashley, *Paupers and the Poor Law* (London, 1852)

Michael Paterson, *Voices from Dickens' London* (Newton Abbott: David and Charles, 2006)

Liza Picard, *Victorian London: The Life of a City 1840–1870* (London: Weidenfeld and Nicolson, 2005)

Stephen Pope, *Gressenhall Farm and Workhouse* (Cromer: Poppyland Publishing, 2006)

Raymond Postgate, *The Life of George Lansbury* (London: Longmans Green, 1951)

Herbert Preston-Thomas, *The Work and Play of a Government Inspector* (Edinburgh: Blackwood, 1909)

Frank Prochaska, *The Voluntary Impulse: Philanthropy in Modern Britain* (London: Faber and Faber, 1988)

June Purvis, *Emmeline Pankhurst* (Routledge, 2002)

Maud Pember Reeves, *A Round about a Pound a Week* (London: Bell, 1913)

Carol Richmond, *Bicester Poor Law Union and Workhouse Records* (Witney: Oxfordshire Black Sheep Publications, 2006)

James C. Riley, *Sick, Not Dead: The Health of the British Workingman During the Mortality Decline* (Baltimore: Johns Hopkins University Press, 1997)

Robert Roberts, *The Classic Slum: Salford Life in the First Quarter of the Century* (London: Penguin, 1978)

Joseph Rogers, *Reminiscences of a Workhouse Medical Officer* (London: T. Fisher Unwin, 1889)

Lionel Rose, *The Erosion of Childhood: Child Oppression in Britain, 1860–1918* (London: Routledge, 1991)

Lionel Rose, *'Rogues and Vagabonds in Britain': Vagrant Underworld in Britain 1815–1985* (London: Routledge, 1988)

B. Seebohm Rowntree, *Poverty: A Study of Town Life* (London: Macmillan, 1901)

Charles Shaw, *When I Was a Child* (Firle: Caliban Books, 1977; first published 1903)

John Shepherd, *George Lansbury at the Heart of Old Labour* (Oxford: University Press, 2002)

Menella B. Smedley, *Boarding Out and Pauper Schools for Girls* (London: Henry S. King, 1875)

Samuel Smiles, *Self-Help, with Illustrations of Conduct and Perseverance* (London: Institute of Economic Affairs, 1996; first published 1859)

Dorothy Stanley (ed.), *The Autobiography of Sir Henry Morton Stanley, GCB* (London: Sampson Low, 1909)

Gareth Stedman Jones, *Outcast London: A Study in the Relationship between Classes in Victorian Society* (London: Penguin, 1984)

Graham Storey (ed.), *The Letters of Charles Dickens, vol. 11* (Oxford: Clarendon Press, 1999)

Anne-Marie Strange, *Death, Grief and Poverty in Britain, 1870–1914* (Cambridge: University Press, 2005)

Brenda Thompson, *Children* (Ripon: Museum Trust, 2003; Life in the Workhouse Booklet 2)

Brenda Thompson, *Food* (Ripon: Museum Trust, 2003; Life in the Workhouse Booklet 6)

Brenda Thompson, *Health and Sickness* (Ripon: Museum Trust, 2003; Life in the Workhouse Booklet 5)

Brenda Thompson, *Old People* (Ripon: Museum Trust, 2003; Life in the Workhouse Booklet 4)

Brenda Thompson, *Vagrants* (Ripon: Museum Trust, 2003; Life in the Workhouse Booklet 3)

James Treble, *Urban Poverty in Britain, 1830–1914* (London: Longman, 1979)

E.S. Turner, *What the Butler Saw: Two Hundred and Fifty Years of the Servant Problem* (London: Michael Joseph, 1962)

Louisa Twining, *Recollections of Life and Work* (London: Edward Arnold, 1893)

David Vincent, *Poor Citizens: The State and the Poor in Twentieth Century Britain* (London: Longman, 1991)

John Waller, *The Real Oliver Twist: Robert Blincoe a Life That Illuminates a Violent Age* (Cambridge: Icon Books, 2005)

James Walvin, *Victorian Values* (London: Cardinal, 1988)

Micky Watkins, *Henrietta Barnett in Whitechapel* (London: Hampstead Garden Suburb Residents Association, 2005)

Katherine A. Webb, *'One of the most useful charities in the City': York Dispensary 1788–1988* (York: Borthwick Paper 74, 1988)

Robert Whelan, *Helping the Poor: Friendly Visiting, Dole Charities and the Dole Queue* (London: Civitas, 2001)

Sarah Wise, *The Italian Boy: Murder and Grave Robbery in 1830s London* (London: Jonathan Cape, 2004)

Peter Wood, *Poverty and the Workhouse in Victorian Britain* (Stroud: Alan Sutton, 1991)

James Woodforde, *The Diary of a Country Parson 1758–1802* (Oxford: University Press, 1978)

John Woodward, *To Do the Sick No Harm: A Study of the British Voluntary Hospital System to 1875* (London: Routledge and Kegan Paul, 1974)

Keith Wrightson, *Earthly Necessities: Economic Lives in Early Modern Britain* (London: Yale University Press, 2000)

ARTICLES

'A Discreet Report' *All the Year Round* (1868) 19, p. 350

'A Country Workhouse' *All the Year Round* (1868) 19, p. 16

Russell Chamberlin, 'Saving the Spike' *Spectator*, 4 February 2006

A.P. Coney, 'Mid-nineteenth Century Ormskirk: Disease, Overcrowding and the Irish in a Lancashire Market Town' *Transactions of the Historic Society of Lancashire and Cheshire* (1990) 139

'James Cropper', *Poor Law Conferences Held in the Year 1901–2* (London: P.S. King, 1902)

B.P. Curle, 'Mr Drouet's Establishment at Tooting: An Essay in Victorian Child Welfare' *Surrey Archaeological Collections* (1969) 66

S.E. De Morgan, 'Recollections of a London Workhouse, Forty Years Ago' *Englishwomen's Review*, 15 February 1889

Charles Dickens, 'A Walk in the Workhouse' *Household Words*, 25 May 1850

David Englander, 'From the Abyss: Pauper Petitions and Correspondence in Victorian London' *London Journal* (2000) 25

Simon Fowler, 'Jenny Foster Newton: "a bonnie fighter"' *Richmond History* (1998) 19

Simon Fowler, 'Vagrancy in Mid-Victorian Richmond, Surrey' *The Local Historian* (1991) 21

David R. Green, 'Pauper Protests: Power and Resistance in Early Nineteenth Century Workhouses' *Social History* (2006) 31

Rosaline Hall, 'A Poor Cotton Weyver: Poverty and the Cotton Famine in Clitheroe' *Social History* (2003) 28

Dick Hunter, 'The Poor Law in Hackney a Century Ago' *The Local Historian* (2004) 34

Dick Hunter, 'Vagrancy in the East and West Ridings of Yorkshire during the Late Victorian Period' *The Local Historian* (2006) 36

Elizabeth T. Hurren, 'Agricultural Trade Unionism and the Crusade against Outdoor Relief: Poor Law Politics in the Brixworth Union, Northamptonshire, 1870–1875' *Agricultural History Review* (2000) 481

Elizabeth T. Hurren, 'Welfare-to-work Schemes and a Crusade against Outdoor Relief on the Brixworth Union, Northamptonshire in the 1880s' *Family and Community History* (2001) 4

Elizabeth Hurren and Steve King, '"Begging for a burial": Form, Function and Conflict in Nineteenth Century Pauper Burial' *Social History* (2005) 30

David G. Jackson, 'The Medway Union Workhouse 1876–1881: A Study Based on the Admission and Discharge Registers and the Census Enumerators Books' *Local Population Studies* (2005) 75

Keith Laybourn, 'The Guild of Help and the Community Response to Poverty 1904–c1914' in Keith Laybourn (ed.), *Social Conditions, Status and Community 1860–c1920* (Thrupp: Sutton, 1997)

Marjorie Levine-Clark, 'Engendering Relief: Women, Ablebodiedness, and the New Poor Law in Early Victorian England' *Journal of Women's History* (2000) 11

Lynn MacKay, 'A Culture of Poverty? The St. Martin in the Fields Workhouse, 1817' *Journal of Interdisciplinary History* (1995) 26

Ann Morton, 'Contracting out Cruelty' *Ancestors* (2005) 29

Brian Owen, 'The Newtown and Llanidloes Poor Law Union Workhouse, Caersws, 1837–1847' *Montgomeryshire Collections* (1990) 78

L.R. Phelps, 'Poor Law and Charity', *Poor Law Conferences Held in the Year 1901–2* (London: P.S. King, 1902)

Ruth Richardson, 'Middlesex Hospital Outpatients Wing/the Strand Union Workhouse' *History Today* (September 1993) 43

David Roberts, 'How Cruel Was the Victorian Poor Law?' *Historical Journal* (1963) 6

Southwell Workhouse Research Group, 'Penny Pinching Parishes' *Ancestors* (2006) 49

Spencer Thomas, 'Power, Paternalism, Patronage and Philanthropy: the Wyndhams and the New Poor Law in Petworth' *The Local Historian* (2002) 32

Kathryn Thompson, 'Apprenticeship and the New Poor Law: a Leicester Example' *The Local Historian* (1989) 19

Martin Wilcox, 'Opportunity or Exploitation? Apprenticeship in the British Trawl Fisheries 1850–1936' *Genealogists' Magazine* (2004) 28

T.W. Wilkinson, 'In a London Workhouse' in George R. Sims, *Living London, Vol. II Section I* (London: Cassell, [1902])

Derek Williams, 'The Ludlow Guardians 1836–1900' *Transactions of the Shropshire Archaeological and Historical Society* (2002) 77

Richard Wiltshire, 'Asylums for London's Poor and Sick' *Ancestors* (2005) 31

NEWSPAPERS

Bethnal Green Standard, 31 March 1866

The Guardian, 5 and 6 July 2006

Household Words, 13 July 1850

The Times, 22 September 1836; 15 March 1837; 10 December 1838; 3 December 1842; 5 September 1843; 9 September 1843; 21 June 1844; 22 June 1844; 15 January 1845; 26–8 August 1845; 17 September 1845; 12 August 1850; 26 August 1856; 14 October 1856; 18 November 1856; 25 October 1867; 30 October 1867; 1 November 1867; 7 November 1867; 3 February 1871; 19 December 1889; 20 May 1897; 17 December 1891; 22 September 1894; 7 April 1908; 26 February 1910; 15 April 1910; 10 December 1915; 24 May 1922; 12 September 1925; 31 August 1926; 1 September 1926; 28 October 1926; 9 March 1927; 16 January 1928; 22 November 1929; 1 April 1930

PARLIAMENTARY PAPERS

1st Annual Report of the Poor Law Commissioners, Appendix A (PP 1835.xxv.167)

2nd Annual Report of the Poor Law Commissioners (PP 1836.xxix Part II.1)

3rd Annual Report of the Poor Law Board, 1850 (PP 1852.xiii.1)

22nd Annual Report of the Poor Law Board, 1869 (PP 1870.xxxv.1 C.123)

2nd Annual Report of Local Government Board, Appendix 32 Outdoor relief – report of committee of Brixworth union (PP 1872–3. xxix, 1, C.748)

19th Annual Report of the Local Government Board (PP 1890.xxxiii.1)

27th Annual Report of the Local Government Board 1897–8 (PP 1898.xxxix.1 C. 8978)

Bedwellty: Report of the Guardians appointed by the Ministry of Health, period ending 30 September 1927 (PP 1927.xi.1111 Cmd 2976)

Chester-Le-Street Union: Report of the Board of Guardians, 1 July–31 December 1927 (PP 1928.xii.123 Cmd 3072)

Committee of the Council on Education: Schools of Parochial Unions (PP 1849.xlii.24)

Depositions Taken by Mr Weale in an Inquiry into the Treatment of Aged Paupers in the Barrow Workhouse (PP 1846.xxxvi.219)

Dietaries for the Inmates of Workhouses: Report of Dr Edward Smith, FRCS (PP 1866.xxxv.321)

Education and Training of Pauper Children (PP 1851.xlix.31)

Farnham Union: Report on State and Management (PP 1867–68.lx.37)

Investigation into the Coalfields of South Wales and Monmouth (Cmd 3272)

Letter and General Rule Issued Relative to Bone Pounding (PP 1846.xxxvi.77)

Letters from the Guardians of Strand Union Relative to Mr George Catch (PP 1867–1868.lxi.249)

Metropolitan Districts, etc.: Relief to the Lunatic Poor; Workhouses (Infirmary Wards) by H.B. Farnall, Poor Law Inspector (PP 1866.lxi.1)

Observations on the Report of Mrs Senior to the Local Government Board as to the Effect on Girls of the System of Education at Pauper Schools (PP 1875.lxiii.299)

Poor Law (Out Relief) Copy of a Memorandum by Local Government Board Relating to the Administration of Out Relief, dated February 1878 (PP 1878.lxv.352)

Poor Law (Walsall) Workhouse (PP 1867–68.lx.547)

Poor Law (Workhouse Inspection) (PP 1867–68.lxi.35)

Proceedings of the Directors and Guardians of the Poor of St Marylebone Relative to the Infant Pauper Children in the Workhouse, 1843 (PP 1843.xx.559)

Report of the Commission of Inquiry into the Administration and Practical Operation of the Poor Laws (PP 1834.xxxvi.1)

Report of a Committee on Workhouse Dietaries, 1898 (PP 1898.li.459)

Report of the Departmental Committee to Inquire into the Nursing of the Sick Poor in Workhouses (PP 1902. xxxix.413 Cd. 1366)

Report of the Departmental Committee to Inquire into Workhouse Accounts (PP 1903.xvii.121 Cd 1440)

Report of the Departmental Committee on the Relief of the Casual Poor (PP 1929–30.xvii.121 Cmd 3640)

Report of the Departmental Committee on Vagrancy (PP 1906.ciii.1 Cd 2852)

Report of Dr Edward Smith on the Infirmary Wards of the Several Metropolitan Workhouses (PP 1866.lxi.171)

Report of Dr Edward Smith on the Sufficiency of the Existing Arrangements for the Care and Treatment of the Sick Poor in Forty-eight Provincial Workhouses in England and Wales (PP 1867–8.lx.4)

Report of H.B. Farnall on the Infirmary Wards of the Several Metropolitan Workhouses (PP 1866.lxi.387)

Report of the Royal Commission on the Poor Laws and Relief of Distress (PP 1909.xxxvii.1 Cd 4499)

Report from the Select Committee on Andover Union; together with the minutes of evidence, appendix and index (PP 1846.v.1)

Reports Made to the President of the Local Government Board by Poor Law Inspectors on Vagrancy (PP 1866.xxxv.1)

Reports by Poor Law Inspectors on Workhouses in Their Districts, in Pursuance of Instructions (PP 1867–68.lxi.1)

Return of Officers Whose Incomes Are Paid from Poor Rates in England and Wales (PP 1849.xlvii.83)

Rotherhithe Workhouse Infirmary: Copies of the Report of the Inquiry Lately Held by the Metropolitan Inspector in the Complaints of Miss Beeton against the Management of the Rotherhithe Workhouse Infirmary (PP 1866.lxi.523)

Royal Commission on the Aged Poor (PP 1895.xiv.1 C. 7684)

Second Report from the Select Committee on Poor Relief (PP 1862.x.230)

Select Committee of the House of Lords on Poor Law Relief (PP 1888.xv.23)

Select Committee on the Abuses at Andover Union (PP 1846.v.1)

Select Committee on the Poor Law Amendment Act: 15th report (PP 1837–38.xxx.210)

The Use of Stimulating Liquors at Wrexham Union (PP 1876.lxiii.405)

West Ham Union: Second Report, 1 November 1926–31 May 1927 (PP 1927.xi.1145 Cmd 2900)

HANSARD

1891 Vol. 178, p. 525

TNA MATERIAL

AST 8/44: printed memorandum from [Charles Frost] on the rational treatment of casual paupers [1903]

KV 2/2322: MI5 file on Fred Copeman

MH 12/12/12478: Lambeth 1869; MH 12/12599: Richmond 1857; MH 12/15356: Ripon 1865; MH 12/15536: Tadcaster 1865; MH 12/6845: Stepney 1850; MH 12/8483: Mitford and Launditch 1874; MH 12/9525: Southwell

MH 25/24: Local Government Board miscellaneous correspondence 1873

MH 57/16: tour of inspection of workhouses in eastern counties by Susan Lawrence, Assistant Secretary of State for Health [Easter 1931]

MH 57/135: appointments of guardians etc. Bedwellty, Chester-le-Street and West Ham unions 1926–9

MH 68/266: Bedwellty correspondence 1926–30

MH 79/264–266: reports on Bedwellty, Chester-le-Street and West Ham unions 1926–9

PROB 11/2202 no. 140: will for Daniel Haybitter

RG 10/641: census entry for George Catch

NON-TNA MATERIAL

Callow Collection Box 3 (Society of Genealogists)

Minute book for Llanfllin, Powys County Archives (http://a-day-in-the-life.powys.org.uk/eng/social/es_workstaff.php)

Minute book Southwell Board of Guardians (Nottinghamshire Archives)

Minute book Tadcaster Board of Guardians (North Yorkshire Record Office G/TD 1424)

Report of the Board of Guardians (Richmond Poor Law Union) Year Ending 31 March 1852 (Richmond Local Studies Library)

WEBSITES

www.workhouses.org.uk – superb resource

www.charlotteville.co.uk – project to restore Guildford

www.en.wikipedia.org – useful reference site

www.institutions.org.uk – another general site on Poor Law institutions, hospitals and the like

www.johnh.co.uk/history/cheesmanbuilders.htm – about the builders of Brighton's first workhouse and the misconduct of the town's guardians in the 1850s

www.judandk.force9.co.uk/workhouse.html – mainly about Stratford-upon-Avon

www.kingston.gov.uk/browse/leisure/museum/kingston_history/ citizenship_in_kingston/welfare_archives.htm – Kingston almshouses and workhouse

I am grateful to Catherine Bradley and her colleagues in the publishing department at the National Archives – Catherine de Gatacre, Mark Hawkins-Dady, Sheila Knight and Nora Talty-Nangle – for giving me the opportunity to study the subject in more detail, and their work on selling and editing the book. In addition, Gwen Campbell researched the pictures and Janet Sacks and Fintan Power edited a somewhat unwieldy text.

Elsewhere at Kew, Paul Carter and the volunteers in the Southwell Workhouse Research Group allowed me to use some of the stories they have unearthed in the course of their work; and Sandra Grant kept *Ancestors Magazine* on the road while its editor was distracted with less pressing things. Several writers for the magazine also provided information and help, including Kathy Chater, Mark Crail, Ian Maxwell and David Webster.

Others helped directly or indirectly: Will Cavendish for details of his great-grandfather, Richard Cavendish; Jill Kell for details of her pauper great-grandmother, Eliza Wright; Margaret Garrod alerted me to the Tadcaster incident of 1865; Philip Jones, at Southwell, and Stephen Pope, at Gressenhall, for their help and hospitality, and Dan Weinbren for suggestions which were not followed up as well as guidance about friendly societies.

Nigel Venus offered reminiscences of Rhayader workhouse, Jess Jenkins at the Record Office for Leicestershire, Leicester and Rutland provided information about Amos Sherriff, members of the Family and Community History Research Society's ill-fated Pauper Emigration Project, particularly Robert Ruegg and Jackie Gore, supplied information about emigration between 1834 and 1871.

And lastly, but above all others, Sylvia Levi who did more, much more, than could have been expected of any author's partner as chauffeur, researcher and slave-driver.

Errors and omissions are of course my own.

Finally, I should like to end with the words of one Poor Law boy made good, Frank Richards, who concluded his autobiography *Old Soldier Sahib* thus: 'I feel… like adjourning to the nearest beer-fountain for a quart or two of purge to celebrate the conclusion of a very severe sentence that I innocently passed on myself.'

= PICTURE SOURCES =

1, 2 People's History Museum 3, 34 Punch 4, 12 TNA: PRO MH 12/15536 5 Norfolk Library Services 6, 27 Hulton Archive/Getty Images 7 MH 14/36 8 NTPL/Ian Shaw 9, 10 City of Westminster Archives Centre 11 Topfoto/HIP 13 NTPL/Andrew Butler 14, 15, 28 Gressenhall Farm and Workhouse 16 Popperfoto 17 TNA: PRO MH 12/1841 18, 26 Museum of English Rural Life/Blackett Collection 19 Chepstow Museum/www.gtj.org.uk 20, 22, 33, 36 TNA: PRO PRO 30/69/1663 21 Brecknock Museum and Art Gallery/www.gtj.org.uk 23, 24 George R. Simms 25 Mary Evans Picture Library 29, 32 www.topfoto.co.uk 30 George Cruikshank 31 TNA: PRO ZPER 34/91 35 TNA: PRO ZPER 34/50